MTEL English

07 Teacher Certification Exam

By Sharon Wynne, M.S.

XAMonline, Inc.

Boston

XAMonline, Inc.
25 First Street, Suite 106
Cambridge, MA 02141
Toll Free 1-800-301-4647
Email: info@xamonline.com
Web www.xamonline.com
Fax: 1-617-583-5552

Library of Congress Cataloging-in-Publication Data

Wynne, Sharon A.
    English 07: Teacher Certification / Sharon A. Wynne. -2nd Ed. ISBN 978-1-60787-350-1
    1. English 07.   2. Study Guides.   3. MTEL
    4. Teachers' Certification & Licensure.   5. Careers

Disclaimer:
The opinions expressed in this publication are the sole works of XAMonline and were created independently from the National Education Association, Educational Testing Service, or any State Department of Education, National Evaluation Systems, or other testing affiliates.

Between the time of publication and printing, state specific standards as well as testing formats and website information may change that is not included in part or in whole within this product. Sample test questions are developed by XAMonline and reflect similar content as on real tests; however, they are not former tests. XAMonline assembles content that aligns with state standards but makes no claims nor guarantees teacher candidates a passing score. Numerical scores are determined by testing companies such as NES or ETS and then are compared with individual state standards. A passing score varies from state to state.

Printed in the United States of America   œ-1

MTEL: English 07
ISBN: 978-1-60787-350-1

Certification Requirements

Educators seeking a first Massachusetts Pre K–12 license must achieve a passing score on the Communication and Literacy Skills test AND any relevant Pre K–12 subject matter test(s). Currently, the MTEL are the only tests that satisfy the communication and literacy skills and subject matter test requirements for a Massachusetts Pre-Kindergarten to Grade 12 license.

Further Information

Further information about Massachusetts Tests for Educator Licensure (MTEL) registration and test administration procedures is available in the current version of the Massachusetts Tests for Educator Licensure Registration Bulletin. Readers may view the registration bulletin via the Internet at **www.mtel.nesinc.com** or **www.doe.mass.edu/mtel** or obtain copies of the registration bulletin from schools of education at Massachusetts's colleges and universities, from the Massachusetts Department of Education, or from the Massachusetts Tests for Educator Licensure program.

About the MTEL English Exam

The English 07 exam is administered on all test dates, during the afternoon session only, from 1:15 pm to 6:00 pm. Performance is evaluated against an establish standard rather than in comparison to other candidates' performances. To provide consistency in reporting scores across tests, the scores are converted to a common scale. The converted scores are called scaled scores. The scaled score is a conversion of the number of points achieved on the test to a score in a range of 0 to 100, with a scaled score of 70 representing the qualifying, or passing, score. Candidates who do not achieve the passing score on a test may retake it at any of the subsequent test administrations at which that test is offered.

There are four domains covered on the exam:

- **Literature and Language:** 51% of the test weight—63-65 multiple choice questions
- **Rhetoric and Composition:** 17% of the test weight—20-22 multiple-choice questions
- **Reading theory, Research, and Instruction:** 12% of the test weight—14-16 multiple-choice questions
- **Integration of Knowledge and Understanding:** 20% of the test weight—2 open-response questions

The first three domains are composed of 100 multiple-choice questions (80% of the points available). The allocation of questions corresponds to the weight of that particular section. For example, the Rhetoric and Composition section, which carries 17% of the test weight, will have 17% of the multiple-choice questions. There is no penalty for guessing.

The Integration of Knowledge and Understanding section consists of two written response answers, approximately 150 to 300 words each. Each prompt will generally include contextual or background information that presents the subject of the written response question, as well as one or more specific directions or assignments that inform you of what you are expected to provide in your response. Each response takes an estimated 30 minutes to complete. Your response to each assignment will be evaluated based on the following criteria.

- **PURPOSE:** the extent to which the response achieves the purpose of the assignment

- **SUBJECT KNOWLEDGE:** appropriateness and accuracy in the application of subject knowledge

- **SUPPORT:** quality and relevance of supporting evidence

- **RATIONALE:** soundness of argument and degree of understanding of the subject area

Table of Contents

Great Study and Testing Tips!

What to study in order to prepare for the subject assessments is the focus of this study guide but equally important is *how* you study.

You can increase your chances of truly mastering the information by taking some simple but effective steps.

Study Tips:

1. Some foods aid the learning process. Foods such as milk, nuts, seeds, rice, and oats help your study efforts by releasing natural memory enhancers called CCKs (*cholecystokinin*) composed of *tryptophan*, *choline*, and *phenylalanine*. All of these chemicals enhance the neurotransmitters associated with memory. Before studying, try a light, protein-rich meal of eggs, turkey, and fish. All of these foods release the memory-enhancing chemicals. The better the connections, the more you comprehend.

Likewise, before you take a test, stick to a light snack of energy boosting and relaxing foods. A glass of milk, a piece of fruit, or some peanuts all release various memory-boosting chemicals and help you to relax and focus on the subject at hand.

2. Learn to take great notes. A by-product of our modern culture is that we have grown accustomed to getting our information in short doses (i.e. TV news sound-bytes or *USA Today*-style newspaper articles.)

Consequently, we've subconsciously trained ourselves to assimilate information better in neat little packages. If you scrawl notes all over the paper, you fragment the flow of the information. Strive for clarity. Newspapers use a standard format to achieve clarity. Your notes can be much clearer through use of proper formatting. A very effective format is called the Cornell Method.

Take a sheet of loose-leaf lined notebook paper and draw a line all the way down the paper about 1-2" from the left-hand edge.

Draw another line across the width of the paper about 1-2" up from the bottom. Repeat this process on the reverse side of the page.

Look at the highly effective result. You have ample room for notes, a left-hand margin for special emphasis items or inserting supplementary data from the textbook, a large area at the bottom for a brief summary, and a little rectangular space for just about anything you want.

3. <u>Get the concept, then the details</u>. Too often we focus on the details and don't gather an understanding of the concept. However, if you simply memorize only dates, places, or names, you may well miss the whole point of the subject.

A key way to understand things is to put them in your own words. If you are working from a textbook, automatically summarize each paragraph in your mind. If you are outlining text, don't simply copy the author's words.

Rephrase them in your own words. You remember your own thoughts and words much better than someone else's, and you subconsciously tend to associate the important details to the core concepts.

4. <u>Ask Why</u>. Pull apart written material paragraph by paragraph--and don't forget the captions under the illustrations.

Example: If the heading is "Stream Erosion," flip it around to read, "Why do streams erode?" Then answer the question.

If you train your mind to think in a series of questions and answers, not only will you learn more but you will also lessen the test anxiety because you are used to answering questions.

5. <u>Read for reinforcement and future needs</u>. Even if you only have ten minutes, put your notes or a book in your hand. Your mind is similar to a computer; you have to input data in order to have it processed. *By reading, you are creating the neural connections for future retrieval.* The more times you read something, the more you reinforce the learning of ideas.

Even if you don't fully understand something on the first pass, *your mind stores much of the material for later recall.*

6. <u>Relax to learn, so go into exile</u>. Our bodies respond to an inner clock called biorhythms. Burning the midnight oil works well for some people, but not everyone.

If possible, set aside a particular place to study that is free of distractions. Shut off the television, cell phone, and pager, and exile your friends and family during your study period.

If you really are bothered by silence, try background music. Light classical music at a low volume has been shown to aid in concentration. Music that evokes pleasant emotions without lyrics are highly suggested. Try just about anything by Mozart. It relaxes you.

7. <u>Use arrows, not highlighters</u>. At best, it's difficult to read a page full of yellow, pink, blue, and green streaks. Try staring at a neon sign for a while and you'll soon see how the horde of colors obscures the message.

A brief dash of color, an underline, and an arrow pointing to a particular passage are much clearer than a horde of highlighted words.

8. <u>Budget your study time</u>. Although you shouldn't ignore any of the material, *allocate your available study time in the same ratio that topics may appear on the test.*

Testing Tips:

1. Get smart, play dumb. Don't read anything into the question. Don't assume that the test writer is looking for something other than what is asked. Stick to the question as written and don't read extra things into it.

2. Read the question and all the choices *twice* before answering the question. You may miss something by not carefully reading and then rereading both the question and the answers.

If you really don't have a clue as to the right answer, leave it blank on the first time through. Go on to the other questions as they may provide a clue on how to answer the skipped questions.

If later on, you still can't answer the skipped ones . . . ***Guess.*** The only penalty for guessing is that you *might* get it wrong. Only one thing is certain; if you don't put anything down, you *will* get it wrong!

3. Turn the question into a statement. Look at the way the questions are worded. The syntax of the question usually provides a clue. Does it seem more familiar as a statement rather than as a question? Does it sound strange?

By turning a question into a statement, you may be able to spot if an answer sounds right, and it may also trigger memories of material you have read.

4. Look for hidden clues. It's actually very difficult to compose multiple-choice questions without giving away part of the answer in the options presented. In most multiple-choice questions you can often readily eliminate one or two of the potential answers. This leaves you with only two real possibilities and automatically your odds go to 50-50 for very little work.

5. Trust your instincts. For every fact that you have read, you subconsciously retain something of that knowledge. On questions that you aren't certain about, go with your basic instincts. **Your first impression on how to answer a question is usually correct.**

6. Mark your answers directly on the test booklet. Don't bother trying to fill in the optical scan sheet on the first pass through the test. *Just be very careful not to incorrectly mark your answers when you eventually transcribe them to the scan sheet.*

7. Watch the clock! You have a set amount of time to answer the questions. Don't get bogged down trying to answer a single question at the expense of 10 questions you can more readily answer.

DOMAIN I.   **LITERATURE AND LANGUAGE**

COMPETENCY 1.0   **UNDERSTAND AMERICAN LITERATURE FROM THE COLONIAL PERIOD THROUGH THE END OF THE NINETEENTH CENTURY**

Skill 1.1   **Understand the significance of writers, works, and movements in the development of American literature from the colonial period through the end of the nineteenth century.**

When compared to other countries, America has had a relatively brief history and thus a comparatively smaller canon of literature. Nevertheless, its fiction and nonfiction have the depth and breadth to tell the story of its people. To study American literature is to study also American history.

The Colonial Period

William Bradford's excerpts from *The Mayflower Compact* relate vividly the hardships of crossing the Atlantic in such a tiny vessel, the misery and suffering of the first winter, the approaches of the American Indians, the decimation of their ranks, and the establishment of the Bay Colony of Massachusetts.

Anne Bradstreet's poetry relates colonial New England life. From her journals, modern readers learn of the everyday life of the early settlers, the hardships of travel, and the responsibilities of different groups and individuals in the community, Early American literature also reveals the commercial and political adventures of the Cavaliers who came to the New World with King George's blessing.

> *"If ever two were one, then surely we.*
> *If ever man were loved by wife, then thee."*
> Read more about
> **Anne Bradstreet**
> http://www.annebradstreet.com/Default.htm

William Byrd's journal, *A History of the Dividing Line,* concerning his trek into the Dismal Swamp separating the Carolinian territories from Virginia and Maryland, makes quite lively reading. A privileged insider to the English Royal Court, Byrd, like other Southern Cavaliers, was given grants to pursue business ventures.

The Revolutionary Period

There were great orations such as Patrick Henry's *Speech to the Virginia House of Burgesses* (the "Give me liberty or give me death" speech) and George Washington's *Farewell to the Army of the Potomac.* Less memorable are Washington's inaugural addresses, which strike modern readers as lacking sufficient focus.

The *Declaration of Independence*, the brainchild predominantly of Thomas Jefferson (along with some prudent editing by Ben Franklin), is a prime example of neoclassical writing—balanced, well crafted, and focused.

Epistles include the exquisitely written, moving correspondence between John Adams and Abigail Adams. The poignancy of their separation—she in Boston, he in Philadelphia—is palpable and real.

The Romantic Period

Nathaniel Hawthorne and Herman Melville are the preeminent early American novelists, writing on subjects definitely regional, specific and American, yet sharing insights about human foibles, fears, loves, doubts, and triumphs.

Hawthorne's writings range from children's stories—his *Cricket on the Hearth* series to adult fare of dark, brooding short stories such as "Dr. Heidegger's Experiment," "The Devil and Tom Walker," and "Rappaccini's Daughter." His masterpiece, *The Scarlet Letter*, takes on the society of hypocritical Puritan New Englanders who ostensibly left England to establish religious freedom but who have become entrenched in judgmental finger wagging. They ostracize Hester and condemn her child, Pearl, as a child of Satan. Great love, sacrifice, loyalty, suffering, and related epiphanies add universality to this tale. *The House of the Seven Gables* deals with kept secrets, loneliness, and societal pariahs, but love ultimately triumphs.

Herman Melville's great opus, *Moby Dick*, follows a crazed Captain Ahab on his Homeric odyssey to conquer the great white whale that has outwitted him and his whaling crews time and again. The whale has even taken Ahab's leg and, according to Ahab, wants all of him. Melville recreates in painstaking detail and with insider knowledge the harsh life of a whaler out of New Bedford by way of Nantucket.

The Life and Works of Herman Melville
http://www.melville.org/

For those who don't want to learn about every guy rope or all parts of the whaler's rigging, Melville offers up the succinct tale of *Billy Budd* and his Christ-like sacrifice to the black-and-white maritime laws on the high seas. An accident results in the death of one of the ship's officers, a slug of a fellow, who has taken a dislike to the young, affable, shy Billy. Captain Vere must hang Billy for the death of Claggert but knows that this is not right. However, an example must be given to the rest of the crew so that discipline can be maintained.

Edgar Allan Poe creates a distinctly American version of romanticism with his 16-syllable lines in "The Raven," his classical "To Helen," and his Gothic "Annabelle Lee." The horror short story can be said to originate from Poe's pen. "The Tell - Tale Heart," "The Cask of Amontillado," "The Fall of the House of Usher," and "The Masque of the Red Death" are exemplary short stories. In addition, the genre of detective story emerges with Poe's "Murders in the Rue Morgue."

American Romanticism has its own offshoot in the transcendentalism of Ralph Waldo Emerson and Henry David Thoreau. Emerson wrote about transcending the complexities of life; Thoreau, who wanted to get to the marrow of life, immersed himself in nature at Walden Pond and wrote an inspiring autobiographical account of his sojourn, aptly titled *On Walden Pond*. Thoreau also wrote passionately regarding his objections to the interference of government imposed on the individual in "On the Duty of Civil Disobedience."

Emerson's elegantly-crafted essays and war poetry still validate several important universal truths. Probably most remembered for his address to Thoreau's Harvard graduating class, "The American Scholar," Emerson defined the qualities of hard work and intellectual spirit required of Americans in their growing nation.

Contemporary American Literature

Twentieth-century American writing can be divided into the following three genres: drama, fiction, and poetry.

American Drama: The greatest and most prolific of American playwrights include these playwrights:

- Eugene O'Neill- *Long Day's Journey into Night, Mourning Becomes Electra,* and *Desire Under the Elms*
- Arthur Miller- T*he Crucible, All My Sons,* and *Death of a Salesman*
- Tennessee Williams. *Cat on a Hot Tin Roof, The Glass Menagerie, and A Street Car Named Desire*
- Edward Albee- *Who's Afraid of Virginia Woolf? Three Tall Women, and A Delicate Balance*

American Fiction: The renowned American novelists of this century include these authors:

- Eudora Welty- *The Optimist's Daughter*
- John Updike- *Rabbit Run* and *Rabbit Redux*
- Sinclair Lewis- *Babbitt* and *Elmer Gantry*
- F. Scott Fitzgerald- *The Great Gatsby* and *Tender Is the Night*
- Ernest Hemingway- *A Farewell to Arms* and *For Whom the Bell Tolls*

- William Faulkner- *The Sound and the Fury* and *Absalom, Absalom*
- Bernard Malamud- *The Fixer* and *The Natural*

American Poetry: The poetry of the twentieth century is multifaceted, as represented by Edna St. Vincent Millay, Marianne Moore, Richard Wilbur, Langston Hughes, Maya Angelou, and Rita Dove. Above all others are the many-layered poems of Robert Frost. His New England motifs of snowy evenings, birches, apple picking, stonewall-mending, hired hands, and detailed nature studies relate universal truths in exquisite diction, polysyllabic words, and rare allusions to either mythology or the Bible.

American Indian Literature

The foundation of American Indian writing is found in story-telling, oratory, autobiographical and historical accounts of tribal village life, reverence for the environment, and the postulation that the earth with all of its beauty was given in trust, to be cared for and passed on to future generations.

Early American Indian Writers

- Hal Barland - *When the Legends Die*
- Geronimo (Apache; edited by Barrett and Turner)- *Geronimo: His Own Story: The Autobiography of a Great Patriot Warrior*
- C. Eastman & E. Eastman- *Wigwam Evenings: Sioux Folktales Retold*
- L. Riggs and Jace Weaver- *Cherokee Night* - drama

Twentieth-Century American Indian Writers

- V. Deloria- *Custer Died for your Sins* (Sioux)
- M. Dorris- *The Broken Cord: A Family's On-going Struggle with Fetal Alcohol Syndrome* (Modoc)
- Linda Hogan- *Mean Spirit* (Chickasaw) - poetry
- C.F. Taylor- *Native American Myths and Legends*
- Leslie Marmon Silko, *Garden in the Dunes* (Laguna Pueblo) – fiction/nonfiction

Afro-American Literature

The three phases of Afro-American literature can be broken down as follows:

- Oppression, slavery, and the re-construction of the post-Civil War/rural South
- Inner-city strife/single parenting, drug abuse, lack of educational opportunities, and work advancement controlled by biased and disinterested factions of society.

- Post-civil rights and the emergence of the Black movement focusing on biographical and autobiographical black heroes and their contribution to Black and American culture.

Pre-Civil War
Memoirs and Poems - Phyllis Wheatley-
Classic Slave Narratives, ed. Henry Louis Gates, Jr.

Post-Civil War and Reconstruction
Frederick Douglass -*Narrative of the Life of Frederick Douglass, An American Slave*
W.E.B. Du Bois-*The Suppression of the African Slave Trade*
-Ernest J. Gaines- *The Autobiography of Miss Jane Pittman*

Twentieth Century to Present
Jean Toomer - *Cane*
Langston Hughes- *I, Too, Sing America*
Richard Wright- *White Man Listen!* and *Native Son*
Mary McLeod Bethune- *Voice of Black Hope*
Ralph Ellison – *Invisible Man*
Gwendolyn Brooks- *A Street in Bronzeville*
Lorraine Hansberry- *A Raisin in the Sun*
Maya Angelou- *I Know Why the Caged Bird Sings*
James Baldwin- *Go Tell It on the Mountain*
Alex Haley- *Roots*
James Haskins- *Diary of a Harlem Schoolteacher, Black Music in America: A History Through Its People*
Nathan Irving Huggins- *Black Odyssey, Harlem Renaissance*
Alice Childress- *A Hero Ain't Nothin' But a Sandwich*
August Wilson – *Fences*

Some works about Black America not written by blacks

Uncle Tom's Cabin- Harriet Beecher Stowe
Nicholas Lemann- *The Promised Land*
Harper Lee -*To Kill a Mockingbird*
*Sounder (*Newberry Medal*)* - William H. Armstrong
Durango Street - Frank Bonham

Latino/a Literature

In the field of literature, we have two new expanding areas, Latino/a and feminist writers. These authors write to retain cultural heritage, share their people's struggle for recognition, independence, and survival, and express their hopes for the future.

Latino/Latina Writers

Lora Dee Cervantes *The First Quartet*
Sandra Cisneros - *The House on Mango Street* and short story collections
Gary Soto - *Tale of Sunlight*
Julia Alvarez - *How the Garcia Girls Lost Their Accents*
Rudolfo Anaya – *Bless Me, Ultima*
Ana Castilla - *So Far From God*
Richard Rodriguez – *Hunger of Memory*

Gabriel Garcia Marquez (Colombian) - *One Hundred Years of Solitude*
A. López Muñoz (Spanish) - *Programas Para Días Especiales*
Pablo Neruda (Chilean) - Nobel Prize winner - Collections of poetry

Feminist / Gender-Concern Literature Written by Women in the United States

American women authors have contributed notably to literature in all genres. Edith Wharton's *Ethan Frome* is a heartbreaking tale of lack of communication, lack of funds, the unrelenting cold of the Massachusetts winter, and a toboggan ride which gnarls Ethan and Mattie just like the old tree which they smash into. The *Age of Innocence*, in contrast to *Ethan Frome*, is set in the upper echelons of fin-de-siècle New York and explores marriage with stifling social protocols.

Willa Cather's work moves the reader to the prairies of Nebraska and the harsh eking-out of existence by the immigrant families who choose to stay there and farm. Her most acclaimed works include *My Antonia* and *Death Comes for the Archbishop,* which is set in New Mexican Territory.

Kate Chopin's regionalism and local color takes her readers to the upper crust Creole society of New Orleans and resort isles off the Louisiana coast. "The Story of an Hour" is lauded as one of the greatest of all short stories. Her feminist liberation novel *The Awakening* is still hotly debated.

Eudora Welty's regionalism and dialect shine in her short stories of rural Mississippi, especially in "The Worn Path."

Modern black female writers who explore the world of feminist/gender issues as well as class prohibitions are Zora Neale Hurston (*Their Eyes Were Watching God*), Alice Walker (*The Color Purple*), and Toni Morrison (*Beloved, Jazz, Song of Solomon*).

Feminists
Louisa May Alcott, *Little Women*
Betty Friedan, *Feminine Mystique* and *The Second Stage*
Elizabeth Janeway, *Man's World, Woman's Place: A Study in Social Mythology*
Adrienne Rich, *Of Woman Born: Motherhood As Experience and Institution* and *Driving into the Wreck*

Skill 1.2   **Knowledge of the changes in literary form and style in American literature**

See Skill 1.3.

Skill 1.3   **Identify the characteristics of major literary periods in American literature (Colonial, Revolutionary, Romantic, Renaissance, Realism, Civil War, post–Civil War).**

American literature is marked by a number of clearly identifiable periods. While these stand alone, they can also be useful as histories across the curriculum.

Native American Works from Various Tribes

These works were originally part of a vast oral tradition that spanned most of continental America from as far back as before the fifteenth century.

Characteristics of native Indian literature include
- Reverence for and awe of nature.
- The interconnectedness of the elements in the life cycle.

Themes of Indian literature often reflect
- The hardiness of the native body and soul.
- Remorse for the destruction of their way of life.
- The genocide of many tribes by the encroaching settlement and Manifest Destiny policies of the U. S. government.

The Colonial Period in both New England and the South

Stylistically, early colonists' writings were neo-classical, emphasizing order, balance, clarity, and reason. Oftentimes schooled in England, their writing and speaking were still decidedly British even as their thinking became entirely American.

Early American literature reveals the lives and experiences of the New England expatriates who left England to find religious freedom.

The Revolutionary Period contains nonfiction genres: essay, pamphlet, speech, famous document, and epistle.

Major Writers and Works of the Revolutionary Period

Thomas Paine's pamphlet, *Common Sense*, though written by a recently transplanted Englishman, spoke to the American patriots' common sense in dealing with the issues in the cause of freedom.

Other contributions are Benjamin Franklin's essays from *Poor Richard's Almanac* and satires such as "How to Reduce a Great Empire to a Small One" and "A Letter to Madame Gout."

The Romantic Period

Early American folktales and the emergence of a distinctly American writing, not just a stepchild to English forms, constitute the next period.

Washington Irving's characters, Icabod Crane and Rip Van Winkle, represent a uniquely American folklore devoid of English influences. The characters are indelibly marked by their environment and

> Find more sites about
> **American Romanticism**
> http://guweb2.gonzaga.edu/faculty/campbell/
> enl311/romanticism.htm

the superstitions of the New Englander. The early American writings of James Fennimore Cooper and his *Leatherstocking Tales* provide readers a window into their uniquely American world through the stirring accounts of drums along the Mohawk, the French and Indian Wars, the futile British defense of Fort William Henry and the brutalities of this period. Natty Bumppo, Chingachgook, Uncas, and Magua are unforgettable characters that reflect the American spirit in thought and action.

The poetry of Fireside Poets—James Russell Lowell, Oliver Wendell Holmes, Henry Wadsworth Longfellow, and John Greenleaf Whittier— was recited by American families and read in the long New England winters. In "The Courtin'," Lowell used Yankee dialect to tell the story. Spellbinding epics by Longfellow (such as *Hiawatha*, *The Courtship of Miles Standish*, and *Evangeline)* told of adversity, sorrow, and ultimate happiness in a uniquely American fashion. "Snowbound" by Whittier relates the story of a captive family isolated by a blizzard, stressing family closeness.

The Transition between Romanticism and Realism

During this period such legendary figures as Paul Bunyan and Pecos Bill rose from the oral tradition. Anonymous storytellers around campfires told tales of a huge lumberman and his giant blue ox, Babe, whose adventures were explanations of natural phenomena like those of footprints filled with rainwater becoming the Great Lakes. Or the whirling-dervish speed of Pecos Bill explained the tornadoes of the Southwest. Like ancient peoples, finding reasons for the happenings in their lives, these American pioneer storytellers created a mythology appropriate to the vast reaches of the unsettled frontier.

The Realistic Period

The late nineteenth century saw a reaction against the tendency of romantic writers to look at the world through rose-colored glasses. Writers including Frank Norris (*The Pit*) and Upton Sinclair (*The Jungle*) used their novels to decry conditions for workers in slaughterhouses and wheat mills.

Upton Sinclair
http://www.online-literature.com/upton_sinclair/

In *The Red Badge of Courage*, Stephen Crane wrote of the daily sufferings of the common soldier in the Civil War. Realistic writers wrote of common, ordinary people and events using realistic detail to reveal the harsh realities of life. They broached taboos by creating protagonists whose environments often destroyed them. Romantic writers would have only protagonists whose indomitable wills helped them rise above adversity. Crane's *Maggie: A Girl of the Streets* deals with a young woman forced into prostitution to survive. In "The Occurrence at Owl Creek Bridge," Ambrose Bierce relates the unfortunate hanging of a Confederate soldier.

Short stories such as Bret Harte's "The Outcasts of Poker Flat" and Jack London's "To Build a Fire," deal with unfortunate people whose luck in life has run out. Many writers, sub-classified as naturalists, believed that man was subject to a fate over which he had no control.

The Modern Era
The twentieth century American writing can be classified into three basic genres: drama, fiction, and poetry.

Skill 1.4 **Understand the historical, social, and cultural contexts of American literature from the colonial period through the end of the nineteenth century.**

Local Color

Local color is defined as the presenting of the peculiarities of a particular locality and its inhabitants. This genre began to be seen primarily after the Civil War although there were certainly precursors such as Washington Irving and his depiction of life in the Catskill Mountains of New

> Read more about
> **Regional Realism**
> http://www.learner.org/amerpass/
> unit08/usingvideo.html

York. However, the local colorist movement is generally considered to have begun in 1865, when humor began to permeate the writing of those who were focusing on a particular region of the country.

Samuel L. Clemens (Mark Twain) is best known for his humorous works such as "The Notorious Jumping Frog of Calaveras County." The country had just emerged from its "long night of the soul," a time when death, despair, and disaster had preoccupied the nation for almost five years. It's no wonder that the artists sought to relieve the grief and pain and lift spirits, nor is it surprising that their efforts brought such a strong response. Mark Twain is generally considered to be not only one of America's funniest writers but also one who also wrote great and enduring fiction.

Other examples of local colorists are George Washington Cable, Joel Chandler Harris, Bret Harte, Sarah Orne Jewett, and Harriet Beecher Stowe.

Slavery

The best-known of the early writers who used fiction as a political statement about slavery is Harriet Beecher Stowe, author of *Uncle Tom's Cabin*. This was her first novel, and it was published first as a serial in 1851, then as a book in 1852. This antislavery book infuriated Southerners. However, Stowe herself had been angered by the 1850 Fugitive Slave Law that made it legal to indict those who assisted runaway slaves. It also took away rights not only of the runaways but also of free slaves. She intended to generate a protest of the law and slavery. It was the first effort to present the lives of slaves from their standpoint.

The novel is about three slaves, Tom, Eliza, and George who are together in Kentucky. Eliza and George are married to each other but have different masters. They successfully escape with their little boy, but Tom does not. Although he has a wife and children, he is sold, ending up finally with the monstrous Simon Legree, where he dies at last.

Stowe cleverly used depictions of motherhood and Christianity to stir her readers. When President Lincoln finally met her, he told her it was her book that started the war.

Many writers used the printed word to protest slavery:
- Frederick Douglass
- William Lloyd Garrison
- Benjamin Lay, a Quaker
- Jonathan Edwards, Connecticut theologian
- Susan B. Anthony

Immigration

Immigration has been a popular topic for literature from the time of the Louisiana Purchase in 1804. The recent *Undaunted Courage* by Stephen E. Ambrose is ostensibly the autobiography of Meriwether Lewis but is actually a recounting of the Lewis and Clark expedition. Presented as a scientific expedition by President Jefferson, the expedition was actually intended to provide maps and information for the opening up of the west. A well-known novel of the settling of the west by immigrants from other countries is *Giants in the Earth* by Ole Edvart Rolvaag, himself a descendant of immigrants.

Skill 1.5   Identify significant genres and themes in American literature from the colonial period through the end of the nineteenth century.

Walt Whitman's poetry was inspired, more often than not, by the Civil War. He is America's greatest romantic poet, and many of his poems are related to and come directly from the conflict between the Northern and Southern states. This is not to say that the war was the only influence; he wrote many poems on topics that are not directly related to it. His major work, *Leaves of Grass,* was revised nine times, the last in 1892 shortly before he died. He was an innovator, using sophisticated linguistic devices previously unexplored. Even though he dealt with a vast, panoramic vision, his style has a personal and immediate effect on readers.

He was born in 1819 on Long Island in New York, a time of great patriotism for the new nation; however, the conflict that presented a serious threat to its survival, the Civil War, became the subject matter for most of his creative output. He began his writing career with newspaper articles and eventually wrote short stories that were published in newspapers. His unconventional techniques were his own creation, and, in *Leaves of Grass,* he intended to speak for all Americans. Whitman is known as the "father of free verse."

He worked as a volunteer in hospitals to help care for soldiers and was deeply affected by first-hand experience with the horrors of war. Some considered his poetry indecent, and he was both praised and vilified during his lifetime. He died in 1892 of tuberculosis.

Some Themes
- Imagination vs. Scientific Process
- Individualism

Emily Dickinson (1830-1886) has been called the "myth of Amherst" because so little is known of her. Her father's stern, puritanical control of his family played a pivotal role in the poetry that his daughter eventually wrote. Although he was severe and controlling, he saw that his daughters received a strong education. Dickinson attended Amherst Academy and then Mount Holyoke Female Seminary. She obtained a copy of Emerson's poems in 1850 and began to develop her own beliefs regarding religion and the severe God that her father represented.

Only a few of her poems were published during her lifetime, and she was unknown until after her death. After she withdrew from school, she became more and more reclusive and after the death of her father in 1874, she never again left her home. She died of Bright's disease in 1886. Her sister Lavinia found roughly 2,000 poems on small pieces of paper, which were published in several editions. The first full three-volume edition was released in 1955. She has come to be known for her superb use of concrete language and imagery to express and evoke abstract issues. Most people have a favorite Dickinson poem.

Some Themes:
- Sanity/insanity
- Doubt
- Death
- Individuality
- Defiance
- Feminism

Willa Cather grew up on the western plains in Nebraska, and much of her best fiction focuses on the pioneering period in that part of the country. She was born in Virginia in 1873 on her family's farm, but in 1884, the family moved to Nebraska where other relatives had settled. Much of the lore that is the basis of her stories came from her visits with immigrant farm women around Red Cloud, where the family eventually made their home.

Willa Cather Foundation
http://www.willacather.org/

When she was sixteen, she enrolled at the University of Nebraska in Lincoln where an essay in her English class was favorably accepted and she began to support herself as a journalist.

She moved to Pittsburgh and was working as a writer and editor when she decided that she wanted to teach school. Even so, she continued to develop her writing career. On a trip back to Nebraska, she witnessed a wheat harvest, which triggered her motive for writing about the pioneer period of American history.

Some Themes
- The American Dream
- Prejudice
- Coming of age
- Nostalgia

Herman Melville was born in 1819 and grew up in upper class New York neighborhoods. His mother was a strict Calvinist Presbyterian and had strong views regarding proper behavior. Melville tended to be a rebellious sort and to some extent his conflicts regarding his mother's viewpoints were never resolved. When Melville was eleven years old, his father's business failed, and he died shortly afterward. Melville tried working in business for a while but soon decided he wanted to go to sea.

Working on ships and traveling, he began to write nonfictional pieces about his experiences. In July 1851, he wrote his most famous work, *Moby Dick*. Before he died, he wrote poems and another well-known novel, *Billy Budd*, which was not published until 1924. Just as he began to write *Moby Dick*, he became friends with Nathaniel Hawthorne, who happened to be his neighbor. Hawthorne's works and friendship became an important influence on his writing.

In *Moby Dick*, the style is indicative of the reportorial writing of the earlier period; however, it is far more than that. It is seen as a great American epic, even though it is not poetry. It was not successful while its author was alive. Its success came much later.

Some Themes
- Man in conflict with the natural world
- Religion and God's role in the universe
- Good and evil
- Cause and effect
- Duty
- Conscience

Skill 1.6 **Identify a range of American authors (John Winthrop, Anne Bradstreet, Jonathan Edwards, Phillis Wheatley, James Fenimore Cooper, Frederick Douglass, Thomas Jefferson, Edgar Allan Poe, Abraham Lincoln, Nathaniel Hawthorne, Ralph Waldo Emerson, Henry David Thoreau, Walt Whitman, Herman Melville, Emily Dickinson, Mark Twain, Stephen Crane, Harriet Beecher Stowe, Kate Chopin, Henry James), their representative works and themes, and their significance in the development of American literature from the colonial period through the end of the nineteenth century.**

The men and women whose writings in turn reflected and shaped the development and direction of American literature from the days of the colonists to the era of the bustling industrialists are many and diverse.

Their voices, recorded on the printed page, tell stories of everyday life, of tragedy and triumph, of progress and failure, and of the never-ending struggle to be heard and to matter in the face of stark prejudices and amidst the chaos of overwhelming change.

One of the first of these voices belonged to **Anne Bradstreet** (1612-1672). In 1630, at the age of 18, Bradstreet left England with her new husband to settle in the Massachusetts Bay Colony. As Puritans, Bradstreet and her family had experienced persecution in England, but there they also had known a comfortable life.

As a child, Bradstreet had had the privilege of tutors and access to her father's extensive library. Her poetry reflects her knowledge and appreciation of the Latin and Greek classics and of the legacy of the British poets. While most Colonial writings were polemics of a political and/or religious nature, Bradstreet's writings stand out as being uniquely personal. Her lyric poetry, such as "A Letter to Her Husband, Absent Upon Public Employment," "For Deliverance from a Fever," and "Here Follow Some Verses upon the Burning of Our House July 10th, 1666. Copied out of a Loose Paper," describes her religion and politics in terms of her family and home. Running through Bradstreet's work can be found the iron will and strength of the settlers and of the emerging American woman who knew her worth:

"I am obnoxious to each carping tongue
Who says my hand a needle better fits;
...Let Greeks be Greeks, and women what they are"
("The Prologue")

Recognized by twentieth-century poet Adrienne Rich as the author of the "first good poems in America," Bradstreet, Rich notes, wrote her poetry "while rearing eight children, lying frequently sick, [and] keeping house at the edge of the wilderness."

Among the eighteenth century's most powerful and influential voices is **Jonathan Edwards** (1703-1758). Considered one of America's first philosophers, Edwards, a Yale graduate, was the son and grandson of New England pastors. A theologian and Congregational clergyman in his own right, Edwards was a leading figure in the religious revival of the 1740s, known as the "Great Awakening." This evangelical movement was in part a response to the growing inclination of the enterprising colonists to leave behind the rigors of Puritanism and embrace theologies that downplayed original sin and exalted an individual's free will. Although the revival was short-lived, the intellectual rigor and vast scope of Edwards' theological vision, recorded in his many sermons and writings, including "Freedom of the Will" and "Christian Doctrine of Original Sin Defended," stand as benchmarks in the development of the American mind.

Abraham Lincoln (1809-1865), the sixteenth president of the United States, remains one of America's most intriguing and revered figures. As the Chief of State who presided over the war to preserve the Union, Lincoln's place in history is secure, yet his legacy goes far beyond his statesmanship in the Civil War.

The writings of Lincoln, including his speeches, debates, and letters, remain unsurpassed for their clarity, simplicity, humility, power, and beauty. Among his most memorable works is the "Gettysburg Address," which begins, "Fourscore and seven years ago" and ends "that this nation, under God, shall have a new birth of freedom; and that government of the people, for the people, and by the people shall not perish from the earth."

The speech, given on November 19, 1863, was part of a dedication ceremony on the site of the Union victory in July, which had cost the lives of several thousand soldiers, North and South. Lincoln's address followed a speech by Edward Everett, a former president of Harvard and leading orator of the day. Everett's speech had lasted nearly two hours. Lincoln then stood and delivered his speech in less than three minutes. Everett was to write Lincoln later, "I should be glad if I could flatter myself that I came as near to the central idea of the occasion in two hours as you did in two minutes."

Read more of
Lincoln's Works at
http://www.thelast
fullmeasure.com/

Lincoln's wisdom, compassion, and sense of destiny were also evident in his second inaugural address, delivered on March 4, 1865, one month before his death by assassination. While Union victory was now inevitable, Lincoln chose against a celebratory tone, opting instead for a conciliatory voice. He ended his second inaugural address with what have become some of the most famous lines in American writings: "With malice toward none, with charity for all, with firmness in the right as God gives us to see the right, let us strive on to finish the work we are in, to bind up the nation's wounds, to care for him who shall have borne the battle and for his widow and his orphan—to do all which may achieve and cherish a just and lasting peace among ourselves and with all nations."

The poetry of **Walt Whitman** (1819-1892) constituted a break from traditional poetry in that it was written in free verse, without rhyme or meter. This

unconventional style was inspired by Whitman's adherence to Ralph Waldo Emerson's transcendental movement of the day and by his desire to capture the spirit and sound of the men and women of the fields and streets of this bustling democracy.

These were the people Whitman celebrated in his most famous work, *Leaves of Grass,* a collection of images and poems that he first published in 1855 and continued to revise until his death in 1892. For its first publication, Whitman, an experienced newspaper journalist, not only wrote and set type for *Leaves of Grass,* but he wrote and published a number of enthusiastic, albeit, anonymous reviews of the work. Other critics were less enthusiastic, but among the few admirers was Emerson who wrote to Whitman that *Leaves of Grass* was "the most extraordinary piece of wit and wisdom that America has yet produced." Emerson

Learn more about
Walt Whitman at
http://web.csustan.edu/eng
lish/

qualified those sentiments later, writing to a friend saying that *Leaves of Grass* was "a nondescript monster which yet had terrible eyes and buffalo strength, and was indisputably American."

In this "indisputably American" piece, Whitman had abandoned the formal vocabulary of traditional literary works, putting into print the language of the people, using such phrases and words as "I recken," "duds," and "folks."

In addition to his career as a journalist, Whitman also held several minor governmental posts, and served as a hospital volunteer during the Civil War. An ardent admirer of Abraham Lincoln, Whitman memorialized the great man's death in 1865 with "When Lilacs last in the Dooryard Bloom'd," a poem that many consider to be Whitman's finest work.

Read more about **Stephen Crane** at http://www.csustan. edu/english/reuben/ pal/

Like Whitman, **Stephen Crane** (1871-1900) was a newspaper journalist; unlike Whitman, Crane's life ended early, dying at age 29 of tuberculosis. In spite of his short career, Crane wrote poetry and several novels, including *Maggie: A Girl of the Streets* (1892) and *Wounds in the Rain* (1900). His most important work, however, is the Civil War novel, *Red Badge of Courage* (1895). In this work, Crane's vivid use of imagery and symbolism focuses on the common man, not as Whitman did in a celebration of everyday life, but as a study of the common man faced with uncommon circumstances and in the grip of the forces of nature.

For Crane, whom critics have dubbed more of an impressionist than a naturalist, the story was in confrontation, not in the unfolding and final resolution of a particular plot. The freshness of this style, considered avant-garde in his day, places Crane at a pivotal point in the development of American literature.

COMPETENCY 2.0   **UNDERSTAND AMERICAN LITERATURE FROM THE TWENTIETH CENTURY TO THE PRESENT**

Skill 2.1   **Understand the characteristics of diverse works of American fiction, nonfiction, poetry, and drama from the early twentieth century to the present.**

See Skill 1.1.

Skill 2.2   **Understand the historical, social, and cultural contexts from which modern and contemporary American literature emerged.**

Civil Rights

Many of the abolitionists were also early crusaders for civil rights. However, the 1960s movement focused attention on the plight of the people who had been "freed" by the Civil War in ways that brought about long overdue changes in the opportunities and rights of African Americans.

David Halberstam, who had been a reporter in Nashville at the time of the sit-ins by eight young black college students that initiated the revolution, wrote *The Children*, published in 1998 by Random House, for the purpose of reminding Americans of their courage, suffering, and achievements. Congressman John Lewis, Fifth District, Georgia, was one of those eight young men who has gone on to a life of public service. Halberstam records that when older black ministers tried to persuade these young people not to pursue their protest, John Lewis responded: "If not us, then who? If not now, then when?"

Some examples of protest literature:

- Langston Hughes, *Fight for Freedom: The Story of the NAACP*
- James Baldwin, *Blues for Mister Charlie*
- Martin Luther King, *Where Do We Go from Here?*
- Eldridge Cleaver, *Soul on Ice*
- Malcolm X, *The Autobiography of Malcolm X*
- Stokely Carmichael and Charles V. Hamilton, *Black Power*
- Leroi Jones, *Home*

Vietnam

An America that was already divided over the civil rights movement faced even greater divisions over the war in Vietnam. Those who were in favor of the war and who opposed withdrawal saw it as the major front in the war against communism. Those who opposed the war and who favored withdrawal of the troops believed that it would not serve to defeat communism and was a quagmire.

Though set in the last years of World War II, *Catch-22* by Joseph Heller was a popular antiwar novel that became a successful movie of the time.

Authors Take Sides on Vietnam, edited by Cecil Woolf and John Bagguley is a collection of essays by 168 well-known authors throughout the world. *Where is Vietnam?* edited by Walter Lowenfels consists of 92 poems about the war.

Many writers were publishing works for and against the war, but the genre that had the most impact was rock music. Bob Dylan was an example of the musicians of the time. His music represented the hippie aesthetic and brilliant, swirling colors and hallucinogenic imagery and created a style that came to be called psychedelic. Some other bands that originated during this time and became well-known for music about the Vietnam War are the Grateful Dead, Jefferson Airplane, Big Brother & the Holding Company, and Sly and the Family Stone. In England, the movement attracted the Beatles and the Rolling Stones.

Immigration

As one of the major movements during the twentieth century, immigration swelled the population, and literature documented the resultant changes in the American culture.

John Steinbeck's *Cannery Row* and *Tortilla Flats* glorify the lives of Mexican migrants in California. Amy Tan's *The Joy Luck Club* deals with the problems faced by Chinese immigrants.

Leon Uris' *Exodus* deals with the social history that led to the founding of the modern state of Israel. It was published in 1958, only a short time after the Holocaust. It also deals with attempts of concentration camp survivors to get to the land that has become the new Israel. In many ways, it is the quintessential work on immigration—causes and effects.

Skill 2.3   **Identify significant genres and themes in modern and contemporary American literature.**

One way to study the significant genres of contemporary literature is to examine the works of its representative authors.

Gwendolyn Brooks was the first African American to receive a Pulitzer Prize for poetry with her acute images of African Americans in the cities of America. Born in 1917 to a schoolteacher and a janitor, she grew up in Chicago. She was named poet laureate of Illinois in 1978 and was the first black woman honorary fellow of the Modern Language Association. Her family was close-knit, and she tended to spend her time reading when she was a child.

She began writing poems when she was very young. She has also had a successful teaching career at several universities including City University of New York where she was Distinguished Professor. Brooks was writing about the experience of being black long before it became the mainstream. She underwent an evolution in subject matter and thinking about being black as a result of the movement of the sixties toward the validity of African Americans. She died of cancer in 2000. She was eighty-three years old.

Learn more about
Gwendolyn Brooks
http://www.english.uiuc.edu/maps/
poets/a_f/brooks/brooks.htm

Some Themes:

- Poverty and racism
- Self-respect
- Heritage
- Community
- Family
- Black unity
- The basic humanness in everyone
- Black solidarity
- Pride

Leslie Marmon Silko is a Laguna Indian of mixed ancestry that includes Cherokee, German, English, Mexican, and Pueblo. Several remarkable women were in her life--grandmothers and aunts who taught her the traditions and stories of the pueblo. At the same time, her father's role in his tribe also made her aware of the abuses her people had experienced at the hands of the government. The major issue was the land that had been stolen from her people. She believed that she could change things by writing about them.

Some Themes:
- Evil
- Reciprocity
- Individual/Community
- Native American traditions
- Native American religion
- Mixed breeds
- Scapegoats, Racism, Prejudice

Maxine Hong Kingston's parents were Chinese immigrants who lived in Stockton, California. Her fiction is highly autobiographical, and she weaves Chinese myths and fictionalized history with the aim of exploring the conflicts between cultures faced by Chinese-Americans. Her writing exposes the ordeals of the Chinese immigrants who were so exploited by American companies, particularly railroad and agriculture industries. She also explores relationships within the Chinese families, particularly between parents who were born in China and children who were born in America. In a 1980 *New York Times Book Review* interview, she said, "What I am doing in this new book [*China Men*] is churning America."

Some Themes:
- Discovery
- The American Dream
- Male/Female roles
- Metamorphosis
- Enforced muteness
- Vocal expression
- Family

Richard Wright was the grandson of slaves and grew up in a time when the lives of African-Americans tended to be very grim. His response to life lived so close to those who had recently risen from bondage permeates his writing.

His writing went through many changes just as his response to the special reality of life as a black person in a white-dominated world went through many changes. He was influenced early by the Russian writer Maxim Gorky, whose own life experience had similarities to Wright's own. Later, another Russian writer, Fyodor Dostoevsky, heavily influenced him as his view changed to universal humanism.

Survival for many blacks and black communities required conformity to whatever white people demanded, and Wright rejected that. He felt profoundly alienated and felt that his individuality had been wounded. He became a "proletarian revolutionary artist" in the earliest years of his career.

The American Communist Party nabbed him as their most illustrious recruit to the newly-established literary standards of proletarian realism. He rejected the "conspicuous ornamentation" of institutions imposed by segregation such as the Harlem Renaissance. He felt that consciousness must draw its strength from the lore of a great people, his own. He sought to integrate the progressive aspects of the folk culture of the African-Americans into a collective myth that would promote a revolutionary approach to reality.

He left the Communist Party in 1944, largely as a result of his own evolution, led in part when white Communists in New York City would not help get him a place to live because of his race. His *Uncle Tom's Children* is fiction about lynching and other violence suffered by American blacks. *Black Boy*, an autobiographical account of his childhood and young manhood, appeared in 1945. Wright settled in Paris as a permanent expatriate shortly after its publication. His first novel *Native Son* is a good example of the naturalist novel where the environment creates the individual's actions by societal expectations.

Some Themes:
- The environment of the South is too small to nourish human beings, especially African-Americans
- Rejection of black militancy
- Violent, battered childhood and victorious adulthood
- Suffocation of instinct and stifling of potential
- Mature reminiscences of a battered childhood
- Black mother's protective nurture and the trauma of an absent or impotent father

His technique and style are not as important as the impact his ideas and attitudes have had on American life. He set out to portray African-Americans to white readers in such a way that the myth of the uncomplaining, comic, obsequious black man might be replaced.

Skill 2.4 **Identify a range of American authors (Charlotte Perkins Gilman, Gertrude Stein, Edith Wharton, Willa Cather, T. S. Eliot, Countee Cullen, William Faulkner, Langston Hughes, Eugene O'Neill, Gwendolyn Brooks, Ernest Hemingway, Saul Bellow, Arthur Miller, Lillian Hellman, James Baldwin, Vladimir Nabokov, N. Scott Momaday, Toni Morrison, Maya Angelou, Rita Dove, Leslie Marmon Silko, Louise Erdrich, Rudolfo Anaya, Amy Tan), their representative works and themes, and their significance in the development of American literature in the twentieth and twenty-first centuries.**

A leading dramatist of the early twentieth century, **Eugene O'Neill** (1888-1953) freely experimented with many forms of drama, drawing on his own dysfunctional family life and experiences as a merchant marine for inspiration. Born in New York City's theater district to an alcoholic, mediocre actor and a devout Catholic mother whose illness led her to a morphine addiction, O'Neill's struggle to accept and escape his past fueled some of his greatest plays.

Writing at a time when American theater was in its infancy, O'Neill used a variety of techniques, including dramatic monologue, as in *Emperor Jones* (1920) and expressionism as in *The Great God Brown* in which the actors wear masks to indicate the disconnect between the inner and outer being. Another play, *Strange Interlude*, is unique because of its length of seven hours.

A recurring theme in all of O'Neill's plays is a deep sense of tragedy, most often expressed in intense, often twisted, and ultimately inescapable family relations. In this vein is one of O'Neill's greatest and most closely autobiographical plays, *Long Day's Journey into Night*. Although completed in 1941, O'Neill would not allow it to be produced until after his death. O'Neill won Pulitzer prizes for four of his plays: *Beyond the Horizon* (1920), *Anna Christie* (1921), *Strange Interlude* (1928), and, posthumously, *Long Day's Journey into Night* (1957). In 1936, O'Neill also was awarded the Nobel Prize in Literature. The body of his work served as a blueprint for future American playwrights as they delved deeply into their psyches and backgrounds for dramatic inspiration.

Born in Oxford, Mississippi, **William Faulkner** (1897-1962) is regarded as one of the great American voices of the twentieth century, and for his work, he received the Nobel Prize for Literature in 1949.

Check out the
**William Faulkner
Society** at
http://www.olemiss
.edu/depts/english/
faulkner/

Faulkner emerged onto the literary scene in the 1920s, writing some of his best known and most highly acclaimed works between 1929 and 1940: *The Sound and the Fury* (1929), *As I Lay Dying* (1930), *Light in August* (1932), *Absalom, Absalom!* (1936), and *The Unvanquished* (1938). In these novels, Faulkner experiments in literature by turning conventional concepts of time, narrations, and dialogue into fluid entities. Dialogues consist of stream-of-consciousness thoughts, while the telling of the story shifts from person to person, and from present to past and back again. Although such devices may at times make his stories difficult to read and to follow, they also shift the reader's prism on reality, allowing an examination from new perspectives on the raw underpinnings of life, with all its tragedy, sorrow, meanness, and beauty. In addition to his novels, Faulkner wrote numerous short stories, as well as a number of screenplays for Hollywood.

A notable twentieth-century playwright, **Lillian Hellman** (1905-1984) was born in New Orleans, Louisiana, and as a child she moved back and forth between Louisiana and New York City with her family. These travels gave the budding playwright exposure to some of the country's most diverse and fascinating cultures. Hellman's experiences with the eccentric characters of her childhood travels attracted her to the Bohemian lifestyle of the 1920s and eventually resulted in a move to Hollywood, where she met like-minded souls and the man with whom she maintained a life-long relationship, mystery-writer, Dashiell Hammet.

Hammet recognized Hellman's talent and strongly encouraged her to write her own plays. With his support and encouragement, she wrote and achieved almost instant notoriety with her first play, *The Children's Hour*, (1936) which tells the tale of two female boarding school teachers who are falsely accused of being lesbians by one of their privileged students. The accusation culminates in the suicide of one of the teachers. The play's unorthodox subject matter did not keep it from being huge hit on Broadway, as it was a gripping, and emotional story--not of sexual orientation but of the abuse of power—an issue not unfamiliar to Hellman.

An outspoken leftist, Hellman helped to establish a writer's union in Hollywood in the 1920s, and in 1952, she was called in front of the House Un-American Committee and asked to "name names" of Communists and possible Communists. Hellman refused, saying in part, "I cannot and will not cut my conscience to fit this year's fashions." For her refusal to cooperate, Hellman was blacklisted in Hollywood for many years. For Hellman, that was a small price to pay to keep her integrity intact. Hellman's life is the chronicle of an independent and successful woman who wrote well and powerfully, who was not afraid to speak her mind, and who was front and center in the artistic scene of her day.

She captured all of this in her memoirs, *An Unfinished Woman* (1969), a work that has been associated with the beginnings of the feminist movement. Other works by Hellman include *Little Foxes* (1939), *Watch on the Rhine* (1940), and *Toys in the Attic* (1959).

Learn more about **James Baldwin** at http://aalbc.com/authors/james.htm

Dealing with "anguish, despair, and beauty" is what novelist **James Baldwin** (1924-1987) has stated turned him into a writer. The son of a strict African-American preacher in New York City's Harlem, Baldwin followed in his father's footsteps and began preaching at the age of 14. That is where he found his voice and witnessed enough human tragedy to solidify his conviction that he would have to use his mind if he were to escape the twin injustices of poverty and racial prejudices.

His first and what many feel is his best work, *Go Tell it on the Mountain* (1953) is a semiautobiographical book about this period in Baldwin's life. During the 1950s he spent years abroad in Europe where he found the distance and freedom to reflect on the American condition. *Notes of a Native Son* (1955) is a collection of essays on these reflections, and *Giovanni's Room* (1956), also written abroad, explicitly explores the taboo subject of homosexuality.

In 1957, Baldwin returned to the States to become part of the Civil Rights movement. His participation resulted in a book of essays, *Nobody Knows My Name* (1961) and the impassioned *The Fire Next Time* (1963). The assassinations of Medgar Evers, Martin Luther King, Jr., and Malcom X, all friends of Baldwin, were devastating to him, and he returned to Europe. There his disillusionment and bitterness found expression in *If Beale Street Could Talk* (1974). In spite of the pain and bitterness, Baldwin never surrendered his pacifist stance and his belief in the power and strength of love and universal brotherhood. His novels are noted for their social relevance, their intrinsic beauty, and penetrating and psychological depth.

A gifted artist in many venues, **Maya Angelou** (1928-) credits include those of a cabaret dancer, novelist, a playwright, an actress, producer, director, and activist in the Civil Rights movement. In addition, she is perhaps the most recognized and honored poet of our day. Born in St. Louis, Missouri, Angelou learned early the painful and humiliating differences that exist in racism. However, racial injustice was not the only pain of her childhood. At age seven, she was raped by her mother's boyfriend, an event that left her mute for five years. *I Know Why the Caged Bird Sing* (1969) is Angelou's autobiographical account of that traumatic experience.

Read about
Maya Angelou at
http://www.poets.org/
poet.php/prmPID/87

Throughout her life that led her from cabarets, to kitchens, to Hollywood and the Broadway stage, Angelou chronicled her progression in a number of autobiographical works, including, "*Gather Together in My Name*" (1974), "*Swingin' and Singin' and Getting Merry Like Christmas*" (1976), "*The Heart of a Woman*" (1981), and "*All God's Children Got Travelin' Shoes*" (1986).

Her books of poetry include *A Brave and Startling Truth* (1995), *I Shall Not Be Moved* (1990), *Oh Pray My Wings Are Gonna Fit Me Well* (1975), *and Just Give Me a Cool Drink of Water 'fore I Die* (1971), which was nominated for the Pulitzer Prize. In 1993, Angelou read her poem "On the Pulse of Morning" at the inauguration of President Bill Clinton. Angelou is described as "a great voice for all who are caged, yet yearn to sing."

COMPETENCY 3.0   UNDERSTAND THE LITERATURE OF GREAT BRITAIN FROM THE ANGLO-SAXON PERIOD THROUGH THE ROMANTIC PERIOD

Skill 3.1   Know the significance of writers, works, and movements in the development of the literature of Great Britain through the Romantic period.

Anglo-Saxon

The Anglo-Saxon period spans six centuries but produced only a smattering of literature. The first British epic is *Beowulf,* from as early as the eighth century. (*Beowulf* was released as a movie in 2007.) It was anonymously written by Christian monks many years after the events in the narrative supposedly occurred. This Teutonic saga relates the hero Beowulf's triumph over the antagonists, Grendel, Grendel's mother, and the dragon.

> Review a
> **Timeline of British Literature**
> http://www.studyguide.org/brit_lit_timeline.htm

A shorter poem "The Seafarer," some history, and some riddles are the rest of the Anglo-Saxon canon.

Medieval

The Medieval period introduces Geoffrey Chaucer, the father of English literature, whose *Canterbury Tales* are written in the vernacular--or street language of England--not in Latin. Thus, the tales are said to be the first work of British literature.

Next, Thomas Malory's *Le Morte d'Arthur* calls together the extant tales from Europe as well as England concerning the legendary King Arthur, Merlin, Guinevere, and the Knights of the Round Table. This work is the generative work that gave rise to the many Arthurian legends that stir the chivalric imagination.

Renaissance and Elizabethan Periods

The Renaissance—nearly synonymous in Great Britain with William Shakespeare--begins with importing the idea of the Petrarchan or Italian sonnet into England. Sir Thomas Wyatt and Sir Philip Sydney wrote English versions. Next, Sir Edmund Spenser invented a variation on this Italian sonnet form (aptly called the Spenserian sonnet). Spenser's masterpiece is the epic, *The Faerie Queene*, honoring Queen Elizabeth I's reign. He also wrote books on the Red Cross Knight, St. George and the Dragon, and a series of Arthurian adventures. Spencer was dubbed the Poet's Poet. He created a nine-line stanza, eight lines iambic pentameter and an extra-footed ninth line, an alexandrine. Thus, he invented the Spenserian stanza as well.

William Shakespeare, the Bard of Avon, wrote 154 sonnets, 39 plays, and two long narrative poems. The sonnets are justifiably called the greatest sonnet sequence in all literature. Shakespeare dispensed with the octave/sestet format of the Italian sonnet and invented his sonnet, comprised of three quatrains and concluding with one heroic couplet. Shakespeare's plays are divided into comedies, history plays, and tragedies. Great lines from these plays are more often quoted than from any other author. The "Big Four" tragedies, *Hamlet*, *Macbeth*, *Othello*, and *King Lear* are acknowledged to be the most brilliant examples of this genre.

Seventeenth Century

John Milton's devout Puritanism was the wellspring of his creative genius. His social commentary in such works as *Aereopagitica*, *Samson Agonistes*, and his elegant sonnets solidified his stature as a great writer. His masterpiece, *Paradise Lost*, based in part on the Book of Genesis, places Milton near the top of the rung of a handful of the most renowned of all writers because of the poem's balanced, elegant, neoclassic form.

The greatest allegory about man's journey to the Celestial City (Heaven) was written at the end of the English Renaissance. John Bunyan's *The Pilgrim's Progress* describes virtues and vices personified. This work for a long time was second only to the Bible in numbers of copies printed and sold.

The **Jacobean Age** gave us the marvelously witty and cleverly constructed conceits of John Donne's metaphysical sonnets as well as his insightful meditations and his version of sermons or homilies. "Ask not for whom the bell tolls" and "No man is an island unto himself" are famous epigrams from Donne's *Meditations*. His most famous conceit (exaggerated comparison) compares lovers to a footed compass--traveling seemingly separate, but always leaning towards one another and conjoined in "A Valediction: Forbidding Mourning."

Another writer during King James I's reign was Ben Jonson, author of the wickedly droll play *Volpone*. King James requested that the Bible be translated into English. The Cavalier *carpe diem* poets preferred a straightforward and erotic style that differed from the metaphysical poets such as John Donne. This movement included Robert Herrick, Sir John Suckling, and Richard Lovelace. Other poets whose works survives are Christopher Marlowe, Andrew Marvell, Robert Herrick, and Sir Walter Raleigh.

Eighteenth Century

The Restoration and Enlightenment reflect the political turmoil during the reign of Charles I, the Interregnum Puritan government of Oliver Cromwell, and the restoring of the monarchy to England by the coronation of Charles II, who had been given refuge by the French King Louis.

Neoclassicism became the preferred writing style, especially for Alexander Pope. New genres, such as *The Diary of Samuel Pepys*, the novels of Daniel Defoe including *Robinson Crusoe*, the periodical essays and editorials of Joseph Addison and Richard Steele, and Alexander Pope's mock epic *The Rape of the Lock* demonstrate the diversity of expression during this time.

Writers who followed were contemporaries of Dr. Samuel Johnson, the lexicographer of *The Dictionary of the English Language*. This period can be called the Age of Johnson. The time period encompasses James Boswell's biography of Dr. Johnson, the Scottish poet Robert Burns' *Auld Lang Syne*, and the mystical pre-Romantic poetry of William Blake. This period concludes with the development of the Romantic Age and its revolution against Neoclassicism.

Romantic Period

The First Generation of Romantic poets includes William Wordsworth and Samuel Taylor Coleridge, who collaborated on *Lyrical Ballads*. The Second Generation includes George Gordon, Lord Byron, Percy Bysshe Shelley, and John Keats. These poets wrote sonnets, odes, epics, and narrative poems, most dealing with homage to nature.

Read about
The Romantic Period
http://www.wwnorton.com/college/
english/nael/romantic/welcome.htm

Wordsworth's most famous other works are "Intimations on Immortality" and "The Prelude." Byron's satirical epic *Don Juan* and his autobiographical *Childe Harold's Pilgrimage* are irreverent, witty, self-deprecating and, in part, cuttingly critical of other writers and critics. Shelley's odes and sonnets are remarkable for sensory imagery. Keats' sonnets, odes, and longer narrative poem *The Eve of St. Agnes* are remarkable for their introspection and the tender age of the poet, who died when he was only twenty-five.

In fact, all of the Second Generation died before their times. Wordsworth, who lived to be eighty, outlived them all, including Coleridge, his friend and collaborator.

Others who wrote during the Romantic Age are the essayist Charles Lamb and the novelist Jane Austin. The Bronte sisters, Charlotte and Emily, wrote one novel each, *Jane Eyre* (Charlotte) and *Wuthering Heights* (Emily). Mary Anne Evans, who wrote under the name George Eliot, wrote several important novels: *Middlemarch*, *Silas Marner*, *Adam Bede*, and *Mill on the Floss*.

Skill 3.2   Identify the characteristics of major literary periods in the development of the literature of Great Britain (Anglo-Saxon, Middle Ages, Renaissance, Restoration and eighteenth-century, Romantic).

See Skill 3.1

Skill 3.3   Understand the historical, social, and cultural contexts of the literature of Great Britain through the Romantic period.

Elizabethan Age

The reign of Elizabeth I ushered in the end of the medieval age. It was a very fertile literary period. The exploration of the new world expanded the vision of all—from royalty to peasant. Additionally, there was rejection of Catholicism by many in favor of Protestantism, and this opened up whole new vistas of thought.

Cloth manufacture increased, driving many people from the countryside into the cities. As a result, the population of London exploded, creating a metropolitan business center. William Caxton had brought printing to England in the 1470s, and literacy increased from 30 percent in the fifteenth century to over 60 percent by 1530.

The Italian Renaissance had a great influence on the Renaissance in England, and early in the sixteenth century, most written works were in Latin. It was assumed that a learned person must express his thoughts in that language.

However, there began to emerge a determination that vernacular English was valuable in writing, and it began to be defended. Elizabeth's tutor, Roger Ascham, for example, wrote in English.

Luther's thesis in 1517, which brought on the Reformation—an attempt to return to pure Christianity—brought on the breakup of western Christendom and eventually the secularization of society and the establishment of the king or queen as the head of this new/old church. This also brought about a new feeling that being religious was also being patriotic; it promoted nationalism.

The ascension of Elizabeth to the throne followed a turbulent period regarding succession, and then she ruled for 45 peaceful years, which allowed arts and literature to flourish.

Queen Elizabeth had shrewd political instincts, and she entrusted power to solid, talented men, most particularly Robert Cecil, her Secretary, and Francis Walsingham, whom she put in charge of foreign policy. She identified with her country as no previous ruler had. That in itself brought on a period of intense nationalism. The defeat of the Spanish armada in 1588 was the direct result of the strong support she had from her own nation during a period of religious rivalry between Catholicism (Spain) and Protestantism (England).

Religious plays had been a part of the life of England for a long time, particularly the courtly life. But in the Elizabethan Age, drama became more secular. By the 1560s, Latin drama, particularly the tragedies of Seneca and the comedies of Plautus and Terence began to wield an influence in England. Courtyards of inns became favorite places for the presentation of plays. Then in 1576, the Earl of Leicester's Men (a dramatic troupe) constructed "The Theatre." Other theatres followed. Each had its own repertory company. Performances were for profit but also for the queen and her court. It is said that Shakespeare wrote *The Merry Wives of Windsor* at the specific command of the queen, who liked Falstaff and wanted to see him in love. It was also for the courtly audience that poetry was introduced into drama.

Shakespeare and Marlowe dominated the literary scene of the late 1500s, and at the turn of the century, only a few years before Elizabeth's death, Ben Jonson began writing his series of satirical comedies.

> Examine links to
> **Renaissance: The Elizabethan World - Related Sites**
> http://elizabethan.org/sites.html

Court favor was notoriously precarious and depended on the whims of the queen and others. Much of the satire of the period reflects the disappointment of writers like Edmund Spenser and John Lyly and the superficiality and treachery of the court atmosphere. "A thousand hopes, but all nothing," wrote Lyly, "a hundred promises, but yet nothing."

Not all literature was dictated by the court. The middle classes were developing and had their own style. Thomas Heywood and Thomas Deloney catered to bourgeois tastes.

The two universities, Oxford and Cambridge, were also sources for the production of literature. The primary aim of the colleges was to develop ministers since there was a shortage brought on by the break with the Catholic Church. However, most university men couldn't make livings as ministers or academics, so they wrote as a way of earning income. Thomas Nashe, Christopher Marlowe, Robert Greene, and George Peele all reveal in their writings how difficult this path was. Making a living came mostly from patrons.

For example, Robert Greene had sixteen different patrons from seventeen books whereas Shakespeare had a satisfactory relationship with the Earl of Southampton and didn't need to seek other support. Publishers would sometimes pay for a manuscript--which they would then own. Unfortunately, if the manuscript did not meet approval with all who could condemn it—the court, the religious leaders, prominent citizens—it was the author who was culpable. Very few became as comfortable as Shakespeare did. His success was not only in writing but also from his business acumen.

Writing was seen more as a craft than as an art in this period. There was not great conflict between art and nature, little distinction between literature, sports of the field, or the arts of the kitchen.

Balance and control were important in the England of this day, and this is reflected in the writing, the poetry in particular. The **sestina**, a form in which the last words of each line in the first stanza are repeated in a different order in each of the following stanzas, became very popular. Verse forms range from the extremely simple four-line **ballad** stanza through the rather complicated form of the **sonnet** to the elaborate and beautiful eighteen-line stanza of Spenser's *Epithalamion.*

Sonnets were called "quatorzains." The term "sonnet" was used loosely for any short poem. Quatorzains are fourteen-line poems in iambic pentameter with elaborate rhyme schemes. That is how sonnets are identified today.

Chaucer's seven-line rhyme royal stanza survived in the sixteenth century. Shakespeare used it in *The Rape of Lucrece*, for example. An innovation was Spenser's nine-line stanza, called the **Spenserian stanza**, which he developed in *The Faerie Queene.*

As to themes, some of the darkness of the previous period can still be seen in some Elizabethan literature, for example Shakespeare's *Richard II*. At the same time, a spirit of joy, gaiety, innocence, and lightheartedness can be seen in much of the most popular literature, and pastoral themes became popular. The theme of the burning desire for conquest and achievement was also significant in Elizabethan thought.

Some Important Writers of the Elizabethan Age
- Sir Thomas More (1478-1535)
- Sir Thomas Wyatt the Elder (1503-1542)
- Edmund Spenser (1552-1599)
- Sir Walter Raleigh (1552-1618)
- Sir Philip Sidney (1554-1586)
- John Lyly (1554-1606)
- George Peele (1556-1596)
- Christopher Marlowe (1564-1593)
- William Shakespeare (1564-1616)

The Industrial Revolution

In England, the Industrial Revolution began with the development of the steam engine. However, the steam engine was only one component of the major technological, socioeconomic, and cultural innovations of the early nineteenth century that began in Britain and spread throughout the world. An economy based on manual labor was replaced by one dominated by industry and the manufacture of machinery. The textile industries also underwent rapid growth and change. Canals were being built, roads were improving, and railways were being constructed.

Steam power (fueled primarily by coal) and powered machinery (primarily in the manufacture of textiles) drove the remarkable amplification of production capacity. All-metal machine tools were developed by 1820 making it possible to produce more machines.

The date of the Industrial Revolution varies according to how it is viewed. Some say that it broke out in the 1780s and wasn't fully perceived until the 1830s or 1840s. Others maintain that the beginning was earlier, about 1760, and began to manifest visible changes by 1830. The effects spread through Western Europe and North America throughout the nineteenth century, eventually affecting all major countries of the world. The impact on society has been compared to the period when agriculture began to develop and the nomadic lifestyle was abandoned.

The first Industrial Revolution was followed immediately by the second Industrial Revolution around 1850 when the progress in technology and world economy gained momentum with the introduction of steam-powered ships and railways and eventually the internal combustion engine and electrical power generation.

In terms of what was going on socially, the most noticeable effect was the development of a middle class of industrialists and businessmen and a decline in the landed class of nobility and gentry. While working people had more opportunities for employment in the new mills and factories, working conditions were often less than desirable. Exploiting children for labor wasn't new but it was more apparent and perhaps more egregious as the need for cheap labor increased. In England, laws regarding employment of children began to be developed in 1833. Another effect of industrialization was the enormous shift from hand-produced goods to machine-produced ones and the loss of jobs among weavers and others, which resulted in violence against the factories and machinery beginning in about 1811.

Eventually, the British government took measures to protect industry. Another effect was the organization of labor. Because laborers were now working together in factories, mines, and mills, they were better able to organize to gain advantages they felt they deserved. Conditions were bad enough in these workplaces that the energy to bring about change was significant and eventually trade unions emerged.

Laborers learned quickly to use the weapon of the strike to get what they wanted. The strikes were often violent and, while the managers usually gave in to most of the demands made by strikers, the animosity between management and labor was endemic.

The mass migration of rural families into urban areas also resulted in poor living conditions, long work hours, extensive use of children for labor, and a polluted atmosphere.

Another effect of industrialization of society was the separation of husband and wife. One person stayed at home and looked after the home and family and the other went off to work, a very different configuration from an agriculture-based economy where the entire family was usually involved in making a living. Eventually, gender roles began to be defined by the new configuration of labor in this new world order.

The application of industrial processes to printing brought about a great expansion in newspaper and popular book publishing. This, in turn, was followed by rapid increases in literacy and eventually in demands for mass political participation.

The literary, intellectual, and artistic movement that occurred along with the Industrial Movement was actually a response to the increasing mechanization of society, an artistic hostility to what was taking over the world. Romanticism stressed the importance of nature in art and language in contrast to the monstrous machines and factories. Blake called them the "dark, satanic mills" in his poem "And Did Those Feet in Ancient Time."

This movement followed on the heels of the Enlightenment period and was, at least in part, a reaction to the aristocratic and political norms of the previous period. Romanticism is sometimes called the Counter-Enlightenment. It stressed strong emotion, made individual imagination the critical authority, and overturned previous social conventions. Nature was important to the Romanticists, who elevated the achievements of misunderstood heroic individuals and artists.

Some British/Scottish Romantic Writers
- William Blake
- Lord George Gordon Byron
- Samuel Taylor Coleridge
- John Keats
- Walter Scott
- Percy Bysshe Shelley
- William Wordsworth

Skill 3.4   Identify significant genres and themes in the literature of Great Britain from the Anglo-Saxon period through the Romantic period.

See Skill 3.1 and 3.3

Skill 3.5   **Identify a range of authors and works from Great Britain (*Beowulf*, the author of "Gawain", Geoffrey Chaucer, Sir Thomas Malory, Christopher Marlowe, William Shakespeare, John Donne, John Milton, Samuel Johnson, Alexander Pope, Jonathan Swift, Robert Burns, William Blake, William Wordsworth, Samuel Taylor Coleridge, Jane Austen, Percy Bysshe Shelley, Mary Wollstonecraft Shelley, Lord Byron, John Keats) and their significance in the development of the literature of Great Britain from the Anglo-Saxon period through the Romantic period.**

The following works and writers are representative of the literature of Great Britain as it developed from the heroic epic poem *Beowulf* to the romantic contemplation of John Keats' "Ode to a Nightingale." This great shift from the mythic struggles of kings and demons to a lyrical mediation on a songbird is told in the poetry and prose of these writers.

Beowulf, an epic poem, taken from the oral tradition and written in Old English on a tenth-century vellum manuscript, is thought to have its origins as far back as the seventh or eighth century. For historians, it marks the beginnings of English literature as it is written in the language of the people rather than in the more formal and universal language of the time, Latin. The poem tells the stories of the battles of Beowulf, a Scandinavian warrior who battles with and defeats Grendel, a ferocious monster, and in turn, Grendel's angry mother.

> Check out this lesson plan
> **An Introduction to Beowulf: Language and Poetics**
> http://www.readwritethink.org/lessons/lesson_view.asp?id=813

Beowulf becomes a hero, is made a prince, and is given his own land and subjects to oversee. After reigning for 50 years, he is called once again into battle, taking on a powerful dragon. Beowulf defeats the dragon, but he is mortally wounded in the process, bringing to end 50 years of peace. The poem is important for not only for its imagery and tale of mythic portions but because it chronicles the emergence of the new Christian faith in a land firmly entrenched in paganism.

Born in London and buried in the Poets' Corner of Westminster Abby, **Geoffrey Chaucer** (1343-1400) is considered one of the greatest writers of the middle ages. Chaucer's background includes service in the King's army and the King's diplomatic core. *The Canterbury Tales*, written in the last years of Chaucer's life, is his most famous work. In it, Chaucer tells the story of 29 men and women on a religious pilgrimage. With humor, respect, reverence, and an eye for detail, Chaucer offers an engaging portrait of the medieval citizens' most important endeavor, that of their journey to unity with God.

Perhaps the most familiar name in the world of Western literature is **William Shakespeare** (1564-1616). His poetry and plays have remained timeless, influencing artists from the time of the Renaissance to modern day Hollywood. In spite of their timeless nature, Shakespeare's plays were closely in tune with the time in which he wrote. The dialogue was that of the street and the tavern, and the stories were those found in the King's court and in the human heart.

One of his most famous works, *Hamlet*, is the story of the Prince of Demark, whose beloved father, the king, is murdered. Following the murder, Hamlet's mother quickly marries his uncle, who then becomes king. To his horror, Hamlet begins to suspect that his mother and his uncle have perpetrated the awful deed. Something indeed is "rotten in Denmark." Like works of the early Middle Ages, Hamlet is concerned with persons of superior stations, kings and princes, yet instead of heroic battles, we find a dysfunctional family whose battles have degenerated into acquisitions of insubstantial and transient earthly power at the expense of the soul. In addition to his 154 sonnets, Shakespeare's other plays include *Romeo and Juliet, Merchant of Venice, A Midsummer Night's Dream, Othello, King Lear,* and *Much Ado about Nothing.*

Born into a close and loving family in Hampton, England, **Jane Austen** (1775-1817) was the sixth of seven children. Her father, the Reverend George Austen, was comfortably prosperous and well-cultivated, and he encouraged such cultivation in his children. Like her siblings, Jane Austin was encouraged to read and to study, and by age 15 had written *Love and Friendship* and "A History of England.*

Austen's world revolved around her family and the busy comings and goings in the family parlor. It was in such a parlor at Chawton, that Austen wrote *Emma* and *Persuasion*. While some critics have found her to be a caustic satirist of social mores, most agree that her greatest gift was in making the very ordinary affairs of everyday life interesting and captivating to all. Other works by Austen include *Pride and Prejudice, Mansfield Park,* and *Sense and Sensibility.*

Regarded as a key figure in the Romantic Movement, **John Keats** (1795-1821) was known and admired by his contemporaries for what poet Matthew Arnold referred to as an "intellectual and spiritual passion for beauty." Such a sentiment clearly defines the Romantic Movement in which feelings, emotions, and passions were emphasized. While the earlier movement of the Enlightenment had focused on an objective view of reality, for Keats, the emotions held the key to a higher perception of reality. He spoke of a "negative capability" in which the artist's sense of self is lost in the object of his contemplation. In this manner, he hoped to "arrive at that trembling, delicate, snail-horn perception of Beauty." Some of his major poetic works include "Endymion," "Hyperion," "Ode to a Nightingale," and Ode on a Grecian Urn."

COMPETENCY 4.0 UNDERSTAND THE LITERATURE OF GREAT BRITAIN FROM THE VICTORIAN PERIOD TO THE PRESENT

Skill 4.1 **Identify the characteristics of significant literary works of Great Britain from the Victorian period to the present.**

Nineteenth Century

The Victorian Period is remarkable for the diversity and proliferation of work in three major areas. Poets who are typified as Victorians include Alfred Tennyson, who wrote *Idylls of the King*, twelve narrative poems about the Arthurian legend; and Robert Browning,

http://www.victorianweb.org/

who wrote chilling, dramatic monologues, such as "My Last Duchess," as well as long poetic narratives such as *The Pied Piper of Hamlin*. Elizabeth Barrett Browning wrote two major works, her epic feminist poem, *Aurora Leigh*, and her deeply moving and provocative *Sonnets from the Portuguese,* in which she details her deep love for Robert (and his reciprocation that resulted in their marriage): "How do I love thee? Let me count the ways."

Gerard Manley Hopkins, a Catholic priest, wrote poetry with sprung rhythm. A. E. Housman, Matthew Arnold, and the Pre-Raphaelites, especially the brother and sister duo, Dante Gabriel Rossetti and Christina Rossetti, contributed much to round out the Victorian Era poetic scene. Inspired by medieval and early Renaissance painters (up to the time of the Italian painter Raphael), the Pre-Raphaelites, a group of nineteenth-century English painters, poets, and critics, reacted against Victorian materialism and the neoclassical conventions of academic art producing earnest, quasi-religious works.

Robert Louis Stevenson, the great Scottish novelist, wrote his adventure/history lessons for young adults. Victorian prose ranges from the incomparable, keenly woven plot structures of Charles Dickens to the deeply moving Dorset/Wessex novels of Thomas Hardy, in which women are repressed, and life is more struggle than euphoria. Rudyard Kipling wrote about colonialism in India in the works *Kim* and *The Jungle Book.* They create exotic locales and a distinct main point concerning the Raj, the British colonial government during Queen Victoria's reign. Victorian drama is a product mainly of Oscar Wilde, whose satirical masterpiece *The Importance of Being Earnest* farcically details and lampoons Victorian social mores.

Twentieth Century

The early twentieth-century is represented mainly by the towering achievement of George Bernard Shaw's dramas: *St. Joan*, *Man and Superman*, *Major Barbara*, and *Arms and the Man,* to name a few.

Novelists are too numerous to list all of them, but some of the best are Polish-born Joseph Conrad (*Heart of Darkness*), E. M. Forster (*A Room With a View*), Virginia Woolf (*To the Lighthouse*), Irish-expatriate James Joyce (Ulysses, Catholic-convert Graham Greene (*The Power and the Glory*), George Orwell (*Animal Farm*), D. H. Lawrence (*Lady Chatterley's Lover*), and, South African Nadine Gordimer (*Occasion for Loving*).

Twentieth-century poets of renown and merit include W. H. Auden, Robert Graves, T. S. Eliot, Edith Sitwell, Stephen Spender, Dylan Thomas, Philip Larkin, Ted Hughes, Sylvia Plath, and Hugh MacDiarmid. This list is by no means complete.

Skill 4.2   Understand the historical, social, and cultural contexts of Victorian, modern, and contemporary literature of Great Britain.

World War I, also known as The First World War, the Great War, and The War to End All Wars, raged from July 1914 to the final Armistice on November 11, 1918. It was a world conflict between the Allied Powers led by Great Britain, France, Russia, and the United States (after 1917) and the Central Powers, led by the German Empire, the Austro-Hungarian Empire, and the Ottoman Empire. It brought down four great empires: The Austro-Hungarian, German, Ottoman, and Russian. It reconfigured European and Middle Eastern maps.

More than nine million soldiers died on the various battlefields and nearly that many more in the participating countries' home fronts as a result of food shortages and genocide committed under the cover of various civil wars and internal conflicts.

Even more people died of the worldwide influenza outbreak at the end of the war and thereafter than had died in the hostilities. The unsanitary conditions engendered by the war, severe overcrowding in barracks, wartime propaganda interfering with public health warnings, and migration of so many soldiers around the world, contributed to the outbreak becoming a pandemic.

The experiences of the war led to a sort of collective national trauma afterwards for all the participating countries. The optimism of the 1900s was entirely gone. Writers who identified with the term "Lost Generation "--those who'd experienced that war or came of age during the war--include Sherwood Anderson, John Dos Passos, Ezra Pound, Ernest Hemingway, and F. Scott Fitzgerald.

> Learn more about
> **Literature of World War One**
> **for Young Adults**
> http://www.geocities.com/Athens/2181/
> Ra.htm?200723#bibliography

Following the war, memorials continued to be erected in thousands of European villages and towns. Certainly a sense of disillusionment and cynicism became pronounced, and nihilism became popular. The world had never before witnessed such devastation, and the depiction in newspapers and on movie screens made the horrors more personal.

War has always spawned creative bursts, and this one was no exception. Poetry, stories, and movies proliferated. In fact, it's still a fertile subject for art of all kinds, particularly literature and movies. In 2006, a young director by the name of Paul Gross created, directed, and starred in *Passchendaele,* based on the stories told him by his grandfather, who was haunted all his life by his killing of a young German soldier in this War to End All Wars.

Some Literature Based on World War I
- "The Soldier," poem by Rupert Brooke
- *Goodbye to All That,* autobiography by Robert Graves
- "Anthem for Doomed Youth" and "Strange Meeting," poems by Wilfred Owen, published posthumously by Siegfried Sassoon in 1918
- "In Flanders Fields," poem by John McCrae
- *Three Soldiers,* novel by John Dos Passos
- *Journey's End*, play by R. C. Sherriff
- *All Quiet on the Western Front*, novel by Erich Maria Remarque
- *Death of a Hero,* novel by Richard Aldington
- *A Farewell to Arms,* novel by Ernest Hemingway
- *Memoirs of an Infantry Officer,* novel by Siegfried Sassoon

The dissolution of the British Empire, the most extensive empire in world history and for a time the foremost global power, began in 1867 with its transformation into the modern Commonwealth.

Although the Allies won the war and Britain's rule expanded into new areas, the heavy costs of the war made it less and less feasible to maintain the vast empire. Economic losses as well as human losses put increasing pressure on the Empire to give up its far-flung imperial posts in Asia and the African colonies. At the same time, nationalist sentiment was growing in both old and new Imperial territories fueled partly by their troops' contributions to the war and the anger of many non-white ex-servicemen at the racial discrimination they had encountered during their service.

The rise of anti-colonial nationalist movements in the subject territories and the changing economic situation of the world in the first half of the twentieth century challenged an imperial power now increasingly preoccupied with issues nearer home. The Empire's end began with the onset of the Second World War when a deal was reached between the British government and the Indian independence movement whereby India would cooperate and remain loyal during the war--but after which they would be granted independence. Following India's lead, nearly all of the other colonies would become independent over the next two decades.

In the Caribbean, Africa, Asia, and the Pacific, post-war decolonization was achieved with almost unseemly haste in the face of increasingly powerful nationalist movements, and Britain rarely fought to retain any territory.

Some Representative Literature
- *Heart of Darkness,* novel by Joseph Conrad
- *Passage to India,* novel by E. M. Forster
- "Gunga Din," poem by Rudyard Kipling

Skill 4.3   Identify significant genres and themes in Victorian, modern, and contemporary literature of Great Britain.

There are four major time periods of writings: Neoclassicism, Romanticism, Realism, and Naturalism. Certain authors, among these Chaucer, Shakespeare, and Donne, though writing during a particular literary period, are considered to have a style all their own.

Neoclassicism

Patterned after the greatest writings of classical Greece and Rome, this type of writing is characterized by balanced, graceful, well-crafted, refined, elevated style. Major proponents of this style are poet laureates, John Dryden and Alexander Pope. The eras in which they wrote are called the Age of Dryden and Age of Pope. The focus is on the group, not the individual, in neoclassic writing.

Romanticism

These writings emphasize the individual. Emotions and feelings are validated. Nature acts as an inspiration for creativity; it is a balm of the spirit. Romantics hearken back to medieval, chivalric themes and ambiance. They also emphasize supernatural, Gothic themes and settings, which are characterized by gloom and darkness. Imagination is stressed. New types of writings include detective and horror stories and autobiographical introspection (William Wordsworth).

There are two generations in British literature:

First Generation includes William Wordsworth and Samuel Taylor Coleridge whose collaboration, *Lyrical Ballads*, defines romanticism and its exponents. Wordsworth maintained that the scenes and events of everyday life and the speech of ordinary people were the raw material of which poetry could and should be made. Romanticism spread to the United States, where Ralph Waldo Emerson and Henry David Thoreau adopted it in their transcendental romanticism, emphasizing reasoning. Further extensions of this style are found in Edgar Allan Poe's Gothic writings.

Second Generation romantics include the ill-fated Englishmen Lord Byron, John Keats, and Percy Bysshe Shelley. Byron and Shelley are often said to epitomize the romantic poet (in their personal lives as well as in their work). They wrote resoundingly in protest against social and political wrongs and in defense of the struggle for liberty in Italy and Greece. The Second Generation romantics stressed that personal introspection and love of beauty and nature are required for inspiration.

Realism

Unlike classical and neoclassical writing that often deal with aristocracies, nobility, or the gods, realistic writers deal with the common man and his socio/economic problems in a non-sentimental way. Muckraking, social injustice, domestic abuse, and inner city conflicts are examples of writings by writers of realism. Realistic writers include Thomas Hardy, George Bernard Shaw, and Henrik Ibsen.

Naturalism

Few writers in Britain joined this movement, but writers in France essentially gave birth to it.

Naturalism is realism pushed to the maximum and is writing that exposes the underbelly of society, usually the lower-class struggles. This is the world of penury, injustice, abuse, ghetto survival, hungry children, single-parenting, and substance abuse—which is scientifically explained. One example is the French writer Émile Zola. Zola was inspired by his readings in history and medicine and attempted to apply methods of scientific observation to the depiction of pathological human character in a series of novels devoted to several generations of one French family. Another French example is Gustav Flaubert (*Madame Bovary*). Influenced largely by Zola was the American naturalist writer Theodore Dreiser (*Sister Carrie*). Jack London (*Call of the Wild*) was another American writer influenced by the naturalism movement.

Skill 4.4   **Identify a range of authors of Great Britain (Charles Dickens, Emily Brontë, Charlotte Brontë, Matthew Arnold, Gerard Manley Hopkins, Thomas Hardy, William Butler Yeats, James Joyce, George Bernard Shaw, D. H. Lawrence, Virginia Woolf, W. H. Auden, Dylan Thomas, Doris Lessing, Seamus Heaney), their representative works, and their significance in the development of the literature of Great Britain from the Victorian period to the present.**

Known as the age of the novel, the Victorian era in Great Britain officially began in 1837 with the ascendance of Queen Victoria to the throne and of Great Britain's unchallenged preeminence as the major world power. The English writers of this new period reflected the tremendous social changes of the time. They exhibited a highly conscious sense of political awareness, self-reflection, and--on one hand--awe at the promise of the industrial age--and on the other-- horror at the unabashed wealth and abject poverty that came with it.

Literary characters and events found in **Charles Dickens'** (1812-1870) novels were inspired by the poverty of his youth, a condition that intensified when his father was thrown into debtor's prison. Family poverty caused Dickens' early entry into the workforce. He began as a warehouse laborer at age 12. Later, he found much more agreeable work as an office boy--and yet later as a newspaper reporter. It was as a reporter that his talent for writing popular material was discovered.

His short articles and observations were eagerly read and digested, so much so that Dickens was approached by his boss to create a series that would attract and retain an appreciative audience. Dickens responded with *The Posthumous Papers of the Pickwick Club* or simply, *The Pickwick Papers*. The adventures and misadventures of the colorful Pickwick Club members were an instant success, and the series was published as a single volume when Dickens was only age 25.

A significant number of Dickens novels began as monthly serials—including *Nicholas Nickleby, Oliver Twist, Bleak House, David Copperfield* (1849-50), *A Tale of Two Cities* (1859), and *Great Expectations* (1860-61). In addition, *A Christmas Carol* was the first in a series of Christmas stories. Dickens was a truly popular novelist whose colorfully drawn caricatures were immediately recognized and affirmed by his reading public. While his popularity was always acknowledged, it was in the twentieth century that his work received serious academic attention and that he was recognized as a master of his craft.

Learn more about
Charlotte Brontë at
http://www.victorianweb.org/

After her mother's death in 1821, **Charlotte Brontë** (1816-1854) and her four sisters were sent to strict boarding school, which she was always to believe ruined her health and caused the early death of her two elder sisters in 1825. (The school did serve, however, as the model for the wretched boarding school she created in her most famous work, *Jane Eyre*.)

She and her two surviving sisters, Emily and Anne, continued their education at home, where they read extensively and where their imaginations were given free reign. The sisters began writing their own material, creating the imaginary kingdoms of Angria (Charlotte's creation) and Gondal (the creation of Emily and Anne).

As young women, the sisters served as governesses, but they never abandoned their writings. In 1845, Charlotte convinced her sisters that they all should publish their poetry. They did so in 1846 under the pseudonyms of Currer, Ellis, and Acton Bell (Charlotte, Emily and Anne, respectively). The volume of poetry did not sell, but by then, Emily and Anne had finished their first mature novels (*Wuthering Heights* and *Agnes Grey*).

These novels were accepted by a publisher in 1847 and were published in1848. Charlotte's *Jane Eyre* which she had begun writing in 1846 was published to immediate acclaim in 1847. However, there was little time for the sisters to celebrate. Emily died in December of 1848, and Anne died in the summer of 1849. Charlotte went on to publish memorial editions of her sisters' novels as well as editions of their unpublished poetry. In 1854, Charlotte was persuaded to marry a friend of her father, and she died a few months later—apparently from complications of a pregnancy. Like Dickens' writings, Charlotte's writings were widely popular during her lifetime. Her work is described as a blend of the Gothic and Romantic styles.

While the novels of Dickens and the Brontës are full of raw and colorful emotions, **George Bernard Shaw** (1856-1950) focused his considerable intellect and wit on creating dramatic conflict not of the passions but of thought and belief. Born into an unloving and unhappy home in Dublin, Ireland, Shaw moved to London in 1876 with his mother, where he began his writing career as a music, art, and drama critic. Throughout his long life, Shaw was tireless worker, with a prodigious output.

Learn more about
George Bernard Shaw at
http://nobelprize.org/
nobel_prizes/
literature/laureates/
1925/shaw-bio.html

He was to write five unsuccessful novels during his first nine years in London, and in his lifetime, he would deliver over 1,000 lectures and would write over 50 plays; *The Quintessence of Ibsenism,* a study of Henrik Ibsen, his personal favorite playwright; and a range of essays and pamphlets detailing his political and intellectual beliefs, including "The Intelligent Woman's Guide to Socialism and Capitalism" (1928) and "Everybody's Political What's What" (1944).

Among his plays, one of the most well known is *Pygmalion* (1913), which during the 1960s was written for the screen in the highly successful film, *My Fair Lady.* Shaw's contributions as a writer were recognized early in his career with the awarding of the 1925 Nobel Prize for Literature. The causes championed by Shaw included women's rights, the abolition of private property, the simplification of English spelling and punctuation, and a reform of the English alphabet. He remained a vegetarian throughout his 94 years and never drank alcohol, coffee, or tea. Holding true to his convictions in lifestyle and in writing, Shaw made audiences realize that passions of the mind could be just as dramatic and absorbing as the passions of the heart.

W.H. Auden (1907-1973), considered a major poet of his own generation, continues to influence poets in each succeeding generation. As a student at Oxford, Auden himself was highly influenced by the early Anglo-Saxon era and the Middle English poetry. His mastery of a broad range of poetic styles and venues, from the traditional to the contemporary, from the urbane to the pastoral, make his work accessible and meaningful to an equally broad and diverse audience.

Read about
W.H. Auden at
http://www.poets.org

Much of his writing, especially in the latter half of his life, returns to the theme of man's essential solitude and how in poetry there is refuge for the "private sphere" amid the "public chaos." In 1940, Auden published *Another Time*, which includes some of his more famous poems, such as "September 1939" and "Lullaby." In 1955, he published what critics consider is best single volume of poetry.

In addition to poetry, Auden also wrote a number of plays, including *The Dance of Death* (1933) and *On the Frontier* (1938). In 1962, he was made a professor of poetry at Oxford, where he had served as the editor of *The Oxford Book of Light Verse* in 1938. In the Hollywood movie, *Three Weddings and a Funeral* Auden's poignant poem, "Funeral Blues" is recited in full.

Born to a cattle farmer in industrial Northern Ireland and the eldest of nine children, **Seamus Heaney** (1939-) notes that the tension between the industrial and the pastoral of his birth place as well as the tension between his verbally sparse father and verbose mother did much to heighten his own sense of inner tension, creating a "quarrel within himself" that has fueled much of his poetry.

As a student at St. Columb's in Derry and later at Queen's University in Belfast, Heaney studied Latin, Gaelic, and Anglo-Saxon dialects. These studies

Learn about
Seamus Heaney at
http://nobelprize.org/
nobel_prizes/literature/la
ureates/1995/heaney-
bio.html

deepened his pride in his heritage and strengthened his growing sense of obligation as a poet not only to preserve his heritage but to be aware of and to speak to the political and social issues of the day. In a land torn for centuries with religious and political violence, this sense of a poet's obligations as a citizen is important to Heaney. Thus, Heaney became part of Ireland's Field Day theatre company and for nearly 15 years, he wrote and toured with the company, whose productions dealt with the political issues affecting his country.

The published volumes of Heaney's poetry include *North* (1975), *The Haw Lantern* (1987), and *Seeing Things* (1991). His prose works include *The Government of the Tongue* (1988) and *The Redress of Poetry* (1995). Heaney has also translated some ancient texts for modern readers. Among his translations are *Sweeney Ashtray* (1982), a Middle Irish story of Suibhne Gealt, and *Beowulf* (2001). Heaney has always supported aspiring poets with workshops and lectures, and he served for five years as the Professor of Poetry at Oxford. For his contributions to his craft, Heaney received the Nobel Prize for Literature in 1995.

COMPETENCY 5.0   UNDERSTAND LITERATURE FROM THE ANCIENT WORLD TO THE FIFTEENTH CENTURY

Skill 5.1   Identify the characteristics of major literary forms, works, and writers associated with literature of the ancient world (African, Asian, European, and Greek and Roman literature; the Bible; world myths and folk tales).

Epic

The epic is one of the major forms of narrative literature, which retells chronologically the life of a mythological person or group of persons. This genre has become uncommon since the early twentieth century although the term has been used to define certain extraordinarily long prose works and films. Usually a large number of characters, multiple settings, and a long span of time are features that lead to its designation as an epic. This change in the use of this term might indicate that some prose works of the past might be called epics although they were not composed or originally understood as such.

The epic was a natural manifestation of oral poetic tradition in preliterate societies where the poetry was transmitted to the audience and from performer to performer by purely oral means. It was composed of short episodes, each of equal status, interest, and importance, which facilitated memorization. The poet recalls each episode and uses it to recreate the entire epic.

Some Ancient Epics
- *The Iliad and the Odyssey,* both ascribed to Homer
- Lost Greek epics ascribed to the Cyclic poets:
- *Trojan War* cycle
- *Theban Cycle*
- *Argonautica* by Apollonius of Rhodes
- *Mahabharata and Ramayana,* Hindu mythologies
- *Aeneid* by Virgil
- *Metamorphoses* by Ovid
- *Argonautica* by Gaius Valerius Flaccus

Some Medieval Epics (500-1500)
- *Beowulf* (Anglo-Saxon mythology)
- *Bhagavata Purana* (Sanskrit "Stories of the Lord")
- *Divina Commedia* (*The Divine Comedy*) by Dante Alighieri
- *The Canterbury Tales* by Geoffrey Chaucer
- *Alliterative Morte Arthure*

Some Modern Epics (from 1500)
- *The Faerie Queene* by Edmund Spenser (1596)
- *Paradise Lost* by John Milton (1667)
- *Paradise Regained* by John Milton (1671)
- *Prince Arthur* by Richard Blackmore (1695)
- *King Arthur* by Richard Blackmore (1697)
- *The Works of Ossian* by James MacPherson (1765)
- *Hyperion* by John Keats (1818)
- *Don Juan by George Gordon Byron, 6th Baron Byron (1824)*

World Folk Epics are poems (or prose sometimes) that are an integral part of the worldview of a people. In many cases, they were original oral texts that were eventually written by a single author or several.

For example, Virgil (Publius Vergilius Maro, later called Virgilius and known in English as Virgil or Vergil) was a Latin poet, author of the *Eclogues,* the *Georgics,* and the *Aeneid.* The *Aeneid* is a poem of twelve books that became the Roman Empire's national epic.

Virgil has had a strong influence on English literature. Edmund Spenser's *The Faerie Queene* reflects that influence. It was also the model for John Milton's *Paradise Lost*, not only in structure but also in style and diction. The Augustan poets considered Virgil's poetry the ultimate perfection of form and ethical content. He was not so popular during the Romantic period, but Victorians such as Matthew Arnold and Alfred, Lord Tennyson rediscovered Virgil and were influenced by the sensitivity and pathos that had not been so appealing to the Romantics.

Some World Folk Epics
- *Soundiata,* an African epic
- *Tunkashila,* an American Indian epic
- *Epic of Gilgamesh*, the oldest epic from Mesopotamia and the Mediterranean world
- *Aeneid,* a Roman epic
- *Moby Dick* is considered by some to be an American folk epic.

Ode

An ode is generally a long lyric poem and as a form or poetry or song has an extensive history. Though odes vary in topic and occasionally structure, three forms have risen to the foreground in literature. The two best-known and best-established ode forms are the Pindaric and the Horatian odes of the Greek and Roman traditions, respectively.

Named after a fifth century B.C.E. Greek poet Pindar, the **Pindaric ode** consists of a triadic structure, which emulates the musical movement of the early Greek chorus. It is irregular—that is, with an inconsistent number of feet in each verse or variations from stanza to stanza. The Roman poet Horace is credited for the Horatian form which typically has equal-length stanzas with the same rhyme scheme and meter. The **Horatian ode**, unlike the Pindaric ode, has a tendency to be personal rather than formal.

Pastoral odes differ from others mostly in subject matter. "Pastoral" designates a literary work that has to do with the lives of shepherds or rural life and usually draws a contrast between the innocence and serenity of the simple life and the discomforts and corruptions of the city and especially court life. The poet's moral, social, and literary views are usually expressed.

In John Keats' short career, his writing shifted from the popular sonnet form to the older form of the ode toward the end of his life. His "Ode on a Grecian Urn," which is about a piece of pottery, is a twist on the pastoral theme. He focuses on the natural scene that is pictured on the urn. Instead of a concern with the disturbing forces of the world as with most pastoral works, he uses the sculptured panel on the urn as a sort of "frozen pastoral" and makes his statement about what is valuable and real.

Some Pastoral Odes
- "Intimations of Immortality" by William Wordsworth
- "Ode to a Nightingale" by John Keats
- "Ode to Psyche" by John Keats
- "Ode to the West Wind" by Percy Bysshe Shelley

Upanishads

The Upanishads are Hindu treatises that deal with broad philosophic problems. The term means "to sit down near" and implies sitting at the feet of a teacher. There are approximately 108 that record views of many teachers over a number of years.

Read chronologically, they exhibit a development toward the concept of a single supreme being and suggest ultimate reunion with it. Of special philosophical concern is the nature of reality.

Their appearance in Europe in the early nineteenth century captured the interest of philosophers, particularly in Germany. The work of Arthur Schopenhauer is reflective of the Upanishads.

National Myth

A national myth is an inspiring narrative or anecdote about a nation's past. These often over-dramatize true events, omit important historical details, or add details for which there is no evidence. It can be a fictional story that no one takes to be true, such as *Paul Bunyan*, which was created by French Canadians during the Papineau Rebellion of 1837, when they revolted against the young English Queen. In older nations, national myths may be spiritual and refer to the nation's founding by God or gods or other supernatural beings.

Some National Myths
- The legend of King Arthur in Great Britain
- Sir Francis Drake in England
- The Pilgrims and the Mayflower in the United States
- Pocahontas, who is said to have saved the life of John Smith from her savage father, Powhatan
- The legendary ride of Paul Revere
- The last words of Nathan Hale
- The person of George Washington and apocryphal tales about him such as his cutting down a cherry tree with a hatchet and then facing up to the truth: "I cannot tell a lie."

Skill 5.2   Understand the historical, social, and cultural contexts from which ancient world literature emerged.

Between 7000 B.C. and 3000 B.C. the domestication of animals, the development of agriculture, and the establishment of an agricultural surplus led to the invention of writing, thus making possible the emergence of literature and the development of human civilization, as well.

Check out
Sumerian Art and Architecture at
http://www.crystalinks.com/sumerart.html

These three developments allowed the small, nomadic groups of hunters and gatherers who had up until then existed in pockets all over the world to evolve into larger, stationary communities. The first of these communities developed in an area in the Middle East called Mesopotamia, meaning "Land Between two Rivers," the Tigris and the Euphrates. This ancestor to civilization as we know it was called Sumer and the Sumerians created the wheel and the first written language.

Perhaps the reason the Sumerians were the first to create so much of what is fundamental to civilization goes back to their unsurpassed ability to create an agricultural surplus. With their position between two flowing rivers, the Sumerians developed an extensive irrigation system, which allowed them to create an abundant surplus. This surplus meant greater economic stability, security, and the ability to support a much larger population within the walls of their cities.

The growing population stimulated the development of governance and specialization. Artisans, governors, builders, regulators, merchants, and priests flourished. Keeping track of all this activity required the development of some kind of record keeping. At first, **pictographs** (images directly representing concrete objects) were etched into soft clay tablets and allowed to dry.

As time went on, the scope of record-keeping grew from recording how many sacks of barley a farmer brought to the temple to describing in great detail and enthusiasm the exploits of the kings. Thus, with the evolution of the city-state and then the nation, pictographs quickly became insufficient to meet the needs of this new societal structure we now call civilization. Eventually, the Sumerians developed symbols to represent abstract qualities such as courage and love.

Skill 5.3   **Identify significant genres and themes in ancient world literature.**

Tales recounting the adventures, exploits, triumphs, and struggles of kings and warriors as well as stories of creation and the meaning of life constitute the major themes in ancient world literature.

While ancient literature began with the **Sumerians** writing and transcribing their epic tales of heroism and of the all-too-human relationship between themselves and their deities, the body of ancient literature most relevant to the modern world is from the period 800 B.C. to 400 A.D. Ancient Hebrew, Greek, and Latin laid the foundation for most of Western secular and religious thought and for the major themes of Western Literature.

The concept (found in **Hebrew** manuscripts dating from the seventh to the second centuries B.C.E.) of a single, all-powerful God is, perhaps, chief among the foundations of Western thought. A wildly revolutionary idea at the time, it set the Hebrew nation apart from the rest of the ancient world. Concurrent with the theme of a single, omnipotent God, the Hebrew manuscripts also carried the less revolutionary idea of the one who suffers for all. Joseph (who suffered for his family and was then rewarded) and Job (who had everything, lost it all, and because he remained faithful, regained his earthly fortune) exemplify this motif. The idea of one suffering for all, or of the innocent serving as a scapegoat for the sins of the many, can be found in the most ancient writings and rituals. However, its most profound expression is found in the innocent Hebrew messiah who, "despised and rejected of men," still sought forgiveness for his executioners and chose to make "his grave with the wicked" (Book of Isaiah).

Two masterpieces of ancient **Greek** literature, the *Iliad* and the *Odyssey*, are attributed to Homer and first existed as part of an oral tradition. War is the graphic subject of the *Iliad*. In this poem, Homer evokes two strong, contradictory, and timeless human emotions: revulsion for war and fascination with violence. In the *Iliad*, Achilles is the ultimate warrior who lives to fight and to die on the battlefield.

The *Odyssey* covers the years after the war described in the *Iliad* and instructs that battles are fought not only on the battlefield but also on the journey home, or on the journey toward a just and honorable life. It is the story of the temptations and obstacles that the soldier Odysseus must overcome before returning to his faithful wife and peaceful home.

The **Romans** chose first to conquer and then to write. In all matters, the Romans paid highest allegiance not to emotions or to questions of right or wrong, but to what was practical, functional, stable, and lasting. A disciplined and highly organized people, the Romans built a great empire, but for their literary inspirations they turned to the Greeks.

Although inspired by the Greeks, the Roman poets created distinctly Roman works. In the Latin manuscripts of the Romans, the highest virtues are those which promote adherence to duty and to discipline, as best expressed in the *Aeneid* by Virgil. In this poem, Aeneas is the ideal Roman ruler, devoted to duty above all else. His god-given mission is to found the city that in time will become the seat of the great Roman Empire. To do this, he sacrifices his one and only love and then his life.

Ancient Literary Genres

The major genres employed in ancient literary works include prose, epic poetry, comedic and tragic plays, and satire. Although ancient novels did exist, with the earliest *Story of Sinuhe*, an Egyptian work, dated between 2000 and 1501 B.C., the novel as a form of literary expression would not come into its own until the Victorian era (1837). The prose that did exist consisted of historical records (such as Thucydides' account of the Peloponnesian Wars) and of the works of philosophers and orators (the speeches of the Greek philosopher Socrates as recorded by his famous student Plato and of the Roman philosopher and orator Cicero).

The popularity of the epic poem in the ancient world stems from its roots in the oral tradition, in which stories and accounts of the wars, kings, warriors, and the gods were shared with the public. While some of the greatest epic poetry is attributed to Homer and Virgil, the Sumerian epic poem *Gilgamesh* is the first of this literary genre.

Absent in ancient Hebrew and Roman literature, **drama** had its birth in the fifth century in Athens. Early Greek plays include tragedies by Aeschylus (*Agamemnon*) and Sophocles (*Oedipus Tyrannus*) and comedies by Aristophanes (*Lysistrata*). These Greek dramas grew out of an ancient ritual, a dance to the god Dionysus. The ritual involved a chorus of dancers who sang the familiar songs of their epic heroes as found in the works of Homer in order to honor and please Dionysus and to ensure a bountiful spring.

After the seventh century B.C., a Greek poet, Thespis, decided to add an "actor" into the chorus. The actor Thespian would stand apart from and answer to the chorus. Thus drama--which in Greek means "thing done"--was born.

While the play was unique to the Greeks, satire was unique to Rome. It was the term the Roman poet Juvenal gave to his poems criticizing the vices and follies of Imperial Rome. According to Juvenal, chief among these follies was blind ambition because it causes those afflicted to pray for anything except "a sound mind in a sound body."

Skill 5.4   **Identify a range of authors and works (the Gilgamesh epic, the Vedas, the Old and New Testaments, the Qur'an, Homer, Lao-Tzu, Sappho, Sophocles, Aristophanes, Virgil, Li Po, Murasaki Shikibu, Omar Khayyám, Rumi, Dante Alighieri) and their significance in the development of ancient world literature.**

Read about **Finding the Tomb of Gilgamesh**
http://news.bbc.co.uk/2/hi/science/nature/2982891.stm

Considered one of the greatest epic poems of all time, the *Gilgamesh* epic (1200 B.C.) is also the first. It was recorded by the Babylonians and is based on the legends and myths that had evolved for generations under the Sumerians. It is the tale of Gilgamesh, a Mesopotamian king who has many adventures, with a significant one being his search for immortality. In this adventure are many elements that are found in the Old Testament account of Noah and the flood.

In this particular adventure, Gilgamesh gains access to the secret of immortality from an elderly couple that the gods had saved from a flood intended to destroy the world. The couple had survived by floating in an ark, yet their message to the hero is quite different from any found in the Old Testament; it is one of resignation—the gods save and destroy whom they please. Nevertheless, the old couple gives Gilgamesh a plant that will return to him his youth. However, while he is sleeping, the plant is eaten by a snake—which is why, according to the epic, each year the snake sheds its old skin. In the end Gilgamesh takes to heart the lesson of the old couple, stating, "When the gods created man, they let death be his share, and life they kept in their own hands."

While *Gilgamesh* may be considered the first recorded epic poem, the first and greatest epic poems of Western civilization are those attributed to **Homer**: the *Iliad* and *Odyssey*. Homer remains significant because of the impact these two epics have had on the development of Western literature. Even with the rise of Christianity, these two Homeric works remain the models for heroic epic poems. Great English writers such as Alexander Pope and John Keats acknowledge their debt to Homer, with Pope writing, "Be Homer's works your study and delight; Read them by day, and meditate by night."

What makes this remarkable is that Homer's view of gods and humankind stand in direct opposition to the Christian view, which has humans made in the image of God. For Homer, the gods and goddesses are made in the image of mortal men and women—in fact, the Homeric gods are not much more than humans made immortal. The daily involvement of the gods and goddesses with their mingling and interferences in human activities was of urgent concern to the Greeks, much more than so than any distant story of creation. Having to deal on a daily basis with the deities had the effect of making the humans more godlike than the gods themselves. It is this essence of the divine as a human attribute that was picked up in Judeo- and Christian-writings and which contributes to the lasting impact and importance of these great epic poems.

Sophocles (496-406 B.C.) was one of the early three great Greek playwrights that included Aeschylus (525-456 B.C.) and Euripides (485-406 B.C.). Sophocles was the ideal Athenian public man of letters- a wealthy man in his own right, he served as one of Athens' ten generals and as a treasurer for the tribute taken from subject states. He was also a prolific and popular playwright, winning first place at least 20 times at the annual Dionysian festivals. To be considered for a prize, the dramatist had to write, not one play, but a **tetrology** (compound work made up of four works) of three tragedies and light **satyr** piece (an ancient Greek form of tragicomedy). Sophocles enhanced the Greek drama by adding a third actor (two had been the standard) and scenery. With Sophocles the spectators saw a more realistic stage for the unfolding of human drama, for along with the song of the chorus, there was now dialogue among the three actors.

It was **Euripides**, however, who is credited with the final development of Greek drama with his innovative "deus ex machina." This innovation involved lowering a god, via a crane, directly into the action of the play to resolve the dramatic problem.

Virgil (70-19 B.C.) is the author of the great Roman epic *Aeneid* which was left unfinished due to the early death of the author. Virgil lived and wrote during the early years of what would become two centuries of stable Roman rule. As a Latin poet, he was deeply indebted to his Greek predecessors, from whom he borrowed extensively. Aeneas, like Achilles, is a warrior, and like Odysseus, he is a wanderer. However, unlike either, Aeneas is bound, not to his passions, which for Achilles is to die in battle and for Odysseus is to reach his home where he can die in comfort and peace, but to a higher mission.

Aeneas is the ideal Roman—whose first and strongest obligation is to public duty. Aeneas has a god-given mission to found the city that would become the seat of the great Roman Empire. To do this and to remain true to his mission, Aeneas forsakes the love of his life, Dido, and in the end, must sacrifice his own life. While describing, through Aeneas, the ideal Roman, Virgil is writing more than a piece of Roman propaganda; his verses are steeped in the sorrow and regret such dedication to obligation entails. It is this understanding of and sympathy for the sacrifices of Aeneas that allows Virgil's *Aeneid* to transcend its historical context to speak to the ages.

Born to into a prosperous family in Florence, Italy, **Dante Alighieri** (1265-1321) studied Latin classics, an affinity for which was encouraged by his mentor,

Learn more about
**Dante Alighieri and
The Divine Comedy** at
http://www.uwm.edu/
Library/special/exhibits/
clastext/clspg064.htm

Brunetto Latini, who was also a leader in the Guelf (papal) political party. Growing up with this dual involvement in the classic literature and politics, Dante traveled to Rome in 1301 to seek support for the independence of Florence from Pope Boniface VIII. Negotiations failed and in 1302, Dante was exiled from his beloved Florence. He was to die in exile, never setting foot in Florence again.

Thus it is in exile that Dante wrote the greatest piece of literature to come to us from the Middle Ages: *The Divine Comedy*. A vividly imaginative piece, it chronicles the journey of the author from the depths of hell to the pinnacle in Paradise. It is the journey of the soul and of the rewards and punishment that await us beyond death's door. It is a journey that occupied the minds of many during the Middle Ages, and it is a journey with its revelations and insights that has much to tell us yet today.

Dante had called this piece a comedy because, unlike a tragedy, which starts out light and ends with horror, he wrote that comedies begin with horror and end with happiness. Dante also noted that the language for comedy differs from tragedy in that "tragedy is lofty and sublime, comedy lowly and humble." Therefore Dante chose to write his great poem not in Latin, but in Italian "because it is the vulgar tongue, in which even housewives hold converse."

While Dante referred to his work as the *Comedy of Dante Alighieri*, the Venice edition printed in 1555 ran it as the *Divine Comedy*, probably because Dante was sometimes referred to as the *Divine Dante*.

In his own words, Dante described the work as a "state of the soul after death." Similar to such ancient classics as the *Odyssey* by Homer and the *Aeneid* by Virgil, the *Divine Comedy* is the story of a wanderer. In this case, the wanderer is Dante himself, and his journey takes into the deepest depths of hell up to the highest point in heaven. Not too surprisingly, the great Latin poet Virgil is Dante's guide in this journey. Remarkable in this work is its total commitment of style and form to the message itself.

The poem has three divisions: Hell, Purgatory, and Heaven. The number three is significant because it corresponds to the Blessed Trinity. Each division is the same length, having 33 cantos, making 99. The first division contains an introductory canto to the entire piece, for a total of 100, which is the square of 10, considered then to be the number of perfection. In addition, the number nine, the square of three, figures centrally in each division.

In Hell, the lost souls are in three groups, occupying nine concentric circles. Purgatory consists of mountain on an island in the sea. The mountain is divided into ante-Purgatory at the base, Purgatory Proper in the middle, and Earthly Summit at the top. Again the number three, with Purgatory Proper being divided into seven subdivisions, Dante achieves another nod to the number nine, the square of three. Heaven's divisions likewise amount to nine with the additional and final division housing the abode of God, making the total 10, corresponding appropriately, to perfection.

Skill 5.5   **Understand the historical, social, and cultural aspects of ancient world literature (the expression of regional, ethnic, and historical values, archetypes, and ideas through literature; ways in which literary works and movements both reflected and shaped culture and history); and characteristics and significance of world mythology and folk literature.**

Of the five ancient civilizations (Babylon and Assyria, Egypt, Greece, Rome, and the Israelite culture), the ones identified as having led directly to the development of Western literature are the Greeks, Romans, and Israelites. However, the Egyptians, the Babylonians, and the Assyrians have left their marks indirectly on papyrus and on clay tablets.

Gilgamesh is recorded on the broken clay tablets of ancient Babylon/Assyria. Written in cuneiform (developed by the Sumerians who preceded the Babylonians), this epic has survived to echo through the ages. The Babylonians also codified a formal set of laws, the Code of Hammurabi, named after a Babylonian king.

Many of these laws were variants on laws inherited from the Sumerians, including the famous *lex talionis*, or "an eye for an eye, a tooth for a tooth, a limb for a limb," which the Sumerians learned from the Semites.

Although not considered to be a civilization of great philosophers, Egypt did provide art and writings as evidence of an advanced and complex system of beliefs in a supernatural world, in an afterlife, and, for a time, in a single god. The Egyptians also had developed high ideals of benevolence and justice. However, these beliefs and standards of behavior were recorded in hieroglyphs on papyrus leaves—neither of which has stood the test of time. Poorly understood by surrounding and subsequent cultures, the direct link between Egyptian literary works and Western thought has been lost.

The independent development and subsequent contact, interaction, and fusion of attitudes of Greece, Rome, and the Israelites do provide us with a direct link to the origins of Western thought and literature.

A significant portion of Western thought is based on these cultures' mythological traditions explaining such matters as creation, the building of civilizations, and the journey one makes from birth to death. In *The Power of Myth* by Joseph Campbell with Bill Moyer (1991), Campbell notes that "Greek and Latin and biblical literature used to be part of everyone's education. Now, when these were dropped, a whole tradition of Occidental mythological information was lost . . . . With the loss of that, we've really lost something because we don't have a comparable literature to take its place."

Mythos is Greek for story, but it not just any story. A myth must involve the relationship between at least one human and a deity. It is this supernatural relationship that has been used to explain the many mysteries of life—the universal truths of love, hate, and fear that have been experienced by humans since the dawn of time. Other characters or archetypes in myths include devils or demons, heroes (almost always male) such as the Greek Hercules, and tricksters (who can be helpful or evil) such as Loki in Norse myths.

Check out the writings of **Joseph Campbell**
http://www.jcf.org/works.php

The Greeks created their Olympian gods and goddesses while the Romans, who always turned to the Greeks for literary inspiration, borrowed almost all their mythology from the Greeks, giving the Olympian gods distinctive Roman names. Thus, Zeus becomes Jupiter; and Aphrodite, the Greek goddess of love, is transformed into Venus.

Greek and Roman myths present gods or goddesses made in the image of humans. Often the only difference is that the god is immortal and the human is destined to die. Living life comfortably and safely into old age in spite of god-like interference was the goal for most Greeks and Romans.

However, in the mythological tradition of the Bible, there is another, more pressing, element. It is the fight between good and evil, the need for the individual to transcend the evil in this life in order to attain the spiritual goodness or wholeness that is his or hers by divine right.

Myths common to almost all cultures deal with the creation of the world, the creation of humans, the human fall from grace, and divine anger resulting in the destruction of the world (usually by a flood) except for a chosen male and female whose children will, it is hoped, have learned their lesson.

In contrast, while the myth has potential for spiritual instruction, folktales are traditional stories told primarily for entertainment, such as the American story of Paul Bunyan. Folktales have been told and retold in the language of the common people: the farmers and peasants, the serfs, and the merchants. Folktales (which can also be instructive) contain heroes, villains, and magical happenings, but they do not involve gods or goddesses.

Taken together, the stories and myths of a people explain and describe their culture with depth, sensitivity, and compassion not possible using mere facts and figures. Myths and folktales describe our common humanity, our origins, and perhaps, if we are careful readers, our destinies.

COMPETENCY 6.0 UNDERSTAND WORLD LITERATURE FROM THE FIFTEENTH CENTURY TO THE PRESENT

Skill 6.1 **Identify the characteristics of major literary forms, works, and writers associated with world literature (African, Asian, European, Latin American) from the fifteenth century to the present.**

In a culture of shrinking global demarcations, the literature of the world enables readers to witness the lives of others, thus increasing our understanding and appreciation of commonalities and differences.

Africa

African literary greats include South Africans Nadine Gordimer (Nobel Prize for literature) and Peter Abrahams, author of *Tell Freedom: Memories of Africa*, an autobiography of life in Johannesburg. Mark Mathabane wrote an

> Learn more about
> **Postcolonial Literature in English**
> http://www.thecore.nus.edu.sg/post/misc/africov.html

autobiography *Kaffir Boy* about growing up in South Africa. Chinua Achebe (*Things Fall Apart*) and the poet, Wole Soyinka, hail from Nigeria. Egyptian writer Naguib Mahfouz and Doris Lessing from Rhodesia (now Zimbabwe), write about race relations in their respective countries. Lessing won the 2007 Nobel Prize for Literature. Because of her radical politics, Lessing was once banned from her homeland as was Alan Paton banned from South Africa when his seemingly simple story, *Cry, the Beloved Country*, brought the plight of blacks and the whites' fear of blacks under apartheid to the rest of the world.

Far East Literature

Asia has many modern writers who are being translated for the western reading public. India's Krishan Chandar has authored more than 300 stories. Rabindranath Tagore won the Nobel Prize for Literature in 1913 (*Song Offerings*). R. K. Narayan, India's most famous writer (*The Guide*), is interested in mythology and legends of India. Santha Rama Rau's work *Gifts of Passage* is her true story of life in a British school where she tries to preserve her Indian culture and traditional home.

Revered as Japan's most famous female author, Fumiko Hayashi (*Drifting Clouds*) by the time of her death had written more than 270 literary works.

In 1968 the Nobel Prize for literature was awarded to Yasunari Kawabata (*The Sound of the Mountain, The Snow Country*). His Palm-of-the-Hand stories take the essentials of Haiku poetry and transform them into the short story genre.

Katai Tayama (*The Quilt*) is touted as the father of the Japanese confessional novel. His works, characterized as naturalism, are definitely not for the squeamish. The "slice of life" psychological writings of Ryunosuke Akutagawa gained him acclaim in the western world. His short stories, especially "Rashamon" and "In a Grove," are greatly praised for style as well as content.

China, too, has given to the literary world. Li Po, the T'ang dynasty poet from the Chinese Golden Age, revealed his interest in folklore by preserving the folk songs and mythology of China. Po further enables his readers to enter into the Chinese philosophy of Taoism and to understand feelings against expansionism during the T'ang dynastic rule. The T'ang dynasty, which was one of great diversity in the arts, saw Jiang Fang help create the Chinese version of a short story. His themes often express love between a man and a woman.

Modern feminist and political concerns are written eloquently by Ting Ling, who used the pseudonym Chiang Ping-Chih. Her stories reflect her concerns about social injustice and her commitment to the women's movement.

Continental European Literature

With its long history of great writers, continental European literature expands the world of students and broadens their exposure to different cultures and values. This category as discussed below excludes British literature as it was covered previously.

Germany

German poet and playwright Friedrich von Schiller is best known for his history plays *William Tell* and *The Maid of Orleans*. He is a leading literary figure in Germany's Golden Age of Literature. Also from Germany, Rainer Maria Rilke, the great lyric poet, is one of the poets of the unconscious, or stream of consciousness. Germany also has given the world Herman Hesse, (*Siddartha*), Gunter Grass (*The Tin Drum*), and the highly respected author of *Faust*, Johann Wolfgang von Goethe.

Scandinavia

Scandinavian literature includes the work of Hans Christian Andersen of Denmark, who advanced the fairytale genre with such wistful tales as "The Little Mermaid" and "Thumbelina." The social commentary of Henrik Ibsen in Norway startled the world through drama exploring such issues as feminism (*The Doll's House* and *Hedda Gabler*) and the effects of sexually-transmitted diseases (*The Wild Duck* and *Ghosts*). In his *Hedda Gabler,* Hedda encourages another to commit suicide and then at the end of the play shoots herself in her temple. The Danish philosopher Kierkegaard is well-known for his development of existentialism, a philosophy that focuses upon the isolation of individual experience in an indifferent universe.

Read more about
Henrik Ibsen
http://www.hf.uio.no/
ibsensenteret/
index_eng.html

Sweden's Selma Lagerlof is the first woman to win the Nobel Prize for literature. Her novels include *Gosta Berling's Saga* and the world-renowned *The Wonderful Adventures of Nils*, a children's work.

Russia

Russian literature is vast and monumental. Who has not heard of Fyodor Dostoevsky's *Crime and Punishment* and *The Brothers Karamazov* or of Count Leo Tolstoy's *War and Peace*? These are examples of psychological realism. Dostoevsky's influence on modern writers cannot be overstressed.

Tolstoy's *War and Peace* is the sweeping account of the invasion of Russia and Napoleon's taking of Moscow. This novel is called the national novel of Russia. Further advancing Tolstoy's greatness is his ability to create realistic and unforgettable female characters, especially Natasha in *War and Peace* and Anna in *Anna Karenina*.

Pushkin is famous for great short stories; Anton Chekhov for drama (*Uncle Vanya, The Three Sisters, The Cherry Orchard*); and Yevgeny Yevtushenko for poetry (*Babi Yar*). Boris Pasternak won the Nobel Prize (*Dr. Zhivago*). Aleksandr Solzhenitsyn (*The Gulag Archipelago*) returned to Russia after years of expatriation in Vermont. Ilya Varshavsky, who creates fictional societies that are dystopias--the opposite of utopias--, represents the genre of science fiction.

France

France has a multifaceted canon of great literature that is universal in scope and that almost always champions some social cause. Examples include the poignant short stories of Guy de Maupassant; the fantastic poetry of Charles Baudelaire (*Fleurs du Mal*); the groundbreaking lyrical poetry of Rimbaud and Verlaine; and the existentialism of Jean-Paul Sartre (*No Exit, The Flies, and Nausea*), Andre Malraux (*The Fall*) and Albert Camus (*The Stranger* and *The Plague*), the recipient of the 1957 Nobel Prize for Literature. Feminist writings include those of Sidonie-Gabrielle Colette, known for her short stories and novels, as well as Simone de Beauvoir.

Learn more about
Jean Paul Sartre
http://www.users.muohio.e
du/shermalw/honors_2001
_fall/honors_papers_2001/
detwilerj_Sartre.htm

Drama in France is best represented by Rostand's *Cyrano de Bergerac* and the neo-classical dramas of Racine and Corneille (*El Cid*). The great French novelists include Andre Gide, Honore de Balzac (*Cousin Bette*), Stendel (*The Red and the Black*), and Alexandre Dumas (*The Three Musketeers* and *The Man in the Iron Mask)*. Victor Hugo is the Charles Dickens of French literature, having penned the masterpieces *The Hunchback of Notre Dame* and *Les Miserables*. The stream of consciousness of Proust's *Remembrance of Things Past* and the Absurdist theatre of Samuel Beckett and Eugene Ionesco (*The Rhinoceros*) attest to the groundbreaking genius of the French writers.

Slavic Nations

Czech writer Franz Kafka (*The Metamorphosis, The Trial,* and *The Castle*) is considered by many to be the literary voice of the first half of the twentieth century. Poet Vaclav Havel also represents the Czech Republic. Slovakia has dramatist Karel Capek (*R.U.R.*). Elie Wiesel (*Night*), Nobel Prize winner, was born in Romania.

Spain

Spain's great writers include Miguel de Cervantes (*Don Quixote*) and Juan Ramon Jimenez. The anonymous national epic, *El Cid*, has been translated into many languages.

Italy

Italy's greatest writers include Virgil (*The Aeneid)*, Giovanni Boccaccio (*The Decameron*), Dante Alighieri (*The Divine Comedy*) and the more contemporary, Alberto Moravia.

Ancient Greece

Greece will always be foremost in literary stature because of Homer's epics, *The Iliad* and *The Odyssey*. No one except Shakespeare is more often cited. The works of Plato and Aristotle in philosophy; of Aeschylus, Euripides, and Sophocles in tragedy, and of Aristophanes in comedy further solidify Greece's pre-eminence. Greece is the cradle not only of democracy but of literature as well.

North American Literature

North American literature is divided between the United States, Canada, and Mexico. Canadian writers of note include feminist Margaret Atwood, (*The Hand Maiden's Tale*); Alice Munro, a remarkable short story writer; and W. P. Kinsella, another short story writer whose two major subjects are North American Indians and baseball. Mexican writers include 1990 Nobel Prize winning poet Octavio Paz (*The Labyrinth of Solitude*) and feminist Rosario Castillanos (*The Nine Guardians*).

Central American/Caribbean Literature

> **The Norton Anthology of World Literature**
> http://www.wwnorton.com/college/english/nawol/

The Caribbean and Central America encompass a vast area and cultures that reflect oppression and colonialism by England, Spain, Portugal, France, and The Netherlands. The Caribbean writers include Samuel Selvon from Trinidad and Armando Valladares of Cuba. Central American authors include dramatist Carlos Solorzano, from Guatemala, whose plays include *Dona Beatriz, The Hapless, The Magician,* and *The Hands of God.*

South American Literature

Chilean Gabriela Mistral was the first Latin American writer to win the Nobel Prize for Literature. She is best known for her collections of poetry, *Desolation and Feeling.* Chile was also home to Pablo Neruda, who, in 1971, also won the Nobel Prize for his poetry. His 29 volumes of poetry have been translated into more than 60 languages, attesting to his universal appeal. *Twenty Love Poems* and *Song of Despair* are justly famous. Isabel Allende is carrying on the Chilean literary standards with her acclaimed novel, *House of Spirits.*

Argentine Jorge Luis Borges is considered by many literary critics to be the most important writer of his century from South America. His collections of short stories, *Ficciones*, brought him universal recognition. Also from Argentina, Silvina Ocampo, a collaborator with Borges on a collection of poetry, is famed for her poetry and short story collections, which include *The Fury* and *The Days of the Night.*

Horacio Quiroga represents Uruguay, and Brazil has Joao Guimaraes Rosa, whose novel, *The Devil to Pay*, is considered first-rank world literature. Paulo Coelho's *The Alchemist* and *The Zahir*, from Brazil, has been translated into more than 50 languages.

Skill 6.2   Understand the historical, social, and cultural contexts of world literature from the fifteenth century to the present.

With the destruction of the Roman Empire in the fifth century, the Roman Catholic Church became the dominant and unifying source in Europe, with the Pope as the supreme authority in all matters. With the ascendancy of the Church and the demise of Rome; the social, political, and artistic achievements of the classical age were effectively "lost" for centuries, and Western civilizations entered a time known as the Dark or Early Middle Ages.

However, by the fifteenth century, the lot of the individual had improved dramatically, and the overwhelming influence of the Catholic Church was challenged.

This period is known as the Renaissance, which started in Italy in the mid-fourteenth century, and is associated with the rediscovery and revival of classical Greek and Latin philosophy, literature, and art.

In the fifteenth and early sixteenth centuries, the invention of the printing press (about 1450) and the revolt of Martin Luther, a German Catholic monk, helped to fuel the revival of classical thought and to fuel challenges to the supremacy of the Catholic Church.

The development of paper gave impetus to the invention of the printing press. Prior to the development of paper, parchment made from the skin of farm animals had been used for writing. Considering that one animal generally produced about 4 leaves or sheets of parchment, reprinting a book the size of the Bible required the slaughter of at least 300 sheep or calves, making it a very expensive process.

With the development of paper from rags and the invention of the printing press, printing books and pamphlets became cheap. In addition, they were printed not only in Greek and Latin (the language of scholars and diplomats) but in the vernacular (the language of the common people). This was important to the revolutionary success of Martin Luther, who in 1517 nailed his famous 95 theses to the door of the castle church of Wittenberg.

Learn more about
Martin Luther at
http://www.educ.msu.edu/h
omepages/laurence/reforma
tion/Luther/Luther.htm

His 95 theses amounted to objections (protestations) regarding the pervasive sale of indulgences (pardons for sins) by the Catholic Church throughout Europe, especially in Germany.

Without the printing press, few would have known or followed Luther's challenge to Roman Catholic authority, but the German monk and his supporters turned immediately to the printing press and sent out hundreds of pamphlets explaining his protests against Rome, which gained the support of German people at all levels of society. As a result, when Luther was excommunicated by the Church in Rome, he and his followers became known as Lutherans, and the first of the Protestant or "protesting" religions was born.

The study of classical texts and advances in science and astronomy aided this break with the Roman Catholic Church by challenging the traditional thinking that had been endorsed and enforced by the Church in Rome for generations. While the Renaissance revived the classics, the subsequent Age of Reason known as The Enlightenment extolled and emulated the clarity and rational thinking of the great classical writers, thinkers, and artists-- especially of the Romans. This is evident in the writings of John Dryden (1631-1700), in the mathematically exact music of the harpsichord, and in the classical ionic and doric architecture exhibited in palaces and stately homes of this period.

By the late 1700s, the Romantics challenged this exclusive admiration for the purely intellectual and logical thinking of the classicists. Instead of looking to science and purely rational thought for answers and inspiration, the Romantics celebrated the emotions and the imagination. Romantic poet William Blake (1757-1827) considered science and mathematics to be soulless disciplines that shackled the imagination and inhibited free expression of thought and feelings.

The Romantics also preferred nature to the city and distrusted most established institutions, especially the church and the government, which, in England, people were finding more and more oppressive. In "The Masque of Anarchy," English poet Percy Shelley (1792-1822) encouraged the people of England to stand up against the enslaving establishment:

> "Rise like Lions after slumber
> In unvanquishable number—
> Shake your chains to earth like dew
> Which in sleep had fallen on you—
> Ye are many—they are few."

For more information on **Percy Bysshe Shelley**, http://www.wam.umd.edu/ ~djb/shelley/home.html

Sentiments such as Shelley's finally led to reforms in England which, among other changes, eliminated seats in Parliament that had been purchased by wealthy families.
Still, it would be 50 years before England passed a reform that allowed men from all economic and social classes to vote and another 50 years before women were granted the same right.

The nineteenth century is considered by many to be the century of greatest change for Western civilization, fueled in large part by the Industrial Revolution, which introduced factories, railroads, and the automobile to civilization.

This revolution radically changed the way people lived, allowing them greater and faster mobility and more economic possibilities. While the growing urbanization created slums and a class of working poor, it also gave rise to a powerful middle class, with surplus wealth and free time in which to spend it.

These developments created a new deity—"progress"—understood as holding out unlimited hope for the future and for the advancement of human civilization.

Religious institutions, which had played such a fundamental role in the public and private lives of peoples in many countries, were forced to take a back seat at this time. The impact of discoveries in astronomy, geology, evolutionary biology, and archeology pushed religion out of the public limelight and into a personal and private sphere.

A majority of the literature of this period celebrated contemporary life and manners, and by the 1850s, it was known as the literature of reality, or "Realism." The novelist was likened to the scientist, who creates and directs the experiment, but is not part of it. The writer is objective and observational, recording the truth of the reality around him or her.

Writers of this movement include Gustave Flaubert (1821-1880) of France (*Madame Bovary*); Fyodor Dostoevsky (1821-1881) of Russia (*Crime and Punishment*); and Henry James (1843-1916) of America (*The Aspen Papers, The Turn of the Screw, Daisy Miller,* and *The Bostonians*).

During the first half of the twentieth century, technological advancements and breakthroughs continued. Henry Ford started the world's first assembly line in Detroit in 1908, mass-producing the famous Model T Ford. The success of this ubiquitous black car was evident because by 1929 over 26 million Model T Fords were registered in the United States.

Radio transmission, telephones, movies, and flying machines all made their debut in the early twentieth century. In the midst of these early advances, the literature produced in these early decades was didactic or instructive in tone. Writers took on issues of the day, such as the function of social classes and professions, female suffrage, the justification of armaments and war, and the morality of empire.

The first half of the twentieth century also witnessed World War I, the end of the supremacy of the British Empire, the onset of the Great Depression, and then World War II.

Modernism is the term used to describe the literary movement up to the First World War. Considered radical and utopian in nature, this movement was inspired by new ideas in anthropology, psychoanalysis, philosophy, and political science. Rejecting styles and forms of the post-Romantic period, writers of this movement include D.H. Lawrence (1885-1930) of England (*The Rainbow, Lady Chatterley's Lover,* and *Women in Love*) and James Joyce (1882-1941) of Ireland (*A Portrait of the Artist as a Young Man, Ulysses*, and *Finnegans Wake*).

D.H. Lawrence's novels that were concerned with relationships in industrial settings were censored. Joyce used symbols, myth, and stream-of-consciousness writing to explore the universality of the human condition and the relationship between the conscious and the unconscious.

The cynicism that followed the horrors of World War I gave rise to a literature that was pessimistic regarding the human potential to survive with dignity the horrors and the conveniences of the modern world. In this vein, Aldous Huxley wrote his inventive, anti-utopian novel *Brave New World*.

The onset of World War II in 1939 in Europe and in 1941 in the United States halted for a time the great literary movements and inventiveness of the first half of the century. The horrors of this second Great War, ending with the use of atomic bombs over Japan, so profoundly affected the human spirit that writer William Golding noted, "We have discovered a limit to literature."

The post-World War II era found the United States and Russia as the new world super powers. Britain was deeply indebted to America and definitely diminished as a world power, and, along with this new world order, styles in literature shifted from "Modernism" to "Postmodernism."

Referred to as a shift, rather than a break, in style, **postmodern literature** is seen as an extension of the Modernist mode of subjective literature—of looking inward, of examining and exploring the inner consciousness of the individual and its connection to the whole.

During the last half of the twentieth century, the assassinations of political and social leaders, the Cold War, Civil Rights movements, the Feminist Movement, the Space Age, the Internet, and all forms of mass media stimulated and heightened the intensity of this inward examination and exploration of self.

> Check out these resources on
> **Contemporary British and American Literature**
> http://vos.ucsb.edu/ browse.asp?id=2741

In an age of mass information and instant messaging, postmodern literature is still evolving, still exploring realities, not just of the inner self and its relation to the exterior world but of multiple realities constructed in time and space at points all over the globe. In spite of the seeming randomness and chaotic nature of such vast and starkly different realties, they remain knowable—and making them so remains the task of the postmodern writer.

Skill 6.3   Identify significant genres and themes in world literature from the fifteenth century to the present.

See Skill 6.1

Skill 6.4   Identify a range of authors (Michel de Montaigne, Miguel de Cervantes Saavedra, Molière, Jean-Jacques Rousseau, Johann Wolfgang von Goethe, Leo Tolstoy, Feodor Dostoevsky, Anton Chekhov, Rabindranath Tagore, Rainer Maria Rilke, Franz Kafka, Federico Garcia Lorca, Isak Dinesen, Albert Camus, Jorge Luis Borges, Primo Levi, Yehuda Amichai, Nadine Gordimer, Aleksandr Solzhenitsyn, Pablo Neruda, Czeslaw Milosz, Wole Soyinka, R. K. Narayan, Margaret Atwood, Derek Walcott, Naguib Mahfouz, Ōe Kenzaburō, V. S. Naipaul), their representative works, and their significance in world literature from the fifteenth century to the present.

As the Middle Ages gave way to the Neoclassical writers and thinkers, the "Great Quarrel" between the writers of antiquity and the modernist began. No longer was an individual's private relation to God an issue. More and more it was the social order and the developing nation-state that were analyzed in light of an individual's development and moral responsibilities.

Jean-Baptiste Poquelin **Molière** (1622-1673), a comic dramatist and one of France's great dramatist of that time, wrote plays that focused on the false values and foibles of the citizens of late seventeenth-century France. Not concerned with the citizen's private relationship with God or perhaps even with the role of Christianity as a whole, Molière examined the mundane hypocrisy of everyday life as well as a lack of good taste and common sense. With his consideration of the individual as foremost a product of his or her social order, Molière was a harbinger of modern thought. His first major success was *The High-Brow Ladies* (1659), which exposed the pretentious nature of high society in France. Included in the nearly two dozen comedies attributed to him are *The School for Husbands* (1665), *Don Juan* (1665), *The Misanthrope* (1666), and *The Imaginary Invalid* (1670).

A religious philosopher, political commentator, psychologist, and novelist of a strong biographical nature, **Feodor Dostoevsky** (1821-1888) has been studied and analyzed from many perspectives. He was born in Moscow, the son of a staff doctor at the Hospital for the Poor. After his father was murdered, Dostoevsky was sent to military school, becoming a draftsman in the St. Petersburg Engineering Corp. Eventually, Dostoevsky's questioning nature would involve him in antigovernment activities and with socialist movements. For these activities he was arrested and condemned to die by firing squad—only to have his life spared at the last minute. Nevertheless, he did earn a four-year stint in a workhouse in Siberia and six years as a common soldier on the Mongolian border. Thus his own life was a rich source of inspiration for his writings—and many of his own experiences, including his epileptic condition—do appear in his works.

Dostoevsky sought out the extreme conditions in society, nature, and human nature to explore in his writings. For in this manner he could reveal the extreme qualities of good and evil—both of which, he believed, struggle for supremacy in each of us. Thus his stories portray the most shocking of crimes in *Crime and Punishment* (1866) and the most angelic of heroes in *The Idiot* (1869). His two other major works are *The Possessed* (1872) and *The Brothers Karamazov* (1880). Preceding these four great works is his *Notes from the Underground* (1864) which serves as a confession and a description of Dostoevsky's methods and thoughts. It speaks of his skepticism of the utopian view of human development and progress that was spreading through Europe at the time and of his belief in the vileness of human nature that can be saved only with Christ-like suffering and pain.

Born in Prague to a successful Jewish merchant, **Franz Kafka** (1883-1924) was to be plagued throughout his life with feelings of inadequacy when comparing himself and his ability to succeed in life with his father's financial achievements. Kafka's writings clearly depict the horror of a grinding reality without even the briefest moment of transcendence—that is, a life in which there is never a sense of understanding or justification for existence or the experience or internalization of the goodness of God. "*The Metamorphosis*" (1812) is the haunting story of the power of a term of abuse in the life of one man who is repeatedly made to feel as useful as an insect. This man, Gregor Samsa, wakes one day to find himself slowly turning into a cockroach. It is every child's nightmare, but for Kafka, it is reality: unrelenting and unforgiving. Other chief writings include *The Judgment* (1913), *The Penal Colony* (1919), *The Trial* (1925), and *America* (1927).

Born into an impoverished family in Algeria, **Albert Camus** (1913-1960) and his Spanish-speaking mother moved to Algiers after his father's death during World War II. As a young man, he worked as a journalist and enjoyed a brief membership with the Communist party and moved to Paris in 1940, where he joined a literary circle. Although a professed unbeliever, Camus struggled with the question of how evil, especially in the form of the suffering of the innocent, can exist in the presence of an all-powerful and loving God. Along with this question, Camus wondered, if indeed there is no God, then does what we do matter at all? Is any type of behavior permitted? For Camus the answer was no. Even without a God, Camus reasoned that we could sin in regard to the way we treat other human beings. Thus, his characters cover the range from the totally selfless to the totally self-absorbed. He first gained recognition as a writer for his contributions to an underground newspaper *Combat*.

His idea of the absurd—of the ceaseless desire of humans to seek and find reason and clarity in a world that offers neither—is a significant contribution to writing and to philosophy. This idea is at play in *The Myth of Sisyphu*s (1942), in which Camus notes that like Sisyphus, who is condemned by the gods to eternally push a boulder up a hill only to have it roll back down again, we should take joy in the task at hand, regardless of its meaning. Other major works include *The Stranger* (1942) *The Plague* (1948), *Exile and the Kingdom* (1957), and *Caligula and Other Plays* (1958). Camus received the Nobel Prize for Literature in 1957 and was killed in a car crash in 1960.

Read more about
**Aleksandr
Solzhenitsyn**
http://nobelprize.org/
nobel_prizes/
literature/laureates/
1970/index.html

Although he always expressed a keen interest in literature, **Aleksandr Solzhenitsyn** (1918-), studied math and physics at Rostov University, graduating in 1941—just in time to be drafted into Stalin's army and sent to the front lines. However, he was arrested in 1945 for speaking disrespectfully of Stalin—a crime for which Solzhenitsyn served eight years in prison. Solzhenitsyn's criticism of "the mustachioed one" (Stalin) may have taken away his freedom and subjected him to the most inhumane of conditions, but it also gave him material for his many writings. His time in a labor camp provided the background for *One Day in the Life of Ivan Denisovich* (1963).

After serving his time, Solzhenitsyn was exiled to southern Kazakhstan, where he taught primary students math and physics and where he continued to write. (Even while in prison, when the physical action of writing was not permitted, Solzhenitsyn would compose poetry in his head.) During a slight thaw in his country's international relations, Solzhenitsyn submitted his *One Day* manuscript for publication. It was an immediate sensation--and the last book he would publish in his country for decades. Although awarded the Nobel Prize for Literature in 1970, Solzhenitsyn was afraid to travel to Stockholm to receive the prize, fearing he would not be allowed to return to his home.

The major work that brought Solzhenitsyn to the attention of the Western world was *The Gulag Archipelago*. Written between 1962 and 1973, it is a book about the Soviet Union's concentration prison camp system, with "Gulag" being an acronym for the Russian term meaning "Chief Administration for Corrective Labor Camps." Based on his own experiences and the testimonies of over 200 other former inmates, the book was published in the West in 1973 and then in the underground press in the Soviet Union. As a result of the book's publication and the reaction of the world to the horrors of the Soviet prison system, Solzhenitsyn was stripped of his Soviet citizenship and deported to West Germany.

Following his deportation, Solzhenitsyn spent some time in Switzerland before moving to the United States and settling in Vermont. Although a severe critic of the Soviet system, Solzhenitsyn never felt comfortable living outside of his native Russia. Following the reinstatement of his Soviet citizenship, he returned to the land of his birth in 1994.

The impact of *The Gulag Archipelago* was immense. The facts and testimonies it presented were irrefutable and damning. While many in the West had attributed the Soviet system of concentration camps to Stalin, Solzhenitsyn traced its origins back to Lenin, who up until then had been idolized by many in the West. The horror of the system and the importance of the slave labor it provided to the Soviet economy were proven greater than imagined. As a result, many European Communist party groups disintegrated under the weight of the evidence, and the moral standing of the Soviet Union in the Western world was destroyed.

Writing with a great "ethical force," Solzhenitsyn is thorough, exact, and scrupulous in detail and design, and a modern example of the best of traditional Russian literature. His other major works include *The First Circle* (1968), *The Cancer Ward* (1969), *For the Good of the Cause*" (1970), and *August 1914* (1972).

Skill 6.5 **Understand social and cultural aspects of world literature from the fifteenth century to the present.**

See Skill 6.2.

COMPETENCY 7.0   UNDERSTAND THE CHARACTERISTICS OF VARIOUS GENRES AND TYPES OF LITERATURE

Skill 7.1   Identify the characteristics of the major literary genres (fiction, nonfiction, poetry, drama).

Prose is divided into two main genres: fiction and nonfiction. Fiction is based on an author's imagination, and nonfiction is based on factual information,

The Difference between Fiction and Nonfiction

Fiction is the opposite of fact and, simple as that may seem, it's the major distinction between fictional works and nonfictional works.

> Learn more about
> **Writing Fiction**
> http://crofsblogs.typepad.com/fiction/
> 2003/07/narrative_voice.html

A work of fiction typically has a central character, called the protagonist, and a character that stands in opposition called the antagonist. The antagonist might be something other than a person. In Stephen Crane's short story, "The Open Boat," for example, the antagonist is a hostile environment, a stormy sea.

Conflicts between protagonist and antagonist are typical of a work of fiction, and climax is the turning point at which those conflicts are resolved. The plot is the sequence of events during which the conflicts occur as the characters and plot move toward resolution.

A fiction writer artistically uses characterization, which depends on dialogue, description, or the attitude or attitudes of one or more characters toward another.

Enjoying fiction depends upon the ability of the readers to suspend disbelief. Readers make a deal with the writer that, for the time the readers take to read the story, the readers will replace their own beliefs with the convictions expressed by the writer and will accept the reality created by the writer.

This is not true in nonfiction. The writer of nonfiction must stick to verifiable facts. Thus, a writer of nonfiction is not free to create a character from imagination, no matter how realistic the author makes that character seem. All nonfiction characters have actually lived. The writer of nonfiction declares in the choice of that genre that the work is reliably based upon reality.

A *bildungsroman* (from the German) means "novel of education" or "novel of formation" and traces the spiritual, moral, psychological, or social development and growth of a main character from childhood to maturity.

Dickens' *David Copperfield* (1850) represents this genre as does Thomas Wolfe's *Look Homeward Angel* (1929).

Types of Fiction (not all):

- Action-adventure
- Erotica
- Mystery
- Thriller
- Crime
- Fantasy
- Romance
- Western
- Detective
- Horror
- Science fiction

Types of Nonfiction (not all):

- Almanac
- Blueprint
- Dictionary
- Essay
- Letter
- Textbook
- Autobiography
- Book report
- Documentary film
- History
- Philosophy
- User manual
- Biography
- Diary
- Encyclopedia
- Journal
- Science book

Poetry

Poetry, one of the densest forms of communications, is embedded with meaning. It is the use of heightened language to convey meaning and music.

Traditionally, a poem is a crafted created in language containing literary conventions such as meter, rhyme, alliteration, imagery, allusion, and versification such as stanza form. In modern times, the definition of poetry has been expanded to use metaphor, unmetered poetry, poetry written like prose but broken into short lines on a page, free verse, and unrhymed poetry. Subjects include personal and autobiographical topics.

Subgenres include the sonnet, elegy, ode, pastoral, and villanelle. Unfixed types of literature include blank verse and dramatic monologue.

Drama

In its most general sense, a drama is any work that is designed to be performed by actors onstage. It can also refer to a literary genre broadly divided into comedy and tragedy.

Contemporary usage, however, denotes drama as a work that treats serious subjects and themes but does not aim for the same grandeur as tragedy. Drama usually deals with characters of a less stately nature than tragedy. A classical example is Sophocles' tragedy *Oedipus Rex,* while a modern example is Eugene O'Neill's *The Iceman Cometh.*

Skill 7.2   Identify elements of fiction (plot, character, setting, theme)

The elements of fiction vary in importance and development from story to story. Some stories are mainly plot-driven while others are character studies. Stories can be so tightly constructed that all elements work together to develop the theme and entertain the reader. Although readers can certainly enjoy a story without an in-depth understanding of these elements, they can develop a deeper appreciation for those works which display the author's talent and writing skill.

Plot is the series of events that give a story its meaning and effect. If the plot does not *move*, the story quickly dies. Therefore, the successful writer of stories uses a wide variety of active verbs in creative and unusual ways. If a reader is kept interested by the movement of the story, the experience of reading it will be pleasurable. That reader will probably want to read more of this author's work. Careful, unique, and unusual choices of active verbs will help to bring about that effect.

William Faulkner is a good example of a successful writer whose stories are lively and memorable because of his use of unusual active verbs. In analyzing the development of plot, analytical readers will look at the verbs. However, the development of believable conflicts is also vital. If there is no conflict, there is no story. In critical thinking readers should ask: What devices does a writer use to develop the conflicts, and are they real and believable? Plot concerns rising actions and complications.

Character is portrayed in many ways: description of physical characteristics, dialogue, interior monologue, the thoughts of the character, the attitudes of other characters toward this one, and so on. Characters may be *round* or *flat*—that is, with an ability to change or one-dimensional.

Characterization can rely on an ability to recreate a sensory experience for the reader. If the description of the character's appearance is a visual one, then the reader must be able to *see* the character. What's the shape of the nose? What color are the eyes? How tall or how short is this character? How does the character move? How does the character walk? What does the character's voice sound like? Writers choose terms that will create a picture for the reader.

A good test of characterization is the level of emotional involvement of the reader in the character. If the reader is to become involved, the description must provide an actual experience—seeing, smelling, hearing, tasting, or feeling. In the following example, Isaac Asimov deftly describes a character both directly and indirectly.

"Undersecretary Albert Minnim was a small, compact man, ruddy of skin and graying, with the angles of his body smoothed down and softened. He exuded an air of cleanliness and smelled faintly of tonic. It all spoke of the good things of life that came with the liberal rations obtained by those high in Administration."

Isaac Asimov, *The Robot Series: The Naked Sun*

Dialogue will reflect characteristics. Is it clipped? Is it highly dialectal? Does a character rely on colloquialisms (*dis me, bling*)? The ability to portray the speech of a character can make or break a story. The kind of person the character is in the mind of the reader is dependent on impressions created by description and dialogue.

How other characters feel about another character is revealed by their treatment of him/her, their discussions of him/her with each other, or their overt descriptions of the character. For example: "John, of course, can't be trusted with another person's possessions." In analyzing a story, it's useful to discuss the devices used to produce character.

Setting may be visual, temporal, psychological, or social. Descriptive words are often used here also. In Edgar Allan Poe's description of the house in "The Fall of the House of Usher" as the protagonist/narrator approaches, the air of dread and gloom that pervades the story is caught in the setting and sets the stage for the story. A setting may also be symbolic, as it is in Poe's story, where the house is a symbol of the family that lives in it. As the house disintegrates, so does the family.

The language used in all of these aspects of a story—plot, character, and setting—work together to create the **mood** of a story. Poe's first sentence establishes the mood of the story: "During the whole of a dull, dark, and soundless day in the autumn of the year, when the clouds hung oppressively low in the heavens, I had been passing alone, on horseback, through a singularly dreary tract of country; and at length found myself, as the shades of the evening drew on, within view of the melancholy House of Usher."

Why did the author write this story? This question will lead to the **theme**—the underlying main idea. Whether a story is escapist or interpretive, it will have a controlling idea that is integral to its development. This idea is more than a topic (love, anger, guilt, jealousy); it is the author's view of the moral.

Sometimes the title of a story will help reveal the theme. For example, in "The Tell-Tale Heart," Poe tells us a story about guilt and the effect it has on one's conscience. The title foreshadows the outcome and helps the reader understand how all these elements contribute to an effective story.

Skill 7.3   Identify characteristic elements of fiction genres (novels, short stories).

Novel

The longest form of fictional prose- novels, contain a variety of characterizations, settings, local color, and regionalism. Most have complex plots, expanded description, and attention to detail. Some of the great novelists include Jane Austin, Charlotte Brontë, Mark Twain, Leo Tolstoy, Victor Hugo, Thomas Hardy, Charles Dickens, Nathaniel Hawthorne, E.M. Forster, and Gustave Flaubert.

Short Story

This is typically a terse narrative, with fewer contexts and more foregrounding than a novel. It may rely on fewer characters, and its success often focuses on a single conflict and the resolution. Ernest Hemingway, William Faulkner, Mark Twain, James Joyce, Shirley Jackson, Flannery O'Connor, Guy de Maupassant, Saki (H.H. Munro), Edgar Allen Poe, and Alexander Pushkin are considered to be great short story writers.

> Learn more about
> **Elements of the Short Story**
> http://www.yale.edu/ynhti/curriculum/
> units/1983/3/83.03.09.x.html

Skill 7.4   Describe types of fictional narratives (folk legend, fantasy, mystery, realistic novel) and their characteristics.

Authors can tell their stories in a variety of narrative styles. Some types are centuries old while others are recent innovations. A technique of starting a narrative at a significant point in the action and then developing the story through flashbacks is called *in medias res*. *Heart of Darkness by* Joseph Conrad is an example.

An **allegory** is a story in verse or prose with characters representing virtues and vices. There are two meanings, symbolic and literal. John Bunyan's *The Pilgrim's Progress* is the most renowned of this genre.

A **fable** is a terse tale offering up a moral or exemplum. Chaucer's "The Nun's Priest's Tale" is a fine example of a *bete fabliau,* or beast fable, in which animals speak and act characteristically human, illustrating human foibles. *Collection of Aesop's Fables* is best known.

A **folk legend** is a traditional narrative or collection of related narratives, popularly regarded as historically factual but actually including a mixture of fact and fiction. An example is Washington Irving's "The Legend of Sleepy Hollow."

In a **myth**, the story is more or less universally shared within a culture to explain its history and traditions. From Zeus to Spider Man, mythological characters represent our search for answers about reality and our place in the cosmos.

A **romance** is a highly imaginative tale set in a fantastical realm dealing with the conflicts between heroes, villains, and/or monsters. "The Knight's Tale" from Chaucer's *Canterbury Tales, Sir Gawain and the Green Knight,* and Keats' "The Eve of St. Agnes" are prime representatives romance tales.

Many of the themes found in **modern fantasy** are similar to those in traditional literature. The stories start out based in reality, enabling readers to suspend disbelief and enter worlds of unreality. Little people live in the walls in *The Borrowers,* and time travel is possible in *The Trolley to Yesterday.* Including some fantasy tales in the curriculum helps students develop their imaginations. Fantasies often appeal to ideals of justice and good and evil and, because students tend to identify with the characters, the message is more likely to be retained.

Robots, spacecraft, mystery, and civilizations from other ages often appear in **science fiction**. Most anticipate advances in science on other planets or in a future time. Most children like these stories because of their interest in space and the "what if" aspect of the stories. Other science fiction examples include *Outer Space and All That Junk* and *A Wrinkle in Time.*

Modern realistic fiction stories are about real problems that real people face. By finding that their hopes and fears are shared by others, student readers can find insight into their own problems. Young readers also tend to experience a broadening of interests as the result of this kind of reading. It's good for them to know that someone like them can be brave and intelligent and can solve difficult problems.

Historical fiction uses historical settings, events, and characters as a backdrop for storytelling. *Rifles for Watie* is an example of this kind of story. Presented in a historically accurate setting, it's about a young boy of sixteen who serves in the Union army. He experiences great hardship but discovers that his enemy is an admirable human being. It provides a good opportunity to study history in a beneficial way.

Mystery fiction, also known as detective fiction, marks its beginnings with Poe's short story "The Murders in the Rue Morgue." Faced with a puzzle or crime, a detective searches for answers. This motif has appealed to all ages and many readers have advanced from the Hardy Boys and Nancy Drew to Sherlock Holmes and Agatha Christie's Hercule Poirot and Miss Marple. Various twists on the genre include the thriller and the use of the supernatural.

Skill 7.5 **Describe genres of nonfiction (biography, autobiography, letters, essays, reports) and their characteristic elements and structures.**

Nonfiction

Nonfiction has many subgenres. Students should be introduced to these as writings that can be informative as well as enjoyable.

Biography: A biography is the story of someone's life written by someone else. The earliest biographical writings were probably funeral speeches and inscriptions, usually praising the life and example of the deceased. Early biographies evolved from this and were almost invariably uncritical, even distorted, and always laudatory.

Beginning in the eighteenth century, this form of literature saw major developments; an eminent example is James Boswell's *Life of Johnson*, which is very detailed and even records conversations. Eventually, the antithesis of the grossly exaggerated tomes praising an individual, usually a person of circumstance, developed. This later form is denunciatory, debunking, and often inflammatory. A famous modern example is Lytton Strachey's *Eminent Victorians* (1918).

Autobiography: A form of biography, an autobiography is written by the subject himself or herself. Autobiographies can range from the very formal to intimate writings made during one's life that were not intended for publication. These include letters, diaries, journals, memoirs, and reminiscences. Autobiography, generally speaking, began in the fifteenth century; one of the first examples is one written in England by Margery Kempe. There are four kinds of autobiography: thematic, religious, intellectual, and fictionalized. Some "novels" may be thinly disguised autobiography, such as the novels of Thomas Wolfe.

> Read more about
> **Nonfiction Reading Strategies
> for High School Students**
> http://www.madison.k12.wi.us/sod/car/
> abstracts/98.pdf

Informational Books and Articles: These types of nonfiction make up much of the reading of modern Americans. Magazines became popular in the nineteenth century in this country, and while many of the contributors to those publications intended to influence the political, social, or religious convictions of their readers, many simply intended to pass on information.

A book or article whose purpose is simply to be informative, that is, not to persuade, is called exposition (adjectival form: expository). An example of an expository book is the *MLA Style Manual*. The writers do not intend to persuade their readers to use the recommended stylistic features in their writing; they are simply making them available in case a reader needs such a guide. Articles in magazines such as *Time* may be persuasive in purpose, such as Joe Klein's regular column, but for the most part, they are expository; they expand upon television news coverage.

Newspaper Accounts of Events: Newspaper stories are expository in nature, because they explore, however briefly, the happenings of breaking stories. That happening might be a school board meeting, an automobile accident that sent several people to a hospital and accounted for the death of a passenger, or the election of the mayor. Such articles are not intended to be persuasive although the bias of a reporter or of an editor must be considered. Reporters are expected to be unbiased in their coverage, and most of them will defend their disinterest fiercely, but what a writer *sees* in an event is inevitably shaped to some extent by the writer's beliefs and experiences.

A newspaper's editorial stance is often openly declared, and it may be reflected in such stories as news reports. Editorial cartoons, however, may not reflect the editor's stance.

Skill 7.6   **Identify genres of drama (serious drama and tragedy, comic drama, melodrama, farce) and their characteristic elements and structures.**

Since the days of the Greeks, drama has undergone many permutations. Definitions which were once rigid have softened as theater has become a more accurate picture of the lives it depicts.

Tragedy: The classic definition dating back to Aristotle is that tragedy is a work of drama written in either prose or poetry, telling the story of a brave, noble hero who, because of some tragic character flaw (*hamartia*), brings ruin upon himself. It is characterized by serious, poetic language that evokes pity and fear.

In modern times, dramatists have tried to update drama's image by drawing its main characters from the middle class and showing their nobility through their nature instead of their standing. Sophocles' *Oedipus Rex* is the classic example of tragedy, while works of Henrik Ibsen and Arthur Miller epitomize modern tragedy.

Read more about
Greek Tragedy
http://depthome.brooklyn.cuny.e
du/classics/dunkle/studyguide/
tragedy.htm

Comedy: The comedic form of dramatic literature is meant to amuse and often ends happily. It uses techniques such as satire or parody, and can take many forms, from farce to burlesque. Examples include Dante Alighieri's *The Divine Comedy,* Noel Coward's play *Private Lives,* some of Geoffrey Chaucer's *Canterbury Tales,* and some of William Shakespeare's plays, such as *A Midsummer's Night Dream.*

Comic Drama: As the name suggests, this form of theater is a combination of serious and light elements. It originated in the Middle Ages under the auspices of the Catholic Church when it tried to reach the common people in mystery and morality plays. The modern equivalent would be the television's "dramedies" that present a serious plot with comic elements.

Melodrama: This is a form of extreme drama that has a somewhat formulaic structure. The hero saves the day from the dastardly villain and wins the heart of the wholesome heroine. The word is a combination of *melody* and *drama* because music was used to heighten the emotions. Although the term is sometimes used as a critical pejorative, it is a true art form with stereotyped characters and plot manipulations. Oftentimes, various operas are melodramatic, so it should be no surprise that soap operas are considered part of this genre.

Farce: This is an extreme form of comedy marked by physical humor, unlikely situations, and stereotyped characters. It is often considered a form of low comedy and is represented by the Three Stooges, Charlie Chaplin, Harold Lloyd, and Buster Keaton. Today's students might easily recognize farce with movies like *Dumb and Dumber, There's Something About Mary, Talladega Nights,* and *Walk Hard: The Dewey Cox Story.*

Skill 7.7   Describe genres of poetry (lyric, concrete, dramatic, narrative, epic) and their characteristic elements and structures.

Lyric Poetry

Remembering that lyrics are words put to music, you can see why lyric poetry is characterized by its musical qualities. As a song expresses the singer's feelings and emotions, so too does a lyric poem convey the same of a poet.

Examples of lyric poetry are discussed in Skill 7.8.

Concrete Poetry

Popular during the 1950s and 1960s, concrete poetry appeals to the senses with its visual approach. Instead of relying on words alone, this form of poetry takes an actual shape. It depends on graphic and typographical elements to match meaning with form.

Narrative Poetry

The greatest difficulty in analyzing narrative poetry is that it partakes of many genres. It can have all the features of poetry: meter, rhyme, verses, and stanzas, but it can have all the features of prose, not only fictional prose but also nonfictional. It can have a protagonist, characters, conflicts, action, plot, climax, theme, and tone. It can also be a persuasive discourse and have a thesis (real or derived) and supporting points. The arrangement of an analysis will depend to a great extent upon the peculiarities of the poem itself.

```
the
    sky
         was
can  dy  lu
minous
         edible
spry
        pinks shy
lemons
greens   coo   l choc
olate
s.

   un   der,
   a   lo
co
mo
      tive   s   pout
                 ing
                    vi
                     o
                     lets
```

Concrete Poetry
"the sky was candy luminous"
by e.e. cummings

Narrative poetry has been very much a part of the output of modern American writers totally apart from attempts to write epics. Many of Emily Dickinson's poems are narrative in form and retain the features that we look for in the finest of American poetry. The first two verses of "A Narrow Fellow in the Grass" illustrate the use of narrative in a poem:

> A narrow fellow in the grass
> Occasionally rides;
> You may have met him—did you not?
> His notice sudden is.
>
> The grass divides as with a comb,
> A spotted shaft is seen;
> And then it closes at your feet
> And opens further on. . . .

This is certainly narrative in nature and has many of the aspects of prose narrative. At the same time, it is a poem with rhyme, meter, verses, and stanzas and can be analyzed as such.

Learn more about
Narrative Poetry
http://www.poetry-portal.com/styles9.html

Dramatic Poetry

A dramatic poem is one that is to be declaimed aloud. It began as the earliest form of Greek drama where one character or chorus recited the verse for the audience. An adaptation is the dramatic monologue, a speech given by an actor as if talking to himself or herself, but actually intended for the audience. It reveals key aspects of the character's psyche and sheds insight on the situation at hand. The audience takes the part of the silent listener, passing judgment and giving sympathy at the same time. This form was invented and used predominantly by Victorian poet Robert Browning.

Epic

In an epic, the conflicts take place in the social sphere rather than a personal life, and it will have a historical basis or one that is accepted as historical. The conflict will be between opposed nations or races and will involve diverging views of civilization that are the foundation of the challenge. Often it will involve the pitting of a group that conceives itself as a higher civilization against a lower civilization. More often than not, divine will determines that the higher one will win, exerting its force over the lower, barbarous, and profane enemy.

Examples are the conflict of Greece with Troy, the fates of Rome with the Carthaginian and the Italian, the Crusaders with the Saracen, or even of Milton's Omnipotent versus Satan. In analyzing these works, protagonist and antagonist need to be clearly identified, the conflicts established, the climax and an outcome that sets the world right in the mind of the writer clearly shown.

At the same time, the form of the epic as a poem must be considered. What meter, rhyme scheme, verse form, and stanza form have been chosen to tell this story? Is it consistent? If it varies, where does it vary and what does the varying do for the poem/story? What about figures of speech? Is there alliteration or onomatopoeia?

The epic is a major literary form historically although it had begun to fall out of favor by the end of the seventeenth century. There have been notable efforts to produce an American epic, but they always seem to slide over into prose. The short story and the novel began to take over the genre. Even so, some would say that *Moby Dick* is an American epic.

Skill 7.8   Identify types of patterned lyric poetry (sonnet, ballad, limerick, haiku).

The Greek poets used to sing their poetry and accompany their songs by playing a lyre. This musical quality characterizes the many types of lyric poetry.

> Learn more about
> **Lyric Poetry:**
> **Poetry's Many Forms**
> http://poetry.suite101.com/
> article.cfm/lyric_poetry

Sonnet

The sonnet is a fixed-verse form of Italian origin, which consists of 14 lines that are typically five-foot iambics rhyming according to a prescribed scheme. Popular since its creation in the thirteenth century in Sicily, it spread at first to Tuscany, where Petrarch adopted it. The Petrarchan sonnet generally has a two-part theme. The first eight lines, the octave, state a problem, ask a question, or express an emotional tension. The last six lines, the sestet, resolve the problem, answer the question, or relieve the tension. The rhyme scheme of the octave is abba abba; that of the sestet varies.

Sir Thomas Wyatt and Henry Howard, Earl of Surrey, introduced this form into England in the sixteenth century. It played an important role in the development of Elizabethan lyric poetry, and a distinctive English sonnet developed, which was composed of three quatrains, each with an independent rhyme-scheme, and it ended with a rhymed couplet.

A form of the English sonnet created by Edmond Spenser combines the English form and the Italian. The Spenserian sonnet follows the English quatrain and couplet pattern but resembles the Italian in its rhyme scheme, which is linked: abab bcbc cdcd ee. Many poets wrote sonnet sequences, where several sonnets were linked together, usually to tell a story. Considered to be the greatest of all sonnet sequences is one of Shakespeare's, which are addressed to a young man and a "dark lady" wherein the love story is overshadowed by the underlying reflections on time and art, growth and decay, and fame and fortune.

The sonnet continued to develop, more in topics than in form. When John Donne in the seventeenth century used the form for religious themes, some of which are almost sermons, or on personal reflections ("When I consider how my light is spent"), there were no longer any boundaries on the themes it could take.

That it is a flexible form is demonstrated in the wide range of themes and purposes it has been used for—all the way from more frivolous concerns to statements about time and death. William Wordsworth, John Keats, and Elizabeth Barrett Browning used the Petrarchan form of the sonnet. A well-known example is Wordsworth's "The World Is Too Much With Us." Rainer Maria Rilke's *Sonnette an Orpheus* (1922) is a well-known twentieth-century sonnet.

Analysis of a sonnet should focus on the form—does it fit a traditional pattern or does it break from tradition? If so, why did the poet choose to make that break? Does it reflect the purpose of the poem? What is the theme? What is the purpose? Is it narrative? If so, what story does it tell and is there an underlying meaning? Is the sonnet appropriate for the subject matter?

Ballad

A ballad is a story told or sung, usually in verse and accompanied by music. Literary devices found in ballads include the refrain, or repeated section, and incremental repetition, or anaphora, for effect. Earliest forms were anonymous folk ballads. Later forms include Coleridge's Romantic masterpiece "The Rime of the Ancient Mariner."

Limerick

The limerick probably originated in County Limerick, Ireland, in the eighteenth century. It is a form of short, humorous verse, often nonsensical, and often ribald. Its five lines rhyme aabbaa with three feet in all lines except the third and fourth, which have only two. Rarely presented as serious poetry, this form is popular because almost anyone can write it.

In the nineteenth century, Edward Lear popularized the limerick in *A Book of Nonsense*. Here's an example:

> There was an Old Man with a beard,
> Who said, "It is just as I feared!
> Two Owls and a Hen,
> Four Larks and a Wren,
> Have all built their nests in my beard!"

Analysis of a limerick should focus on its form. Does it conform to a traditional pattern or does it break from the tradition? If so, what impact does that have on the meaning? Is the poem serious or frivolous? Is it funny? Does it try to be funny but does not achieve its purpose? Is there a serious meaning underlying the frivolity?

Cinquain

A cinquain is a poem with a five-line stanza. Adelaide Crapsey (1878-1914) called a five-line verse form a cinquain and invented a particular meter for it. Similar to the haiku, there are two syllables in the first and last lines and four, six, and eight in the middle three lines. It has a mostly iambic cadence. Her poem, "November Night," is an example:

> Listen…
> With faint dry sound
> Like steps of passing ghosts,
> the leaves, frost-crisp'd, break from the trees
> And fall.

Haiku

Haiku is a very popular unrhymed form that is limited to seventeen syllables arranged in three lines thus: five, seven, and five syllables. This verse form originated in Japan in the seventeenth century where it is accepted as serious poetry and is Japan's most popular form. Originally, a haiku was to deal with the season, the time of day, and the landscape although as it has come into more common use, the subjects have become less restricted. The imagist poets and other English writers used the form or imitated it. It's a form much used in classrooms to introduce students to the writing of poetry.

Here's an example by Japanese poet Kobayashi Issa, translated by American poet Robert Haas.

> New Year's morning--
> everything is in blossom!
> I feel about average.

Analysis of a cinquain and a haiku poem should focus on form first. Does the haiku poem conform to the seventeen-syllables requirement and are they arranged in a five, seven, and five pattern? For a cinquain, does it have only five lines? Does the poem distill the words so as much meaning as possible can be conveyed? Does it treat a serious subject? Is the theme discernable? Short forms like these seem simple to dash off; however, they are not effective unless the words are chosen and pared so the meaning intended is conveyed. The impact should be forceful, and that often takes more effort, skill, and creativity than longer forms. Students should consider all of this in their analyses.

Villanelle is a form of poetry that was designed in France is the villanelle, which uses just two rhymes, while also repeating two lines throughout the poem. The first five stanzas are triplets, and the last stanza is a quatrain. Dylan Thomas' "Don't Go Gentle into that Good Night" is probably the most famous villanelle in English.

Skill 7.9   Understand criteria for evaluating prose, dramatic, and poetic works of various types

When we speak of form with regard to poetry, we usually mean one of three attributes:

- The pattern of the sound and rhythm
- The visible shape it takes
- The type of rhyme or verse

> Learn more about
> **Teaching Poetry**
> http://www.poets.org/page.php/prmID/85

The Pattern of the Sound and Rhythm

Knowing the history of this characteristic is helpful. History was passed down in oral form almost exclusively until the invention of the printing press and was often set to music. A rhymed story is much easier to commit to memory. Adding a tune makes it even easier to remember, so not surprisingly much of the earliest literature-- epics, odes, and the like--are rhymed and were probably sung. When we speak of the pattern of sound and rhythm, we are referring to verse form and stanza form.

The verse form is the rhythmic pattern of a single verse. An example would be any meter: blank verse, for instance, is iambic pentameter. A stanza is a group of a certain number of verses (lines), having a rhyme scheme. If the poem is written, there is usually white space between the verses although a short poem may be only one stanza. If the poem is spoken, there will be a pause between stanzas.

The Visible Shape It Takes

In the seventeenth century, some poets shaped their poems to reflect the theme. A good example is George Herbert's *Easter Wings*. Since that time, poets have occasionally played with this device; it is, however, generally viewed as nothing more than a demonstration of ingenuity. The rhythm, effect, and meaning are often sacrificed to the forcing of the shape.

Rhyme and Free Verse

Poets also use devices to establish form that will underscore the meanings of their poems. A very common one is alliteration. When the poem is read (which poetry is usually intended to be), the repetition of a sound may not only underscore the meaning, but it may also pleasure to the reading. Poets may create alliteration with vowels rather than consonants.

Following a strict rhyming pattern can add intensity to the meaning of the poem in the hands of a skilled and creative poet. On the other hand, the meaning can be drowned out by the steady beat-beat-beat of it.

Shakespeare very skillfully used the regularity of rhyme in his poetry, breaking the rhythm at certain points to very effectively underscore a point. For example, in Sonnet #130, "My mistress' eyes are nothing like the sun," the rhythm is primarily iambic pentameter. It lulls the reader (or listener) to accept that this poet is following the standard conventions for love poetry, which in that day reliably used rhyme and more often than not iambic pentameter to express feelings of romantic love along conventional lines. However, in Sonnet #130, the last two lines sharply break from the monotonous pattern, forcing the reader or speaker to pause:

> And yet, by heaven, I think my love as rare
> As any she belied with false compare

Shakespeare's purpose is clear: he is not writing a conventional love poem; the object of his love is not the red-and-white conventional woman written about in other poems of the period. This is a good example where a poet uses form to underscore meaning.

Poets eventually began to feel constricted by the rhyming conventions and began to break away and make new rules for poetry. When poetry was only rhymed, it was easy to define. When free verse, or poetry written in a flexible form, came upon the scene in France in the 1880s, it quickly began to influence English-language poets such as T. S. Eliot, whose memorable poem *The Wasteland* had an alarming but desolate message for the modern world. It's impossible to imagine that it could have been written in the soothing, lulling rhymed verse of previous periods. Those who first began writing in free verse in English were responding to the influence of the French *vers libre*. However, free verse could be loosely applied to the poetry of Walt Whitman, writing in the mid-nineteenth century, in the first stanza of *Song of Myself*:

> I celebrate myself, and sing myself,
> And what I assume you shall assume,
> For every atom belonging to me as good belongs to you.

When poetry was no longer defined as a piece of writing arranged in verses that had a rhyme scheme of some sort, distinguishing poetry from prose became a point of discussion. Merriam Webster's *Encyclopedia of Literature* defines poetry as "Writing that formulates a concentrated imaginative awareness of experience in language chosen and arranged to create a specific emotional response through its meaning, sound and rhythm."

A poet chooses the form of poetry deliberately, based upon the emotional response being evoked and the meaning being conveyed. Robert Frost, a twentieth-century poet who chose to use conventional rhyming verse to make his point is a memorable and often-quoted modern poet. Who can forget his closing lines in "Stopping by Woods"?

> But I have promises to keep,
> And miles to go before I sleep,
> And miles to go before I sleep.

Would they be as memorable if the poem had been written in free verse?

Skill 7.10   Understand literary devices (figurative language, imagery, irony, symbolism, ambiguity, rhythm, rhyme, sensory detail) and ways in which they contribute to meaning and style.

Poetry, one of the densest forms of communications, is embedded with meaning. For students to enjoy and appreciate poetry, they should be able to peel away the layers to find the depth of meaning. One way they can do this is by understanding the techniques poets use.

> Share this website with your students
> **NewsHour Extra: Poetry**
> http://www.pbs.org/newshour/ extra/poetry/#

Figurative Language

Figurative language is also called figures of speech. If all figures of speech that have ever been identified were listed, it would be a very long list. However, for purposes of analyzing poetry, a few are sufficient.

Alliteration: The repetition of either vowels or consonant sounds in two or more neighboring words or syllables. In its simplest form, it reinforces one or two consonant sounds. Example: Shakespeare's Sonnet #12:

> When I do count the clock that tells the time.

Some poets have used more complex patterns of alliteration by creating consonants both at the beginning of words and at the beginning of stressed syllables within words. Example: Shelley's "Stanzas Written in Dejection Near Naples"

> The City's voice itself is soft like Solitude's

Allusion: An allusion is very much like a symbol, and the two sometimes tend to run together. An allusion is defined by Merriam Webster's *Encyclopedia of Literature* as "an implied reference to a person, event, thing, or a part of another text." Allusions are based on the assumption that there is a common body of knowledge shared by poet and reader and that a reference to that body of knowledge will be immediately understood. Allusions to the Bible and classical mythology are common in western literature on the assumption that they will be immediately understood. This is not always the case, of course.

T. S. Eliot's *The Wasteland* requires research and annotation for understanding. He assumed more background on the part of the average reader than actually exists. However, when Michael Moore headlines an article on the war in Iraq: "Déjà Fallujah: Ramadi surrounded, thousands of families trapped, no electricity or water, onslaught impending," we understand immediately that he is referring first of all to a repeat of the human disaster in New Orleans although the "onslaught" is not a storm but an invasion by American and Iraqi troops. The use of allusion is a sort of shortcut for poets. They can use an economy of words and count on meaning to come from the reader's own experience.

Bathos: A ludicrous attempt to portray pathos—that is, to evoke pity, sympathy, or sorrow. It may result from inappropriately dignifying the commonplace, elevated language to describe something trivial, or greatly exaggerated pathos.

Climax: A number of phrases or sentences are arranged in ascending order of rhetorical forcefulness. Example from Melville's *Moby Dick*:

> All that most maddens and torments; all that stirs up the lees of things; all truth with malice in it; all that cracks the sinews and cakes the brain; all the subtle demonisms of life and thought; all evil, to crazy Ahab, were visibly personified and made practically assailable in Moby Dick.

Climax in fiction is the moment of great intensity that results in a turning point.

Euphemism: The substitution of an agreeable or inoffensive term for one that might offend or suggest something unpleasant. Many euphemisms are used to refer to death to avoid using the real word such as "passed away," "crossed over," or "passed."

Hyperbole: Deliberate exaggeration for effect or comic effect. An example from Shakespeare's *The Merchant of Venice*:

> Why, if two gods should play some heavenly match
> And on the wager lay two earthly women,
> And Portia one, there must be something else
> Pawned with the other, for the poor rude world
> Hath not her fellow.

Irony: Expressing something other than and particularly opposite the literal meaning such as words of praise when blame is intended. In poetry, it is often used as a sophisticated or resigned awareness of contrast between what is and what ought to be and expresses a controlled pathos without sentimentality. It is a form of indirection that avoids overt praise or censure. An early example: the Greek comic character Eiron, a clever underdog who by his wit repeatedly triumphs over the boastful character Alazon.

Malapropism: A verbal blunder in which one word is replaced by another similar in sound but different in meaning. This derives from Sheridan's Mrs. Malaprop in *The Rivals* (1775). Thinking of the geography of contiguous countries, she spoke of the "geometry" of "contagious countries." Meaning the "pinnacle of perfection," she describes someone as "the pineapple of perfection."

The Pineapple of Perfection!

Metaphor: Indirect comparison between two things. It is the use of a word or phrase denoting one kind of object or action in place of another to suggest a comparison between them. While poets use them extensively, they are also integral to everyday speech. For example, chairs are said to have "legs" and "arms" although we know that humans and other animals have these appendages.

Parallelism: The arrangement of ideas in phrases, sentences, and paragraphs that balance one element with another of equal importance and similar wording or syntax. An example from Francis Bacon's *Of Studies:* "Reading maketh a full man, conference a ready man, and writing an exact man."

Personification: Human characteristics are attributed to an inanimate object, an abstract quality, or animal. Examples: John Bunyan wrote characters named Death, Knowledge, Giant Despair, Sloth, and Piety in his *Pilgrim's Progress.* The metaphor of an arm of a chair is a form of personification. Carl Sandburg, in his poem "Fog," writes "The fog comes / on little cat feet. // It sits looking / over harbor and city / on silent haunches / and then moves on."

Onomatopoeia: The naming of a thing or action by a vocal imitation of the sound associated with it such as buzz or hiss or the use of words whose sound suggests the sense. A good example: from "The Brook" by Tennyson:

> I chatter over stony ways,
> In little sharps and trebles,
> I bubble into eddying bays,
> I babble on the pebbles.

Oxymoron: A contradiction in terms deliberately employed for effect. It is usually seen in a qualifying adjective whose meaning is contrary to that of the noun it modifies such as "wise folly."

Simile: Direct comparison between two things using "like," "as," such as." For example: "My love is like a red-red rose."

Poets use figures of speech to sharpen the effect and meaning of their poems and to help readers see things in ways they have never seen them before. Marianne Moore observed that a fir tree has "an emerald turkey-foot at the top." Her poem makes us aware of something we probably had never noticed before. The sudden recognition of the likeness yields pleasure in the reading.

Figurative language allows for the statement of truths that more literal language cannot. Skillfully used, a figure of speech will help the reader see more clearly and focus upon particulars. Figures of speech add many dimensions of richness to our reading and understanding of a poem; they also allow many opportunities for worthwhile analysis.

The approach to take in analyzing a poem on the basis of its figures of speech is to ask the question: What does it do for the poem? Does it underscore meaning? Does it intensify understanding? Does it increase the intensity of our response?

Imagery

Imagery can be described as a word or sequence of words that refers to any sensory experience—that is, anything that can be seen, tasted, smelled, heard, or felt. Writers intend to make an experience available to the reader. In order to do that, they must appeal to the senses. The most-often-used one, of course, is the visual sense. The poet will deliberately paint a scene in such a way that the reader can see it. However, the purpose is not simply to stir the visceral feeling but also to stir the emotions. A good example is "The Piercing Chill" by Taniguchi Buson (1715-1783):

> The piercing chill I feel:
> My dead wife's comb, in our bedroom,
> Under my heel . . .

In only a few short words, the reader can feel many things: the shock that might come from touching the corpse, a literal sense of death, the contrast between her death and the memories he has of her when she was alive. Imagery might be defined as speaking of the abstract in concrete terms, a powerful device in the hands of a skillful poet.

Symbolism

A **symbol** is an object or action that can be observed with the senses in addition to its suggesting many other things. The lion is a symbol of courage; the cross a symbol of Christianity; the color green a symbol of envy.

These can almost be defined as metaphors because society agrees on the one-to-one meaning of them. Symbols used in literature are usually of a different sort. They tend to be private and personal; their significance is only evident in the context of the work where they are used. A good example of a symbol is poetry is the mending wall in Frost's poem. A symbol can certainly have more than one meaning, and the meaning may be as personal as the memories and experiences of the particular reader. In analyzing a poem or a story, students should identify the symbols and their possible meanings.

Looking for symbols is often challenging, especially for novice poetry readers. However, these suggestions may be useful: First, pick out all the references to concrete objects such as a newspaper, black cats, or other nouns. Note any that the poet emphasizes by describing in detail, by repeating, or by placing at the very beginning or ending of a poem.

Ask yourself, what is the poem about? What does it add up to? Paraphrase the poem and determine whether the meaning depends upon certain concrete objects. Then ponder what the concrete object symbolizes in this particular poem.

Look for a character with the name of a prophet who does little but utter prophecy or a trio of women who resemble the Three Fates. A symbol may be a part of a person's body such as the eye of the murder victim in Poe's story "The Tell-Tale Heart" or a look, a voice, or a mannerism.

Some things a symbol is not: an abstraction such as truth, death, and love; in narrative, a well-developed character who is not at all mysterious--or the second term in a metaphor. In Emily Dickenson's "The Lightning Is a Yellow Fork," the symbol is the lightning, not the fork.

Ambiguity

Ambiguity opens a piece of literature to several interpretations, adding both depth and breadth to the work's meaning. Poets may intend more than one understanding or readers may bring to the poem their own insights. However, any interpretation must be supported by the correct interpretation of the poem. To offer an alternative viewpoint without substantiation is a misunderstanding of the term and the work. Pun and double entendres are the basest forms of ambiguity.

Rhythm and Rhyme

Rhythm in poetry refers to the recurrence of stresses at equal intervals. A stress (accent) is a greater amount of force given to one syllable in speaking than is

For more information, consult
Glossary of Poetry Terms
http://www.infoplease.com/spot/
pmglossary1.html

given to another. For example, we put the stress on the first syllable of such words as father, mother, daughter, and children. The unstressed or unaccented syllable is sometimes called a slack syllable. All English words carry at least one stress except articles and some prepositions such as "by," "from," or "at." Indicating where stresses occur is to scan; doing this is called scansion.

Very little is gained in understanding a poem or making a statement about it by merely scanning it. The pattern of the rhythm—the meter—should be analyzed in terms of its overall relationship to the message and impression of the poem.

Slack syllables, when they recur in pairs, cause rhythmic trippings and bouncings; on the other hand, recurrent pairs of stresses will create a heavier rocking effect. The rhythm is dependent on words to convey meaning. Alone, they communicate nothing.

When examining the rhythm and meaning of a poem, a good question to ask is whether the rhythm is appropriate to the theme. A bouncing rhythm, for example, might be dissonant in a solemn elegy.

Stops are those places in a poem where the punctuation requires a pause. An end-stopped line is one that *ends* in a pause. A line that has no punctuation at its end is read with only a slight pause. Called a run-on, the running on of its thought into the next line is called enjambment. These are used by a poet to underscore, intensify, and communicate meaning.

Rhythm, then, is a pattern of recurrence. In poetry it is made up of stressed and relatively unstressed syllables. The poet can manipulate the rhythm by making the intervals between stresses regular or varied, by making lines short or long, by end-stopping lines or running them over, by choosing words that are easier or less easy to say, or by choosing polysyllabic words or monosyllables. What's important to remember about rhythm is that it conveys meaning.

The basic unit of rhythm is called a foot and is usually one stressed syllable with one or two unstressed ones or two stressed syllables with one unstressed one. A foot made up of one unstressed syllable and one stressed one is called an iamb. If a line is made of five iambs, it is iambic pentameter. A rhymed poem typically establishes a pattern such as iambic pentameter, and even though there will be syllables that don't fit the pattern, the poem, nevertheless, will be said to be in iambic pentameter. In fact, a poem may be considered weak if the rhythm is too monotonous.

Common Feet in English Poetry

- Iamb: -'
- Trochee: '-
- Monosyllabic: '
- Pyrrhic foot: --
- Anapest: --'
- Dactyl: '--
- Spondee: "

Iambic and anapestic are said to be rising because the movement is from slack to stressed syllables. Trochaic and dactylic are said to be falling.

Meters in Poetry

- Monometer: a line of one foot
- Trimeter: a line of three feet
- Pentameter: a line of five feet
- Heptameter: a line of seven feet
- Dimeter: a line of two feet
- Tetrameter: a line of four feet
- Hexameter: a line of six feet
- Octameter: a line of eight feet

Longer lines are possible, but a reader will tend to break it up into shorter lengths. A caesura is a definite pause within a line. In scansion, it is indicated by a double line: ||

A stanza is a group of a certain number of lines with a rhyme scheme or a particular rhythm or both, typically set off by white space.

Some Typical Patterns of English Poetry

- **Alexandrine**: a line of iambic hexameter.
- **Ballad Stanza**: four iambic feet in lines 1 and 3, three in lines 2 and 4. Rhyming is abcb.
- **Blank Verse**: unrhymed iambic pentameter.
- **Couplet**: two-line stanza, usually rhymed and typically not separated by white space.
- **Free Verse**: no conventional patterns of rhyme, stanza, or meter.
- **Heroic Couplet or Closed Couplet**: two rhymed lines of iambic pentameter, the first ending in a light pause, the second more heavily end-stopped.
- **Quatrain**: four-line stanza, the most popular in English.
- **Refrain**: a line or lines repeated in a ballad as a chorus.
- **Sonnet**: a fourteen-line poem in iambic pentameter.
  - **English Sonnet**: sometimes called a Shakespearean sonnet. Rhymes cohere in four clusters: abab cdcd efef gg
  - **Italian or Petrarchan** sonnet: first eight lines (the octave), abba abba; then the sestet, the last six lines add new rhyme sounds in almost any variation; does not end in a couplet.
- **Tercet**: a three-line stanza, which, if rhymed, usually keeps to one rhyme sound.
- **Terminal Refrain**: follows a stanza in a ballad.

- o Five-line stanzas occur, but not frequently.
- o Six-line stanzas are more frequent than five-line ones.
- o The sestina: six six-line stanzas and a tercet. Repeats in each stanza the same six end-words in a different order.
- o Rime royal: seven-line stanza in iambic pentameter with rhyme ababbcc.
- o Octava rima: eight-line stanza of iambic pentameter rhyming abababcc.
- o Spenserian stanza: nine lines, rhyming ababbcbcc for eight lines then concludes with an Alexandrine.
- **Terza Rima**: At the middle line of the tercet rhymes with the first and third lines of the next tercet.

COMPETENCY 8.0   UNDERSTAND LITERARY THEORY AND CRITICISM

Skill 8.1   Understand various critical approaches to literature (New Criticism, structuralism, deconstructionism, New Historicism, Marxist criticism, feminism, reader response).

Teachers should be familiar with professional resources that aid them in recognizing reader responses and teaching students the process of assessing their responses. One exceptional tool is Laurence Perrine's *Sound and Sense*, cited in the bibliography. Both the text itself and the teacher manual that accompanies it provide excellent activities that contribute to the student's ability to make interpretive and evaluative responses.

In addition, a variety of good student resources are available in most school and public libraries that provide models of critical analyses. The Twayne publications are book-length critiques of individual titles or of the body of work of a given author. *The Modern Critical Interpretations* series, edited by Harold Bloom, offers a collection of critical essays on individual titles in each book. Gale Research Company also provides several series: *Nineteenth Century Literature Criticism, Twentieth Century Literature Criticism*, and *Contemporary Literary Criticism*, to name a few. These encyclopedic sets contain reprints of literary magazine articles that date from the author's own lifetime to the present. Students doing independent research will find these are invaluable tools.

The New Criticism

New Criticism treats literary texts as independent entities requiring little or no consideration of external factors such as the identity of the author or the society in which

> **Resources for Literary Theory**
> http://vos.ucsb.edu/browse.asp?id=2718

he or she lives. Proponents of the New Criticism believe that the literary text itself is the paramount concern.

Works are analyzed, evaluated, and interpreted through what is called "close reading." Close reading emphasizes genre and literary form; a work's theme and a writer's rendition of it; plot and character development; poetic meter, rhythm, and, if applicable, rhyme; metaphor, simile, and other figurative or literal imagery; evaluation of literary quality; analysis and interpretation of a work's meaning.

The goal of close reading is to arrive, without biographical or sociological distractions, at an objective understanding and appreciation of a literary work

The New Criticism's approach is summed up in two key literary anthologies: *Understanding Poetry* (4th ed.) and *Understanding Fiction*, both edited by Cleanth Brooks and Robert Penn Warren. Either one of these would be suitable as assigned texts for high school literature courses.

Structuralism and Deconstructionism

The structural approach is to examine the structure of a literary work without regard for external influences. This is an attempt to quantify objectively certain criteria that a work must follow. Emphasis is placed on the work as a whole and its place within its genre.

In deconstruction theory, only the text itself is examined. This is done through a very close reading. Formulated by Jacques Derrida in the 1960s, it has been unjustly called "destruction criticism" because of its detailed analytical approach.

Both of these theories are much more complex that explained here and require further study.

Marxist Criticism

Based on the ideas of Karl Marx, some of the key components of this critical theory follow:

- Class conflict drives the history of human civilization.
- The capitalists or bourgeoisie (those who possess and control economic capital) exploit and oppress the proletariat (the working classes) for their own economic and political benefit.
- The workers must therefore unite to overthrow the capitalists and their socio-economic system. This will result in a "dictatorship of the proletariat" that will create a classless society in which most, if not all, private property is abolished in favor of collective ownership. The result will be a "workers' paradise"; eventually the nation-states themselves will dissolve and be replaced by a unitary, worldwide communist society free of class conflict.
- Marxist orthodoxy holds that the triumph of communism is inevitable, and that Marxist doctrine is validated by its scientific and materialist approach to history.
- Therefore the Marxist critic uses these ideas to scrutinize literary works, which are analyzed and interpreted to determine their "revolutionary" or "proletarian," "bourgeois" or "reactionary," character.
- Works focused primarily on social injustice and abuses of power have drawn sustained attention from Marxist critics. These include: *The Jungle* by Upton Sinclair; Stephen Crane's *Maggie, a Girl of the Streets*; Theodore Dreiser's *Sister Carrie* and *An American Tragedy*; John Steinbeck's *Grapes of Wrath*; Virginia Woolf's *A Room of One's Own*; and Dostoevsky's *Crime and Punishment* and *The Brothers Karamazov*.

Feminist Criticism

Feminist critics emphasize the ways that literary works are informed and inspired by an author's gender, by an author's ideas about gender and gender roles, and by social norms regarding gender. Of prime concern to the feminist critical enterprise is the advocacy of women as intellectual, social, and artistic equals to men. Feminist criticism is not limited to works by women, nor is it hostile or opposed to male writers or males in general.

"Feminism" could just as easily be referred to as "feminisms." There are a variety of schools of thought that make the plural form more accurate than the singular. Some feminists emphasize class, others race, still others sexual orientation, when critiquing texts or social norms and conditions affecting women's lives.

When introducing feminist writing and criticism to high school students, teachers should consider giving a comprehensive summary of what feminism is, and when, where, and why it arose. Some students will likely have the impression that feminism originated in the 1960s, despite the fact that it has existed for over 200 years. To counter any such misconceptions, teachers can assign excerpts or entire works by these eighteenth or nineteenth-century authors:

- Mary Wollstonecraft
- Margaret Fuller
- Sojourner Truth
- Susan B. Anthony
- Elizabeth Cady Stanton
- Frederick Douglass

Some popular twentieth-century works relevant to feminist thought and suitable for high school students are listed below.

- *A Room of One's Own* by Virginia Woolf (nonfiction)
- *The Yellow Wallpaper* by Charlotte Perkins Gilman (novella)
- *The Color Purple* by Alice Walker (novel)
- *Beloved* by Toni Morrison (novel)
- *Good Woman* by Lucille Clifton (poems)
- *She Had Some Horses* by Joy Harjo (poems)
- *The Joy Luck Club* by Amy Tan (novel)
- *The Secret Life of Bees* by Sue Monk Kidd (novel)

There are numerous up-to-date anthologies of women's literature and feminist criticism available through major publishers. The groundbreaking anthology, *The New Feminist Criticism*, edited by Elaine Showalter, offers an excellent variety of feminist essays on Western literature. Some of these essays are rather dated, but the collection does give a solid overview of key concerns that animated "second wave" feminism in the 1960s and 70s.

Students who seem uninterested in feminist thought might benefit from teachers giving written assignments based on questions such as: Should men and women have equality in today's society? How has life in America been affected by women's campaigns for equal rights? What are your thoughts about gender-based roles, norms, and social expectations in today's America? Once such assignments have been completed, teachers can assign readings and essays in which students compare and contrast their ideas with some of those expressed in a literary work or works listed above.

Psychoanalytic, or Freudian, criticism

Based initially on the works of Sigmund Freud, this theory has been expanded to include the ideas of other psychoanalysts.

Freudian psychoanalysis holds that the human mind is a tripartite structure (divided into three parts) composed of the *id*, which generates and seeks to satisfy all of a person's urges and desires; the *superego*, which "polices" and counters the id; and the *ego*, which is the psychic result of the id/superego conflict. The ego is characterized by a person's thoughts and behaviors.

The formation of human character—including sexual behavior—begins at birth. The infant is said to pass through various stages—the oral stage, the anal stage, and so on—as its needs and urges arise and are either satisfied or frustrated; and as it learns (or doesn't learn) to master human relationships and bodily functions.

All humans are said to have inexorable conflicts between drives such as Eros (the sex drive) and Thanatos (the death wish), which are also played out in the contests between id and superego.

Neurotic behavior results from fixations on one of the above physical factors, or from an imbalance in the powers of the id and superego, or from deeply embedded (unconscious) memories of pleasant or unpleasant experiences, or from a combination of these. Neurosis is usually rooted in infancy or early childhood.

To discover the nature of a person's mind, the psychoanalyst looks for recurrent thoughts, images, speech patterns, and behaviors evident in the person being analyzed. By carefully observing (especially listening to) a patient, the psychoanalyst uncovers previously unknown truths about the hows and whys of the patient's predicament.

The psychoanalytic literary critic applies Freudian theories to writings and authors in order to better understand the psychological underpinnings of literary works, writers, and, sometimes, society itself.

Writers that have garnered much attention from Freudian critics include Edgar Allen Poe, the Marquis de Sade, Moses, Madame de Stahl, and William S. Burroughs. Not surprisingly, sex and violence feature prominently in these writers' works. Representative examples of psychoanalytic criticism include "Moses and Monotheism" by Sigmund Freud, and *Edgar Allen Poe* by Marie Bonaparte.

Note: For high school-level literature courses, short works would probably be best for any psychoanalytic critical ventures. Especially "Freud friendly" are stories and poems by Poe that directly relate to one or another facet of Freudian thought: "The Tell-Tale Heart," "The Black Cat," "The Fall of the House of Usher," "The Premature Burial," "The Cask of Amontillado," "The Raven," and "Annabelle Lee," among others. Some of these works share subject matter that makes it appropriate to cluster them in single assignments.

Reader-Response

In this critical theory, the readers create meaning through their individual understandings and responses. Some critics focus solely on the readers' experiences; other critics experiment on defined groups to determine reader response.

Skill 8.2   Understand the role of major works in classical literary criticism and the theories associated with them.

See Skill 8.1

Skill 8.3   Identify characteristics of Neoclassic and Romantic literary theory as developed in major writings associated with each movement.

The time between 1660 and 1798 is identified as the Neoclassic Period and is associated with such authors as John Dryden (1631-1700) and Alexander Pope (1688-1744). Following on the heels of the Renaissance, the period in which the great Greek and Roman classics had been rediscovered and revered, the Neoclassic Period was the time of the "Quarrel with the Ancients and the Moderns." The Neoclassicists argued that the classics were not the last word in literature, only a foundation upon which to develop an even higher art form.

The classical ideals of proportion, common sense, and reason were still preferred over raw emotion and imagination, yet the purpose of prose and poetry was not to extol these ideals but to use them to instruct and teach. Writings took the form of the essay in prose and the ode in poetry. These writers were critics of their age and employed wit and satire to expose the foibles and of human nature. Few did this better than Pope, who in his "Essay on Man" finds that although capable of reason, the sentient human being does not always employ this attribute. Not using this God-given gift gives rise to a form of evil, which Pope identifies as coming from humankind's failure to live up to its divine potential, making humanity "The glory, jest, and riddle of the world."

The Romantic Movement (1798-1870) is perhaps best defined by what poet Matthew Arnold referred to as an "intellectual and spiritual passion for beauty." During this period of literature a great emphasis was placed on feelings, emotions, and passions. While the writers of the Neoclassic Period still honored the classical ideals of reason and common sense, the Romantics believed the emotions held the key to a higher perception of reality. John Keats (1795-1821), one of the great Romantic poets, spoke of a "negative capability" in which the artist's sense of self is lost in the object of his contemplation. In this manner, he hoped to "arrive at that trembling, delicate, snail-horn perception of Beauty." Some of his major poetic works include" Hyperion" and "Ode on a Grecian Urn."

Another Romantic, William Blake (1757-1827), viewed the rationalism of the preceding period as cold, analytical, and essentially, inhumane. Believing that the imagination was the sole route to reviving a world that had been lost to reason, Blake argued for the supremacy of the emotions and imagination—to the point of mysticism.

"Imagination," he wrote is "the real and eternal world of which this Vegetable Universe is but a faint shadow … The whole business of man is the arts." Some of his major works include "Songs of Innocence," "Songs of Experience," and "Mock on, Mock on, Voltaire, Rousseau."

Skill 8.4   Apply the use of various critical perspectives to analyze given literary passages.

Reading literature involves a reciprocal interaction between the reader and the text.

Types of Responses

Emotional: In an emotional response, readers can identify with the characters and situations so as to project

> Learn more about
> **Reading Response Journals**
> http://www.education-world.com/a_curr/profdev/profdev085.sh
> tmlreading%20strategies%20index.htm

themselves into the story. They feel a sense of satisfaction by associating aspects of their own lives with the people, places, and events in the literature. Emotional responses are observed in readers' verbal and non-verbal reactions—laughter, comments on its effects, and retelling or dramatizing the action.
Interpretive: Interpretive responses result in inferences about character development, setting, or plot; analysis of style elements, such as metaphor, simile, allusion, rhythm, tone; outcomes derivable from information provided in the narrative; and assessment of the author's intent. Interpretive responses are made verbally or in writing.

Critical: Critical responses involve making value judgments about the quality of a piece of literature. Reactions to the effectiveness of the writer's style and language use are observed through discussion and written reactions.

Evaluative: Some reading response theorists add a response that considers the readers' considerations of such factors as how well the piece of literature represents its genre, how well it reflects the social/ethical mores of society, and how well the author has approached the subject for freshness and slant.

Middle school readers will exhibit both emotional and interpretive responses. Naturally, making interpretive responses depends on the degree of knowledge the student has of literary elements. Students show critical reactions on a fundamental level when they are able to say why a particular book was boring or why a particular poem was sad. Adolescents in ninth and tenth grades should begin to make critical responses by addressing the specific language and genre characteristics of literature.

Evaluative responses are harder to detect and are rarely made by any but a few advanced high school students. However, a teacher who knows what to listen for can recognize evaluative responses and incorporate them into discussions.

For example, if a student says, "I don't understand why that character is doing that," she is making an interpretive response to character motivation. However, if she goes on to say, "What good is that action?" she is giving an evaluative response that should be explored in terms of "What good should it do and why isn't that positive action happening?"

At the emotional level, another student might say, "I almost broke into a sweat when the author was describing the heat in the burning house." An interpretive response says, "The author used descriptive adjectives to bring his setting to life." Critically, the student adds, "The author's use of descriptive language contributes to the success of the narrative and maintains reader interest through the whole story." If he goes on to wonder why the author allowed the grandmother in the story to die in the fire, he is making an evaluative response.

Levels of Response

The levels of reader response will depend largely on the reader's level of social, psychological, and intellectual development. Most middle school students have progressed beyond merely involving themselves in the story enough to be able to retell the events in some logical sequence or describe the feeling that the story evoked. They are aware to some degree that the feeling evoked was the result of a careful manipulation of good elements of fiction writing.

They may not explain that awareness as successfully as a high school student, but they are beginning to grasp the concepts and not just the personal reactions. They are beginning to differentiate between responding to the story itself and responding to a literary creation.

Fostering Self-esteem and Empathy for Others and the World in Which One Lives

All-important is the use of literature as bibliotherapy that allows the reader to identify with others and become aware of alternatives while not feeling directly betrayed or threatened. For the high school student, the ability to empathize is an evaluative response, a much desired outcome of literature studies. Use of these books either individually or as a thematic unit of study allows for discussion or writing. The titles are grouped by theme, not by reading level.

Abuse
Blair, Maury and Doug Brendel. *Maury, Wednesday's Child*
Dizenzo, Patricia. *Why Me?*
Parrot, Andrea. *Coping with Date Rape and Acquaintance Rape*

Natural World Concerns
Caduto, M. and J. Bruchac. *Keepers of Earth*
Gay, Kathlyn. *Greenhouse Effect*
Johnson, Denis. *Fiskadaro*
Madison, Arnold. *It Can't Happen to Me*

Eating Disorders
Arnold, Caroline. *Too Fat? Too Thin? Do You Have a Choice?*
DeClements, Barthe. *Nothing's Fair in Fifth Grade*
Snyder, Anne. *Goodbye, Paper Doll*

Family
Cormier, Robert. *Tunes for Bears to Dance To*
Danzinger, Paula. *The Divorce Express*
Neufield, John. *Sunday Father*
Okimoto, Jean Davies. *Molly by Any Other Name*
Peck, Richard. *Don't Look and It Won't Hurt*
Zindel, Paul. *I Never Loved Your Mind*

Stereotyping
Baklanov, Grigory. (Trans. by Antonina W. Bouis) *Forever Nineteen*
Greene, Betty. *Summer of My German Soldier*
Kerr, M.E. *Gentle Hands*
Reiss, Johanna. *The Upstairs Room*
Taylor, Mildred D. *Roll of Thunder, Hear Me Cry*
Wakatsuki-Houston, Jeanne and James D. Houston. *Farewell to Manzanar*

Suicide and Death
Blume, Judy. *Tiger Eyes*
Bunting, Eve. *If I Asked You, Would You Stay?*
Gunther, John. *Death Be Not Proud*
Mazer, Harry. *When the Phone Rings*
Peck, Richard. *Remembering the Good Times*
Richter, Elizabeth. *Losing Someone You Love*
Strasser, Todd. *Friends Till the End*

Caution

Teachers should always use caution with reading materials that have a sensitive or controversial nature. A child who has known a recent death in his family or circle of friends may need to distance himself from classroom discussion. Whenever open discussion of a topic brings pain or embarrassment, the child should not be further subjected to it Older children and young adults will be able to discuss issues with greater objectivity without making blurted, insensitive comments.

Teachers must be able to gauge the level of emotional development of the students when selecting subject matter and the strategies for studying it. Students or parents may consider some material objectionable. Should a student choose not to read an assigned material, it is the teacher's responsibility to allow the student to select an alternate title. It is always advisable to notify parents if a particularly sensitive piece is to be studied.

COMPETENCY 9.0 UNDERSTAND THE STRUCTURE AND DEVELOPMENT OF THE ENGLISH LANGUAGE

Skill 9.1 Recognize structural features of languages (phonological, morphological, syntactic, semantic).

Phonological Awareness

Phonological awareness means the ability of the reader to recognize the sound of spoken language. This recognition includes how these sounds can be blended together, segmented (divided up), and manipulated (switched around). This awareness then leads to phonics, a method for teaching students to read. It helps them "sound out words."

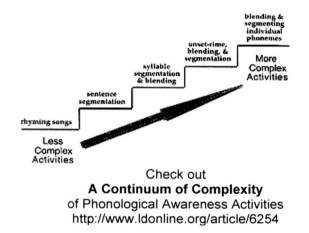

Check out
A Continuum of Complexity
of Phonological Awareness Activities
http://www.ldonline.org/article/6254

Instructional methods to teach phonological awareness may include any or all of the following: auditory games and drills during which students recognize and manipulate the sounds of words, separate or segment the sounds of words, take out sounds, blend sounds, add in new sounds, or take apart sound to recombine them in new formations. These are good ways to foster phonological awareness.

Identification of Common Morphemes, Prefixes, and Suffixes

This aspect of vocabulary development is to help students look for structural elements within words that they can use independently to help them determine meaning.

The terms listed below are generally recognized as the key structural analysis components.

Root Words: A root word is a word from which another word is developed. The second word can be said to have its "root" in the first. This structural component nicely lends itself to the illustration a tree with roots so that students can use a concrete image for an abstract concept.

An example of a root word is "bene" which means "good" or "well." English words from this Latin root include "benefit," "beneficial," "beneficent," and "beneficiary."

Students may also want to construct root words literally by using cardboard trees and/or actual roots from plants to create word family models. This is an effective way to help students own their root words.

Base Words: A base word is a stand-alone linguistic unit which cannot be deconstructed or broken down into smaller words. For example, in the word "re-tell," the base word is "tell."

Contractions: These are shortened forms of two words in which a letter or letters have been deleted. These deleted letters have been replaced by an apostrophe. For example, "hasn't" is the contraction for "has not."

Prefixes: These are beginning units of meaning which can be added (the vocabulary word for this type of structural adding is "affixed") to a base word or root word. They cannot stand alone. They are also sometimes known as "bound morphemes," meaning that they cannot stand alone as a base word. Some examples of prefixes are "pre," "ex," "trans," and "sub."

Suffixes: These are ending units of meaning that can be "affixed" or added on to the ends of root or base words. Suffixes transform the original meanings of base and root words. Like prefixes, they are also known as "bound morphemes," because they cannot stand alone as words. Some examples of suffixes are "ing," "ful," "ness," and "er."

Inflectional endings: These are types of suffixes that impart a new meaning to the base or root word. These endings in particular change the gender, number, tense, or form of the base or root words. Just like other suffixes, these are also termed "bound morphemes." Some examples are "ette," "es," and "ed."

> Learn more about
> **Word Analysis**
> http://www.orangeusd.k12.ca.us/
> yorba/word_analysis.htm

Compound Words: These occur when two or more base words are connected to form a new word. The meaning of the new word is in some way connected with that of the base word. "Bookkeeper," besides being the only English word with three double letters in a row, is an example of a compound word.

Syntax

Sentence Completeness

Avoid fragments and run-on sentences. Recognize the sentence elements necessary to make a complete thought and use independent and dependent clauses properly. Proper punctuation will correct such errors.

Sentence Structure
Recognize simple, compound, complex, and compound-complex sentences. Use dependent (subordinate) and independent clauses correctly to create these sentence structures.

Simple   Joyce wrote a letter.
Compound   Joyce wrote a letter, and Dot drew a picture.
Complex   While Joyce wrote a letter, Dot drew a picture.
Compound/Complex When Mother asked the girls to demonstrate their new-found skills, Joyce wrote a letter, and Dot drew a picture.

Note: Do **not** confuse compound sentence elements with compound sentences.

Simple sentence with compound subject
Joyce and Dot wrote letters.
The girl in row three and the boy next to her were passing notes across the aisle.

Simple sentence with compound predicate
Joyce wrote letters and drew pictures.
The captain of the high school debate team graduated with honors and studied broadcast journalism in college.

Simple sentence with compound object of preposition
Coleen graded the students' essays for style and mechanical accuracy.

Skill 9.2   **Understand the historical, social, cultural, and technological influences shaping English language structure and use.**

Historical Influences

English is an Indo-European language that evolved through several periods. The origin of English dates to the settlement of the British Isles in the fifth and sixth centuries by Germanic tribes called the Angles, Saxons, and Jutes. The original Britons spoke a Celtic tongue while the Angles spoke a Germanic dialect. Modern English derives from the speech of the Anglo-Saxons who imposed not only their language but also their social customs and laws on their new land. From the fifth to the tenth century, Britain's language was the tongue we now refer to as Old English. During the next four centuries, the many French attempts at English conquest introduced many French words to English. However, the grammar and syntax of the language remained Germanic.

Learn more about the
History of the English Language
http://ebbs.english.vt.edu/hel/hel.html

English   109

Middle English, most evident in the writings of Geoffrey Chaucer, dates loosely from 1066 to 1509. William Caxton brought the printing press to England in 1474 and increased literacy. Old English words required numerous inflections to indicate noun cases and plurals as well as verb conjugations. Middle English continued the use of many inflections and pronunciations that treated these inflections as separately pronounced syllables. English in 1300 would have been written "Olde Anglishe" with the e's at the ends of the words pronounced as our short *a* vowel. Even adjectives had plural inflections: "long dai" became "longe daies" pronounced "long-a day-as." Spelling was phonetic, thus every vowel had multiple pronunciations, a fact that continues to affect the language.

Modern English dates from the introduction of The Great Vowels Shift because it created guidelines for spelling and pronunciation. Before the printing press, books were copied laboriously by hand; the language was subject to the individual interpretation of the scribes. Printers and subsequently lexicographers like Samuel Johnson and America's Noah Webster influenced the guidelines. As reading matter was mass produced, the reading public was forced to adopt the speech and writing habits developed by those who wrote and printed books.

Despite many students' insistence to the contrary, Shakespeare's writings are in Modern English. Teachers should stress to students that language, like customs, morals, and other social factors, is constantly subject to change. Immigration, inventions, and cataclysmic events change language as much as any other facet of life is affected by these changes.

The domination of one race or nation over others can change a language significantly. Beginning with the colonization of the New World by England and Spain, English and Spanish became dominant languages in the Western hemisphere.

American English today is somewhat different in pronunciation and sometimes vocabulary from British English. The British call a truck a "lorry," baby carriages a "pram," short for "perambulator," and an elevator a "lift." The two languages have very few syntactical differences, and even the tonal qualities that were once so clearly different are converging.

Though Modern English is less complex than Middle English, having lost many unnecessary inflections, it is still considered difficult to learn because of its many exceptions to the rules. It has, however, become the world's dominant language by reason of the great political, military, and social power of England from the fifteenth to the nineteenth century and of America in the twentieth century.

Modern inventions—the telephone, phonograph, radio, television, and motion pictures—have especially affected English pronunciation. Regional dialects, once a hindrance to clear understanding, have fewer distinct characteristics. The speakers from different parts of the United States of America can be identified by their accents, but more and more as educators and media personalities stress uniform pronunciations and proper grammar, the differences are diminishing.

The English language has a more extensive vocabulary than any other language. Ours is a language of synonyms, words borrowed from other languages, and coined words—many of them introduced by the rapid expansion of technology.

Students should understand that language is in constant flux. They can demonstrate this when they use language for specific purposes and audiences. Negative criticism of a student's errors in word choice or sentence structures will inhibit creativity. Positive criticism that suggests ways to enhance communication skills will encourage exploration.

Geographical influences

Dialect differences are basically in pronunciation. Bostoners say "pahty" for "party" and Southerners blend words such as "you all" into "y'all." Besides the dialectal differences, the biggest geographical factors in American English stem from minor word choice variances. Depending on the region where you live, when you order a carbonated, syrupy beverage most generically called a soft drink, you might ask for a "soda" in the South, or a "pop" in the Midwest. If you order a soda in New York, then you will get a scoop of ice cream in your soft drink, while in other areas you would have to ask for a "float."

Social Influences

Social influences are mostly those imposed by family, peer groups, and mass media. The economic and educational levels of families determine language use. Exposure to adults who encourage and assist children to speak well enhances readiness for other areas of learning and contributes to their ability to communicate their needs. Historically, children learned language, speech patterns, and grammar from members of the extended family just as they learned the rules of conduct within their family unit and community. In modern times, the mother in a nuclear family became the dominant force in influencing children's development. With increasing social changes, many children are not receiving the proper guidance in all areas of development, especially language.

Those who are fortunate to be in educational-day-care programs like Head Start or in certified preschools often develop better language skills than those whose care is entrusted to untrained care providers. Once children enter elementary school, they are also greatly influenced by peer language. This peer influence becomes significant in adolescence as the use of teen jargon gives teenagers a sense of identity within their chosen group(s) and independence from the influence of adults. In some lower socio-economic groups, children use Standard English in school and street language outside the school. Some children of immigrant families become bilingual by necessity if no English is spoken in the home.

Research has shown a strong correlation between socio-economic characteristics and all areas of intellectual development. Traditional measurement instruments rely on verbal ability to establish intelligence. Research findings and test scores reflect that children reared in nuclear families providing cultural experiences and individual attention become more language-proficient than those who are denied that security and stimulation.

Personal Influences

The rate of physical development and identifiable language disabilities also influence language development. Nutritional deficiencies, poor eyesight, and conditions such as stuttering or dyslexia can inhibit children's ability to master language. Unless diagnosed early, they can hamper communication into adulthood. These conditions also stymie the development of self-confidence and, therefore, the willingness to learn or to overcome the handicap. Children should receive proper diagnosis and positive corrective instruction.

In adolescence, children's choice of role models and decisions about their future determine the growth of identity. Rapid physical and emotional changes and the stress of coping with the pressure of sexual awareness make concentration on any educational pursuits difficult. The easier the transition from childhood to adulthood, the better the competence will be in all learning areas.

Middle school and junior high school teachers are confronted by a student body ranging from fifth-graders who are still childish to eighth- or ninth-graders who, if not in fact, at least in their minds, are young adults. Teachers must approach language instruction as a social development tool with more emphasis on vocabulary acquisition, reading improvement, and speaking/writing skills. High school teachers can deal with the more formalized instruction of grammar, usage, and literature meant for older adolescents whose social development allows them to pay more attention to studies that will improve their chances for a better adult life.

As a tool, language must have relevance to students' real environment. Many high schools have developed practical English classes for business/ vocational students whose specific needs are determined by their desire to enter the workforce upon graduation. More emphasis is placed upon accuracy of mechanics and understanding verbal and written directions because these are skills desired by employers. Writing résumés, completing forms, reading policy and operations manuals, and generating reports are some of the desired skills.

Emphasis is placed on higher-level thinking skills, including inferential thinking and literary interpretation, in literature classes for college-bound students. In overcrowded classrooms, students are divided into small groups to foster intellectual development.

Skill 9.3 **Understand significant historical events influencing the development of the English language (Anglo-Saxon migrations; the Norman Conquest).**

See Skill 9.2

Perhaps the most basic principle about language in understanding its changes and variations is a simple one: language inevitably changes over time. If a community that speaks a homogeneous language and dialect are for some reason separated with no contact between the two resulting communities, they will be speaking different dialects within a few generations and eventually will have difficulty understanding each other.

Language changes in all its manifestations: At the phonetic level, the sounds of a language will change as will its orthography (spelling). The vocabulary level will probably manifest the greatest changes. Changes in syntax are slower and less likely to occur.

For example, English has changed in response to the influences of many other languages and cultures as well as internal cultural changes such as the development of the railroad and the computer; however, its syntax still relies on word order—it has not shifted to an inflected system even though many of the cultures that have impacted it do, in fact, have an inflected language, such as Spanish.

The most significant influence on a language is the blending of cultures. The Norman Conquest that brought the English speakers in the British Isles under the rule of French speakers changed the language, but the fact that English speakers did not adopt the language of the ruling class is significant—they did not become speakers of French. Even so, many vocabulary items entered the language in that period. The Great Vowel Shift that occurred between the fourteenth and sixteenth centuries is somewhat of a mystery although it's generally attributed to the migration to Southeast England following the plague of the Black Death. The Great Vowel Shift largely accounts for the discrepancy between orthography and speech—the difficult spelling system in modern English.

Colonization of other countries has also brought new vocabulary items into the language. Indian English has its own easily recognizable attributes as does Australian and North American English, and these cultural interactions have added to items in the usages of each other and in the language at large. Since English is the most widely spoken and understood language all over the world, it implies that it is constantly being changed by the globalized world.

Other influences, of course, impact language. The introduction of television and its domination by the United States has had great influence on the English that is spoken and understood all over the world. The same is true of the computerizing of the world (Tom Friedman called it "flattening" in his *The World is Flat: A Brief History of the Twenty-first Century*). New terms have been added ("blog"), old terms have changed meaning ("mouse"), and nouns have been verbalized ("prioritize").

Skill 9.4   **Identify additions to the lexicon of the English language throughout its development (words from Latin and French, regional and social dialects in the United States, words derived from technology).**

Just as countries and families have histories, so do words. Knowing and understanding the origin of a word, where it has been used down through the years, and the history of its meaning as it has changed is an important component of the writing and language teacher's tool kit.

> Check out the
> **Learning Resources of the OED**
> hhttp://www.oed.com/learning/

Never in the history of the English have had the forms and meanings of words changed so rapidly. When America was settled originally, immigration from many countries made it a "melting pot." Immigration accelerated rapidly within the first hundred years, resulting in pockets of language throughout the country. When trains began to make transportation available and affordable, individuals from those various pockets came in contact with each other, shared vocabularies, and attempted to converse. From that time forward, every generation brought the introduction of a technology that made language interchange not only more possible but more important.

Radio began the trend to standardize dialects. A Bostonian might not be understood by a native of Louisiana, who might not be interested in turning the dial to hear the news or a drama or the advertisements of the vendors that had a vested interest in being heard and understood. Soap and soup producers knew a goldmine when they saw it and created a market for radio announcers and actors who spoke without a pronounced dialect. In return, listeners began to hear the English language in a dialect very different from the one they spoke, and as it settled into their thinking processes, it eventually made its way to their tongues, and spoken English began to lose some of its local peculiarities.

It has been a slow process, but most Americans can easily understand other Americans, no matter where they come from. They can even converse with a native of Great Britain with little difficulty. The introduction of television carried the evolution further as did the explosion of electronic communicating devices over the past fifty years.

An excellent example of the changes that have occurred in English is a comparison of Shakespeare's original works with modern translations. Without help, twenty-first-century Americans are unable to read the *Folio*. On the other hand, teachers must constantly be mindful of the vocabularies and etymologies of their students, who are on the receiving end of the escalation brought about by technology and increased global influence and contact.

DOMAIN II.   **RHETORIC AND COMPOSITION**

COMPETENCY 10.0   **UNDERSTAND PRINCIPLES OF RHETORIC AS THEY APPLY TO VARIOUS FORMS AND PURPOSES OF ORAL AND WRITTEN COMMUNICATION**

Skill 10.1   **Trace the development of rhetoric from a classical art of persuasive oratory to a modern discipline concerned with the analysis and interpretation of spoken, written, and media communications.**

The art of rhetoric was first developed in Ancient Greece. Its pioneer was Socrates, who recognized the crucial role that rhetoric played in education, politics, and storytelling. Socrates argued that, effectively, speech could evoke any desired emotion or opinion. His method of dialectic syllogism, known today as the Socratic Method, pursued truth through a series of questions. Socrates established three types of appeals used in persuasive speech:

Types of Appeal

Ethos: Refers to the credibility of the speaker. It establishes the speaker as a reliable and trustworthy authority by focusing on the speaker's credentials.

Pathos: Refers to the emotional appeal made by the speaker to the listeners. It emphasizes the fact that the audience responds to ideas with emotion. For example, when the government is trying to persuade citizens to go to war for the sake of "the fatherland," it is using the appeal to *pathos* to target their love of their country.

Logos: Refers to the logic of the speaker's argument. It uses the idea that facts, statistics, and other forms of evidence can convince an audience to accept a speaker's argument. Remember that information can be just as, if not more, persuasive than appeal tactics.

Today, rhetoric's evolution can be traced back to ancient Athens in many facets of our society. The structure of many governments and judicial systems reflect rhetorical tactics established by the Greeks so long ago. The media has taken rhetoric to a whole new level and has refined it to a very skilled art. Every word as well as the method of presentation is carefully planned. The audience is taken into account and speech tailored to their needs and motivations. Though the content has changed, this concept has been around since Socrates contemplated it thousands of years ago.

Skill 10.2   Understand modern and contemporary theories of rhetoric.

Throughout history, theories of rhetoric have been developed, adopted, modified, and discarded. Here are three variations of persuasive speech.

Fact: Similar to an informative speech, a persuasive speech on a question of fact seeks to find an answer where there isn't a clear one. The speaker evaluates evidence and attempts to convince the audience that their conclusion is correct. The challenge is to accept a certain carefully crafted view of the facts presented.

Value: This kind of persuasion tries to convince the audience that a certain thing is good or bad, moral or immoral, valuable or worthless. It focuses less on knowledge and more on beliefs and values.

Policy: This speech is a call to action, arguing that something should be done, improved, or changed. Its goal is action from the audience, but it also seeks passive agreement with the proposition proposed. It appeals to both reason and emotion, and tells listeners what they can do and how to do it.

Skill 10.3   Effective application of modern rhetorical principles (unity, coherence, emphasis) to produce a desired result in an audience

In writing or speaking, you can be persuasive if you follow the three basic principles of unity, coherence, and emphasis.

Unity: All ideas must relate to the controlling thesis. At the simplest level, this means that all sentences must develop the topic sentence of a paragraph. By extension, then, all paragraphs must develop the thesis statement of the essay; all chapters must develop the main idea of the book. All ideas must develop the argument.

Coherence: One way to achieve unity is to show the relationship of ideas by using transitional words, phrases, sentences, and paragraphs. Using coordinating conjunctions (for, and, nor, but, or, yet, so), subordinating conjunctions (because, since, whenever), or transitional adverbs (however, therefore) is an effective way to show logical order and thus create coherence. Another way to show the relationship of ideas is to use an appropriate strategy (spatial, chronological, cause and effect, classification, comparison/contrast) to arrange details.

Emphasis: By placing your stronger arguments in areas of importance, you emphasize the significance of the ideas. In direct order, the main ideas are stated first and then supported by reasons or details. In indirect order, the support is provided first (in either increasing or decreasing order of importance) so that the end is a well-defended argument.

The classical argument structure below uses unity, coherence, and emphasis effectively.

Classical Argument

In its simplest form, the classical argument has five main parts:

The **introduction**, which warms up the audience, establishes goodwill and rapport with the readers, and announces the general theme or thesis of the argument.

The **narration**, which summarizes relevant background material, provides any information the audience needs to know about the environment and circumstances that produce the argument, and set up the stakes—what's at risk in this question.

The **confirmation**, lays out in a logical order (usually strongest to weakest or most obvious to most subtle) the claims that support the thesis, providing evidence for each claim.

The **refutation** and concession, which looks at opposing viewpoints to the writer's claims, anticipating objections from the audience, and allowing as much of the opposing viewpoints as possible without weakening the thesis.

The **summation**, which provides a strong conclusion, amplifies the force of the argument and shows the readers that this solution is the best at meeting the circumstances.

Skill 10.4   Possess consideration of subject, subject knowledge, purpose, and audience in producing a communication

To convey effective written and oral messages, you must have a clear idea of your purpose and audience.

Establish a Purpose

All messages are basically informative in that they relay ideas, but many go beyond this and are intended to analyze, convince, motivate, entertain, or any combination. As a communicator, you must gather and organize your information to fulfill that purpose.

To gather that information, you will evaluate your knowledge of the subject and then probably conduct additional research to verify and gather new data. Unless you are an expert in the field, you will want to rely on the credibility of others.

Guidelines for Assessing your Audience

Now that you know your purpose and have the information, you need to assess your audience. What does your audience know and what does it need to know? Here are some questions to consider.

Values: What is important to this group of people? What is their background and how will that affect their perception of your speech?

Needs: Find out in advance what the audience's needs are. Why are they listening to you? Find a way to satisfy their needs.

Constraints: What might hold the audience back from being fully engaged in what you are saying, or agreeing with your point of view, or processing what you are trying to say? These could be political reasons, which make them wary of your presentation's ideology from the start, or knowledge reasons, in which the audience lacks the appropriate background information to grasp your ideas. Avoid this last constraint by staying away from technical terminology, slang, or abbreviations that may be unclear to your audience.

Demographic Information: Take the audience's size into account as well as the location of the presentation. Demographics could include age, gender, education, religion, income level and other such countable characteristics.

Skill 10.5   Use of appropriate arrangement and organization (logical ordering of ideas), style and tone (lexical choices, word order, cadence), and form of delivery.

A logical argument consists of three stages. First, **state the premises** of the argument. These are the propositions which are necessary for the argument to continue. They are the evidence or reasons for accepting the argument and its conclusions.

Premises (or assertions) are often indicated by phrases such as "because," "since," "obviously," and so on. (The phrase "obviously" is often viewed with suspicion, as it can be used to intimidate others into accepting suspicious premises. If something doesn't seem obvious to you, don't be afraid to question it. You can always say, "Oh, yes, you're right, it is obvious" when you've heard the explanation.)

Next, **use the premises** to derive further propositions by a process known as inference. In inference, one proposition is arrived at on the basis of one or more other propositions already accepted. There are various forms of valid inference. The propositions arrived at by inference may then be used in further inference. Inference is often denoted by phrases such as "implies that" or "therefore."

Finally, **conclude the argument** with the proposition that is affirmed on the basis of the premises and inference. Conclusions are often indicated by phrases such as "therefore," "it follows that" "we conclude" and so on. The conclusion is often stated as the final stage of inference.

Delivery Techniques

As a teacher, you recognize the importance of delivering your message. While written communications is discussed in later sections, let's consider oral communications now. Instruct your students on the ways that verbal and non-verbal communication can affect the way a presentation is understood. You can model these techniques.

Posture: Maintain a straight, but not stiff posture. Instead of shifting weight from hip to hip, point your feet directly at the audience and distribute your weight evenly. Keep shoulders towards the audience. If you have to turn your body to use a visual aid, turn 45 degrees and continue speaking towards the audience.

Movement: Instead of staying glued to one spot or pacing back and forth, stay within four to eight feet of the front row of your audience. Take a step or half-step to the side every once in a while. If you are using a lectern, feel free to move to the front or side of it to engage your audience more. Avoid distancing yourself from the audience; you want them to feel involved and connected.

Gestures: Gestures can maintain a natural atmosphere when speaking publicly. Use them just as you would when speaking to a friend. They shouldn't be exaggerated, but they should be used for added emphasis. Avoid keeping your hands in your pockets or locked behind your back, wringing your hands and fidgeting nervously, or keeping your arms crossed.

Eye Contact: Many people are intimidated by using eye contact when speaking to large groups. Interestingly, eye contact usually *helps* the speaker overcome speech anxiety by connecting with the attentive audience and easing feelings of isolation. Instead of looking at a spot on the back wall or at your notes, scan the room and make eye contact for one to three seconds per person.

In addition to the content of your presentation, you want to use a strong delivery. As with most skills, the key is practice, practice, practice. Record and play back your presentation to hear how you sound.

Voice: Many people fall into one of two traps when speaking: using a monotone or talking too fast. These are both caused by anxiety. A monotone restricts your natural inflection but can be remedied by releasing tension in upper and lower body muscles. Subtle movement will keep you loose and natural.

> Learn more about
> **Using Your Voice**
> http://www.longview.k12.wa.us/mmhs
> /wyatt/pathway/voice.html

Talking too fast, on the other hand, is not necessarily bad if you are exceptionally articulate. If you are not a strong speaker or if you are talking about very technical items, the audience will easily become lost. When you talk too fast and begin tripping over your words, consciously pause after every sentence you say. Don't be afraid of brief silences. The audience needs time to absorb what you are saying.

Volume: Problems with volume, whether too soft or too loud, can usually be overcome with practice. If you tend to speak too softly, have someone stand in the back of the room and signal you when your volume is strong enough. If possible, have someone in the front of the room as well to make sure you're not overcompensating with excessive volume. Conversely, if you have a problem with speaking too loud, have the person in the front of the room signal you when your voice is soft enough and check with the person in the back to make sure it is still loud enough to be heard. In both cases, note your volume level for future reference. Don't be shy about asking your audience, "Can you hear me in the back?" Suitable volume is beneficial for both you and the audience.

Pitch: Pitch refers to the length, tension, and thickness of your person's vocal bands. As your voice gets higher, the pitch gets higher. In oral performance, pitch reflects the emotional arousal level. More variation in pitch typically corresponds to more emotional arousal but can also be used to convey sarcasm or highlight specific words.

While these skills are essential for you to be an effective teacher, you want your students to develop these techniques as well. By encouraging the development of proper techniques for oral presentations, you are enabling your students to develop self-confidence for higher levels of communication.

Skill 10.6   Understand similarities and differences between language structures in spoken and written English

Although widely different in many aspects, written and spoken English share a common basic structure or syntax (subject, verb, and object) and the common purpose of fulfilling the need to communicate—but there, the similarities end.

Spoken English does follow the basic word order mentioned above (subject, verb object) as does written English. We would write as we would speak, "I sang a song." It is usually only in poetry or music that that word order or syntax is altered: "Sang I a song." However, beyond that, spoken English is freed from the constraints and expectations imposed upon the written word.

Because of these restraints in the form of rules of grammar and punctuation, learning to read and write occupy years of formal schooling whereas learning to speak is a natural developmental stage, much like walking, that is accomplished before the tedious process of learning to write what we speak is endured.

These rules are imposed upon the written language, in part because of necessity. Written English is an isolated event. The writer must use an expected, ordered structure, complete with proper spacing and punctuation in order to be understood by an audience that the writer may never see.

In contrast, the speaker of English can rely on hand gestures, facial expressions, and tone of voice to convey information and emotions beyond that which is conveyed in words alone. In addition, speaking is not usually an isolated event. A speaker has a listener who can interrupt, ask questions, or provide additional information, ensuring that the communication is understood. Thus, spoken English is a much more fluid form of communication and is more directly suited to meeting the needs of the particular audience.

This gives rise to regional dialects and forms of expressions that with time and usage may find their way into formal written English.

However, with technology, there are new avenues for communication that are resulting in a synthesis of these two forms of communication: text messaging and chat room dialogues. In these forms, written English is not bound by the formal rules of spelling, grammar, and punctuation—rather it is free to more closely mimic its spoken counterpart.

Want to shout your answer? USE ALL CAPS! Saying something with a smile? Then show it! ☺ The limited space on cell phones and the immediacy of Internet chat rooms have also led to adaptations in spelling, where, for example, "text message" becomes "*txt msg*." Other abbreviated spellings and expressions have gained reached such popular usage that in 2005, the world's first *dxNRE & glosRE* (dictionary and glossary), "*transl8it!*" (Translate!) was published to help in the translation of standard English into text speak. Although these unorthodox forms of communication may frighten formal grammarians, this brave new world of communicating, as employed online and via cell phones, is far from being the death knell for "proper" English. Rather it is just one more indication of the versatility of our language and the ingenuity and creativity of the individuals who employ it.

Skill 10.7   Know how to interpret and apply English grammar and language conventions in oral and written contexts.

Let's review some of the mechanics of English Grammar.

Capitalization

> Check out this
> **Guide to Grammar and Writing**
> http://grammar.ccc.commnet.edu/grammar/

Capitalize all proper names of persons (including specific organizations or agencies of government); places (countries, states, cities, parks, and specific geographical areas); and things (political parties, structures, historical and cultural terms, and calendar and time designations); and religious terms (any deity, revered person or group, sacred writings).

> Percy Bysshe Shelley, Argentina, Mount Rainier National Park, Grand Canyon, League of Nations, the Sears Tower, Birmingham, Lyric Theater, Americans, Midwesterners, Democrats, Renaissance, Boy Scouts of America, Easter, God, Bible, Dead Sea Scrolls, Koran

Capitalize proper adjectives and titles used with proper names.

> California Gold Rush, President John Adams, French fries, Homeric epic, Romanesque architecture, Senator John Glenn

Note: Some words that represent titles and offices are not capitalized unless used with a proper name.

Capitalized	Not Capitalized
Congressman McKay	the congressman from Florida
Commander Alger	commander of the Pacific Fleet
Queen Elizabeth	the queen of England

Capitalize all main words in titles of works of literature, art, and music.

Spelling

Concentration in this section will be on spelling plurals and possessives. If the multiplicity and complexity of spelling rules based on phonics, letter doubling, and exceptions to rules are not mastered by adulthood, writers should use a good dictionary to achieve correctness. Since spelling mastery is usually difficult for adolescents, our recommendation for them is the same. Learning the use of a dictionary and thesaurus will be a more rewarding use of time than laboring to master each obscure rule and exception.

Most plurals of nouns that end in hard consonants or hard consonant sounds followed by a silent *e* are made by adding *s*. Some words ending in vowels only add *s*.

fingers, numerals, banks, bugs, riots, homes, gates, radios, bananas

Nouns that end in soft consonant sounds *s, j, x, z, ch,* and *sh*, add *es*. Some nouns ending in *o* add es.

dresses, waxes, churches, brushes, tomatoes, potatoes

Nouns ending in *y* preceded by a vowel just add *s*.

boys, alleys

Nouns ending in *y* preceded by a consonant change the *y* to *i* and add *es.*

babies, corollaries, frugalities, poppies

Some nouns plurals are formed irregularly or remain the same.

sheep, deer, children, leaves, oxen

Some nouns derived from foreign words, especially Latin, may make their plurals in two different ways--one of them Anglicized. Sometimes, the meanings are the same; other times, the two plurals are used in slightly different contexts. It is always wise to consult the dictionary.

appendices, appendixes   criterion, criteria
indexes, indices   crisis, crises

Make the plurals of closed (solid) compound words in the usual way except for words ending in *ful* which make their plurals on the root word.

> timelines, hairpins

Make the plurals of open or hyphenated compounds by adding the change in inflection to the word that changes in number.

> fathers-in-law, courts-martial, masters of art, doctors of medicine

Make the plurals of letters, numbers, and abbreviations by adding *s*.

> fives and tens, 1990s, *p*s and *q*s (Note that letters are italicized.)

When in doubt, consult a dictionary.

Skill 10.8   Understand the role of cultural factors in oral and written communication

The knowledge that teachers need to be effective in the multicultural English classroom can be broken into seven broad areas:

1. The nature of human language
2. The components of language
3. The process of language acquisition
4. Language and culture
5. Linguistics and literacy
6. TESOL methodologies
7. Language pathology

Human language is creative in that it allows speakers to form an unlimited number of sentences from the vocabulary and operations base they build when they learn language. Noam Chomsky called language the "human essence" which means that this distinction is, so far as we know, unique to man.

The basics of linguistics are phonology, morphology, syntax, semantics, and pragmatics, and all languages are rule-governed, not the rules we "teach," but the rules that have become embedded in the brain processes of the user. The rule embedded in the mind of a native speaker of English that the nominative is different from the accusative is well known to a three-year-old speaker. If he is told that Mommy bit the dog, he will laugh; he will have a quite different response if he is told that the dog bit Mommy.

A native learning the language as a child will progress through predictable stages. A speaker of another language learning to speak and use English will also go through predictable though different stages, and the age of the learner is significant. Younger children will learn a foreign language much more quickly than older ones. Learning to read is very different from learning to understand and speak the language.

Language is tied to culture and carries with it very strong emotions. The very heated discussions over whether Black English is a different language or a different dialect demonstrate how emotional it is. It involves not just language usage but also cultural, social, and political matters.

Variations in language are manifested in the phonology, lexicon, morphology, syntax, and semantics of a language and can even be related to gender, ethnicity, social class, geography, and age. Not only are there variations in language, but also all languages change over time, including English.

The English spoken by our parents is not the English being spoken today by high school students. To assume that variations and changes are somehow flaws, wrong, or problematic is to misunderstand the very nature of language.

TESOL—teaching English to speakers of other languages—requires specialized training, knowledge, and experience. While most English teachers are not required to have that training and experience, they do need to understand the needs of students in their classroom who are not native speakers of English. In the same way, teachers should have enough linguistic training to be able to recognize when language or speech production is atypical and when specialists, either speech pathologists or therapists, should be consulted.

Skill 10.9   Apply strategies for evaluating the content and effectiveness of written and spoken messages

Language Skills to Evaluate

- The ability to talk at length with few pauses and fill time with speech
- The ability to call up appropriate things to say in a wide range of contexts
- The size and range of a student's vocabulary and syntax skills
- The coherence of their sentences, the ability to speak in reasoned and semantically dense sentences
- Knowledge of the various forms of interaction and conversation for various situations
- Knowledge of the standard rules of conversation
- The ability to be creative and imaginative with language, and express oneself in original ways
- The ability to invent and entertain, and take risks in linguistic expression

Methods of Evaluation

- Commercially designed language assessment products
- Instructor observation using a rating scale from 1 to 5 (where 1=limited proficiency and 5=native speaker equivalency)
- Informal observation of students' behaviors

> Check out this
> **Oral Presentation Rubric**
> http://www.tcet.unt.edu/START/
> instruct /general/oral.htm

Uses of Language Assessment

- Diagnosis of language strengths and weaknesses
- Detection of patterns of systematic errors
- Appropriate bilingual/ESL program placement if necessary

Common Language Errors

- Application of rules that apply in a student's first language but not in the second
- Using pronunciation that applies to a student's first language but not in the second
- Applying a general rule to all cases even when there are exceptions
- Trying to cut corners by using an incorrect word or syntactic form
- Avoiding use of precise vocabulary or idiomatic expressions
- Using incorrect verb tense

Skill 10.10   Understand principles of effective speaking and listening for various purposes (for information and understanding, literary response and expression, critical analysis and persuasion, debate)

Different Methods of Oral Communication

Different from the basic writing forms of discourse is the art of **debating, discussion, and conversation**. The ability to use language and logic to convince the audience to accept your reasoning and to side with you is an art. This form of writing/speaking is extremely confined or structured,

> Learn more about
> **Oral Communication Skills**
> http://www.glencoe.com/sec/teachingt oday/weeklytips.phtml/88

and logically sequenced with supporting reasons and evidence. At its best, it is the highest form of propaganda. A position statement, evidence, reason, evaluation and refutation are integral parts of this writing schema.

Interviewing provides opportunities for students to apply expository and informative communication. It teaches them how to structure questions to evoke fact-filled responses. Compiling the information from an interview into a biographical essay or speech helps students list, sort, and arrange details in an orderly fashion.

Speeches that encourage them to describe persons, places, or events in their own lives or oral interpretations of literature help them sense the creativity and effort used by professional writers.

Listening

Communication skills are crucial in a collaborative society. In particular, a person cannot be a successful communicator without being an active listener.

Focus on what others say, rather than planning on what to say next. By listening to everything another person is saying, you may pick up on natural cues that lead to the next conversation move without so much added effort.

> **Reasons to Improve Listening Skills**
> To avoid saying the wrong thing, being tactless
> To dissipate strong feelings
> To learn to accept feelings (yours and others)
> To generate a feeling of caring
> To help people start listening to you
> To increase the other person's confidence in you
> To make the other person feel important and recognized
> To be sure you both are on the same wavelength
> To be sure you both are focused on the same topic
> To check that you are both are on target with one another
> *http://www.coping.org/dialogue/listen.htm*

Facilitating

It is quite acceptable to use standard opening lines to facilitate a conversation. Don't agonize trying to come up with witty "one-liners" as the main obstacle in initiating conversation is just getting the first statement over with. After that, the real substance begins. A useful technique may be to make a comment or ask a question about a shared situation. This may be anything from the weather to the food you are eating to a new policy at work. Use an opener you are comfortable with because your partner in conversation will be comfortable with it as well.

Stimulating Higher Level Critical Thinking Through Inquiry

Many people rely on questions to communicate with others. However, most fall back on simple clarifying questions rather than open-ended inquiries. For example, if you paraphrase a response by asking "Did you mean . . . ." you may receive merely a "yes" or "no" answer. On open-ended inquiry would ask "What did you mean when you said . . . . ?"

Try to ask open-ended, deeper-level questions since those tend to have the greatest reward and lead to a greater understanding. With answers to those questions, you can make more complex connections and achieve more significant information.

Skill 10.11 Know techniques for interpreting and analyzing media messages

More money is spent each year on advertising to children than educating them. Thus, the media's strategies are considerably well thought out and effective. They employ large, clear letters, bold colors, simple line drawings, and popular symbols to announce upcoming events, push ideas and advertise products. By using attractive photographs, brightly colored cartoon characters, or instructive messages, they increase sales, win votes, or stimulate learning. The graphics are designed to communicate messages clearly, precisely, and efficiently. Some even target subconscious yearnings for sex and status.

Because so much effort is being spent on influencing students through media tactics, just as much effort should be devoted to educating those students about media awareness. A teacher should explain that artists and the aspects they choose to portray as well as the ways in which they portray them reflect their attitude and understanding of those aspects. The artistic choices are not entirely based on creative license—they also reflect an imbedded meaning the artist wants to represent. Colors, shapes, and positions are meant to arouse basic instincts for food, sex, and status, and are often used to sell cars, clothing, or liquor.

To stimulate analysis of media strategies, ask students questions such as:
- Where/when do you think this picture was taken/film was shot/piece was written?
- Would you like to have lived at this time in history, or in this place?
- What objects are present?
- What do the people presented look like? Are they happy or sad?
- Who is being targeted?
- What can you learn from this piece of media?
- Is it telling you something is good or bad?
- What message is being broadcast?

> Learn more about
> **Teaching Film,**
> **Television, and Media**
> http://www.tc.umn.edu/~rbeach/
> linksteachingmedia/chapter8/16.htm

Advertising Techniques

Because students are very interested in the types of approaches advertisers use, you can develop high-interest assignments requiring them to analyze commercial messages. What is powerful about Nike's "Just Do It" campaign? What is the appeal of Jessica Simpson's eponymous perfume?

Beauty Appeal: Beauty attracts us; we are drawn to beautiful people, places, and things.

Celebrity Endorsement: This technique associates product use with a well-known person. By purchasing this product we are led to believe that we will attain characteristics similar to the celebrity.

Compliment the Consumer: Advertisers flatter the consumer who is willing to purchase their product. By purchasing the product the consumer is recognized by the advertisers for making a good decision with the selection.

Escape: Getting away from it all is very appealing; you can imagine adventures you cannot have; the idea of escape is pleasurable.

Independence/Individuality: This technique associates product with people who can think and act for themselves. Products are linked to individual decision making.

Intelligence: This technique associates product with smart people who can't be fooled.

Lifestyle: This technique associates product with a particular style of living/way of doing things.

Nurture: Every time you see an animal or a child, the appeal is to your paternal or maternal instincts, so this technique associates products with taking care of someone.

Peer Approval: This technique associates product use with friendship/acceptance. Advertisers can also use this negatively to make you worry that you'll lose friends if you don't use a certain product.

Rebel: This technique associates products with behaviors or lifestyles that oppose society's norms.

Rhetorical Question: This technique poses a question to the consumer that demands a response. A question is asked and the consumer is supposed to answer in such a way that affirms the product's goodness.

Scientific/Statistical Claim: This provides some sort of scientific proof or experiment, very specific numbers, or an impressive sounding mystery ingredient.

Unfinished Comparison/Claim: This technique uses phrases such as "Works better in poor driving conditions!" Works better than what?

COMPETENCY 11.0   UNDERSTAND THE COMPOSITION PROCESS

Skill 11.1   Understand strategies for writing effectively in a variety of forms and for a variety of audiences, purposes, and contexts

Basic expository writing simply gives information not previously known about a topic or is used to explain or define one. Facts, examples, statistics, cause and effect, direct tone, objective rather than subjective delivery, and non-emotional information are presented in a formal manner.

Descriptive writing centers on person, place, or object, using concrete and sensory words to create a mood or impression and arranging details in a chronological or spatial sequence.

Narrative writing is developed using an incident or anecdote or related series of events. Chronology, the 5 *Ws*, topic sentence, and conclusion are essential ingredients.

Persuasive writing implies the writer's ability to select vocabulary and arrange facts and opinions in such a way as to direct the actions of the listener/reader. Persuasive writing may incorporate exposition and narration as they illustrate the main idea.

Journalistic writing is theoretically free of author bias. It is essential when relaying information about an event, person, or thing that it be factual and objective. Provide students with an opportunity to examine newspapers and create their own. Many newspapers have educational programs that are offered free to schools.

Skill 11.2   Understand processes for generating and developing written texts (prewriting, drafting, revising, editing, publishing)

Writing is a recursive process. As students engage in the various stages of writing, they develop and improve not only their writing skills but their thinking skills as well.

Prewriting Strategies

Students gather ideas before writing. Prewriting may include clustering, listing, brainstorming, mapping, free writing, and charting. Providing many ways for students to develop ideas on a topic will increase their chances for success.

Listed below are the most common prewriting strategies students can use to explore, plan, and write on a topic. When teaching these strategies, remember that not all prewriting must eventually produce a finished piece of writing. In fact, in the initial lesson of teaching prewriting strategies, you might have students practice prewriting strategies without the pressure of having to write a finished product.

- Keep an idea book so that they can jot down ideas that come to mind.

- Write in a daily journal.

- Write down whatever comes to mind; this is called free writing. Students do not stop to make corrections or interrupt the flow of ideas. A variation of this technique is focused free writing—writing on a specific topic—to prepare for an essay.

- Make a list of all ideas connected with their topic; this is called brainstorming. Make sure students know that this technique works best when they let their mind work freely. After completing the list, students should analyze the list to see if a pattern or way to group the ideas.

- Ask the questions *who, what, when, where, why and how.* Help the writer approach a topic from several perspectives.

- Create a visual map on paper to gather ideas. Cluster circles and lines to show connections between ideas. Students should try to identify the relationship that exists between their ideas. If they cannot see the relationships, have them pair up, exchange papers and have their partners look for some related ideas.

- Observe details of sight, hearing, taste, touch, and taste.

- Visualize by making mental images of something and write down the details in a list.

- Model their favorite writers.

After they have practiced with each of these prewriting strategies, ask them to pick out the ones they prefer and ask them to discuss how they might use the techniques to help them with future writing assignments. Remind them that they can use more than one prewriting strategy at a time. Also they may find that different writing situations may suggest certain techniques.

Writing

Students compose the first draft. Encourage them to write freely. If they get their ideas down first, then they can move to revising. If they have difficulty, have them write as they speak—perhaps have them dictate to another writer or recorder. It's important to keep in mind that using a computer for writing can be so quick that exploration and contemplation of composing can be inhibited.

Revising

Students examine their work and make changes in sentences, wording, details and ideas. Revise comes from the Latin word *revidere*, meaning, "to see again." This step is often overlooked, unfortunately. Sometimes writers confuse it with proofreading. So students need to understand how important this process is.

Editing

Students proofread the draft for punctuation and mechanical errors.

Publishing

Students may have their work displayed on a bulletin board, read aloud in class, or printed in a literary magazine or school anthology.

These steps are recursive; as students engage in each aspect of the writing process, they may begin with prewriting, write, revise, write, revise, edit, and publish. They do not engage in this process in a lockstep manner; it is more circular.

Skill 11.3   Identify techniques for revising written texts to achieve clarity and economy of expression

Writing that is clear and concise will achieve its purpose more effectively. Here are techniques to enhance interest and ensure understanding of written texts.

Enhancing Interest
- Start out with an attention-grabbing introduction. This sets an engaging tone for the entire piece and will be more likely to pull readers in.
- Use dynamic vocabulary and varied sentence beginnings. Keep the readers on their toes. If they can predict what you are going to say next, switch it up.
- Avoid using clichés (as cold as ice, the best thing since sliced bread, nip it in the bud). These are easy shortcuts, but they are not interesting, memorable, or convincing.

Ensuring Understanding

- Avoid using the words "clearly," "obviously," and "undoubtedly." Often, what is clear or obvious to the author is not as apparent to the readers. Instead of using these words, make your point so strongly that it is clear on its own.
- Use the word that best fits the meaning you intend, even if it is longer or a little less common. Try to find a balance, and go with a familiar, yet precise, word.
- When in doubt, explain further.

Skill 11.4 Describe revision of sentences to eliminate wordiness, ambiguity, and redundancy

Consider revising and editing. This is an extremely important step that often is ignored. Some questions to ask:

- Is the reasoning coherent?
- Is the point established?
- Does the introduction make the reader want to read this discourse?
- What is the thesis? Is it proven?
- What is the purpose? Is it clear? Is it useful, valuable, and interesting?
- Is the style of writing so wordy that it exhausts the reader and interferes with engagement?
- Is the writing so spare that it is boring?
- Are the sentences too uniform in structure?
- Are there too many simple sentences?
- Are too many of the complex sentences the same structure?
- Are the compounds truly compounds, or are they unbalanced?
- Are parallel structures truly parallel?
- If there are characters, are they believable?
- If there is dialogue, is it natural or stilted?
- Is the title appropriate?
- Does the writing show creativity, or is it boring?
- Is the language appropriate? Is it too formal? Too informal? If jargon is used, is it appropriate?

Studies have clearly demonstrated that the most fertile area in teaching writing is this one. If students can learn to revise their own work effectively, they are well on their way to becoming effective, mature writers.

Word-processing is an important tool for teaching this stage in the writing process. For example, Microsoft Word has tracking features that make the revision exchanges between teachers and students more effective than ever before. In WordPerfect, changes are referred to as "annotations", and this method is used to edit and show changes in the manuscript while still maintaining the document's original integrity.

Skill 11.5   Understand development of a thesis

A well-crafted thesis statement can help both writers and readers. Writers can stay on topic and develop their thesis statement with appropriate and relevant details. Readers can better understand the main idea and the supporting ideas. By following these steps, writers can develop the skill to formulate clear and strong thesis statements.

Write the Thesis Statement

First, you should identify the topic.
> I am going to write about the tone and how it is created in the poem "I Hear America Singing" by Walt Whitman.

Second, state your point of view about the topic.

> The upbeat and optimistic tone of Whitman's poem is created by his word choice, structure and imagery.

Third, summarize the main points you will make in your essay.

> Whitman creates an optimistic tone through his choice of words, parallel structure, and images.

Skill 11.6   Understand development of an effective introduction and conclusion

Once you have written the body of the paper, you can write your introduction and conclusion so that they reflect the body of the paper. This is the time to review the organization of your material.

Introductions

Until the body of the paper has been determined—thesis, development—it's difficult to make strategic decisions regarding the introduction. The Greek rhetoricians called this part of a discourse *exordium*, a "leading into."

The basic purpose of the introduction, then, is to lead the audience into the discourse. It can let the reader know what the purpose of the discourse is and it can condition the audience to be receptive to what you want to say. The introduction can be very brief, or it can take up a large percentage of the total word count. Aristotle said that the introduction could be compared to the flourishes that flute players make before their performance—an overture in which the musicians display what they can play best in order to gain the favor and attention of the audience for the main performance.

In order to do this, you must first know what you are going to say; who the readership is likely to be; what the social, political, or economic climate is; what preconceived notions the audience may have about the subject; and how long the discourse is going to be.

Suggestions for Writing an Introduction
- Show that the subject is important.
- Show that although the points you are presenting may seem improbable, they are true.
- Show that the subject has been neglected, misunderstood, or misrepresented.
- Explain an unusual mode of development.
- Forestall any misconception of the purpose.
- Apologize for a deficiency.
- Arouse interest in the subject with an anecdotal lead-in.
- Ingratiate oneself with the readership.
- Establish one's own credibility.

The introduction often ends with the thesis, the point or purpose of the paper. However, this is not mandatory. The thesis may open the body of the discussion, or it may conclude the discourse. What you need to remember is that the purpose and structure of the introduction should be deliberate since it is to serve the purpose of "leading the reader into the discussion."

Conclusions

Writing a conclusion is easier after you have written the introduction. Aristotle taught that the conclusion should strive to do five things:

1. Inspire the reader with a favorable opinion of the writer.
2. Amplify the force of the points made in the body of the paper.
3. Reinforce the points made in the body.
4. Rouse appropriate emotions in the reader.
5. Restate in a summary way what has been said.

The conclusion may be short or may be long--depending on its purpose in the paper. Recapitulation, a brief restatement of the main points--or certainly of the thesis-- is the most common form of effective conclusions. A good example is a court trial where an attorney would review the main points to support the closing argument.

Skill 11.7   Understand effective use of topic sentences.

Now that you have established the overriding purpose of your paper, you can focus on development in the body of the paper. To maintain unity and coherence, you should writer clear and well-organized paragraphs.

Techniques to Maintain Focus

- **Focus on a main point.** The point should be clear to readers, and all sentences in the paragraph should relate to it.
- **Start the paragraph with a topic sentence.** This should be a general, one-sentence summary of the paragraph's main point, relating back to the thesis and forward to the content of the paragraph. (A topic sentence is sometimes unnecessary if the paragraph continues a developing idea clearly introduced in a preceding paragraph, or if the paragraph appears in a narrative of events where generalizations might interrupt the flow of the story.)
- **Stick to the point.** Eliminate sentences that do not support the topic sentence.
- **Be flexible.** If you do not have enough evidence to support the claim of your topic sentence, do not fall into the trap of wandering or introducing new ideas within the paragraph. Either find more evidence, or adjust the topic sentence to corroborate with the evidence that is available.

Skill 11.8   Describe the role of voice and style in writing.

There are at least thirteen possible choices for point of view (voice) in literature as demonstrated and explained by Wallace Hildick in his *13 Types of Narrative*. However, for purposes of helping students write essays about literature, three, or possibly four, are adequate.

Point of view or **voice** is essentially through whose eyes the reader sees the action. The most common is the **third-person objective**. From this point of view, the reader watches the action, hears the dialogue, reads

Learn more about
Writing Fiction
http://crofsblogs.typepad.com/fiction/
2003/07/narrative_voice.html

descriptions, and (in fiction) deduce characterizations. An unseen narrator tells the reader what is happening, using *he, she, it, they*. The author may intrude and evaluate or comment on the ideas being presented, or in fiction, the characters or the action.

The voice of the **first-person** narrator enables the reader to see the action through the eyes of the writer—or in fiction through the eyes of the character who is narrating the story. In fiction then, the narrator must be analyzed as a character. What sort of person is this? What is this character's position in the story—observer, commentator, and actor? Can the narrator be believed, or is he/she biased? The value of this voice is that, while the reader is able to follow the narrator around and see what is happening through that character's eyes, the reader is also able to feel what the narrator feels. For this reason, the writer can involve the reader more intensely in the story itself and move the reader by invoking feelings—pity, sorrow, anger, hate, confusion, disgust. Many of the most memorable novels, such as Charlotte Bronte's *Jane Eyre*, are written in this point of view. For essays, the teacher must decide if the first-person narrative may or may not use the word "I."

Another voice often used may best be titled "**omniscient**" because the reader is able to get into the mind of more than one character or sometimes all the characters. This point of view can also bring greater involvement of the reader in the story. By knowing what a character is thinking and feeling, the reader is able to empathize when a character feels great pain and sorrow, which tends to make a work memorable, such as Leo Tolstoy's *War and Peace*. On the other hand, knowing what a character is thinking makes it possible to get into the mind of a pathological murderer and may elicit horror or disgust.

Omniscient can be broken down into **third-person omniscient** or **first-person omniscient**. In third-person omniscient, the narrator is not seen or known or acting in the story but is able to watch and record not only what is happening or being said but also what characters are thinking. In first-person omniscient on the other hand, the narrator plays a role in the story but can also record what other characters are thinking. That occurs with a first-person narrator rather than an involved character (examples: *Madame Bovary* and *Heart of Darkness*).

It is possible, of course, that the narrator is the pathological murderer, which creates an effect quite different than a story where the thoughts of the murderer are known but the narrator is standing back and reporting his behavior, thoughts, and intents.

Point of view or voice is a powerful tool in the hands of a skillful writer. The questions to be answered in writing an essay about a literary work are: What point of view has this author used? What effect does it have on the story? If it had been written in a different voice, how would the story be different?

Most credible literary works are consistent in point of view but not always, so consistency is another aspect that should be analyzed. Does the point of view change? Where does it vary? Does it help or hurt the effect of the story?

Skill 11.9 Demonstrate effective use of figurative language.

Figurative language is not meant in a literal sense but to be interpreted through symbolism. Figurative language is made up of such literary devices as hyperbole, metonymy, synecdoche, and oxymoron.

Hyperbole: Exaggeration for a specific effect. For example, "I'm so hungry that I could eat a million of these."

Metonymy: Use of an object or idea closely identified with another object or idea to represent the second. "Hit the books" means "go study." *Washington* can mean the U.S. government in general, and the *White House* can mean the U.S. president or administration.

Synecdoche: Figure of speech in which the word for part of something is used to mean the whole; for example, "sail" for "boat," or vice versa.

Oxymoron: A contradictory form of speech, such as jumbo shrimp, unkindly kind, working vacation, peace force, or singer John Mellencamp's "It hurts so good."

Skill 11.10 Demonstrate identification of logical fallacies

Logical Fallacies

A fallacy is, essentially, an error in reasoning. In persuasive speech, logical fallacies are instances of reasoning flaws that make an argument invalid. For example, a premature generalization occurs when you form a general rule based on only one or a few specific cases, which do not represent all possible cases. An illustration of this is the statement, "Bob Marley was a Rastafarian singer. Therefore, all Rastafarians sing."

A common fallacy in reasoning is the *post hoc ergo propter hoc* ("after this, therefore because of this") or the false-cause fallacy. These occur in cause/effect reasoning, which may either go from cause to effect or effect to cause.

They happen when an inadequate cause is offered for a particular effect; when the possibility of more than one cause is ignored; and when a connection between a particular cause and a particular effect is not made.

Learn more about
Fallacies and the Art of Debate
http://www.csun.edu/~dgw6131
5/

An example of a *post hoc*: Our sales shot up thirty-five percent after we ran that television campaign; therefore, the campaign caused the increase in sales. It might have been a cause, of course, but more evidence is needed to prove it.

See also Skill 13.8

Skill 11.11   Identify techniques for improving text organization

In studies of professional writers and the way they produce their successful works, it has been revealed that writing is a process that can be clearly defined although in practice it must have enough flexibility to allow for creativity. The teacher must be able to define the various stages that a successful writer goes through.

First, there must be a discovery stage when ideas, materials, supporting details are deliberately collected. These may come from many possible sources- the writer's own experience and observations, deliberate research of written sources, interviews of live persons, television presentations, or the Internet.

The next stage is organization where the purpose, thesis, and supporting points are determined. Most writers will put forth more than one possible thesis, and in the next stage--writing the paper--will settle on one as the result of trial and error.

Once the first draft is written, the editing stage is necessary and is probably the most important stage. Now the writer evaluates whether the reasoning is cohesive—does it hold together? Is the arrangement the best possible one or should the points be rearranged? Are there holes that need to be filled in? What form will the introduction take? Does the conclusion lead the reader out of the discourse or is it inadequate or too abrupt.

The final stage is polishing.

The best writers engage in all of these stages recursively. They may go back to discovery at any point in the process. They may go back and rethink the organization, and so on. To help students become effective writers, the teacher needs to give them adequate practice in the various stages and encourage them to engage deliberately in the creative thinking that makes writers successful.

Skill 11.12   Possess effective use of transitions to enhance the clarity of an argument.

A mark of maturity in writing is the effective use of transitional devices. For example, a topic sentence can be used to establish continuity. The writer can refer to what has preceded, repeat or summarize it, and then go on to introduce a new topic. An essay by W. H. Hudson uses this device: "Although the potato was very much to me in those early years, it grew to be more when I heard its history." It summarizes what has preceded, makes a comment on the author's interest, and introduces a new topic: the history of the potato.

Another example of a transitional sentence could be, "Not all matters end so happily." This refers to the previous information and prepares for the next paragraph, which will be about matters that do not end happily. This transitional sentence is a little more forthright: "The increase in drug use in our community leads us to another general question."

Another fairly simple and straightforward transitional device is the use of numbers or their approximation: "First, I want to talk about the dangers of immigration; second, I will discuss the enormity of the problem; third, I will propose a reasonable solution."

An entire paragraph may be transitional in purpose and form. In "Darwiniana," Thomas Huxley used a transitional paragraph:

> So much, then, by way of proof that the method of establishing laws in science is exactly the same as that pursued in common life. Let us now turn to another matter (though really it is but another phase of the same question), and that is, the method by which, from the relations of certain phenomena, we prove that some stand in the position of causes toward the others.

The most common transitional device is a single word. Some examples: *and, furthermore, next, moreover, in addition, again, also, likewise, similarly, finally, second.* There are many, but they should be used correctly and judiciously...

Common Transitions

Logical Relationship	Transitional Expression
Similarity	also, in the same way, just as ... so too, likewise, similarly
Exception/Contrast	but, however, in spite of, on the one hand ... on the other hand, nevertheless, nonetheless, notwithstanding, in contrast, on the contrary, still, yet, although
Sequence/Order	first, second, third, next, then, finally, until
Time	after, afterward, at last, before, currently, during, earlier, immediately, later, meanwhile, now, presently, recently, simultaneously, since, subsequently, then
Example	for example, for instance, namely, specifically, to illustrate
Emphasis	even, indeed, in fact, of course, truly
Place/Position	above, adjacent, below, beyond, here, in front, in back, nearby, there
Cause and Effect	accordingly, consequently, hence, so, therefore, thus, as a result, because, consequently, hence, if...then, in short
Additional Support or Evidence	additionally, again, also, and, as well, besides, equally important, further, furthermore, in addition, moreover, then
Conclusion/Summary	finally, in a word, in brief, in conclusion, in the end, in the final analysis, on the whole, thus, to conclude, to summarize, in sum, in summary
Statement support	most important, more significant, primarily, most essential
Addition	again, also, and, besides, equally important, finally, furthermore, in addition, last, likewise, moreover, too
Clarification	actually, clearly, evidently, in fact, in other words, obviously, of course, indeed

In marking student papers, a teacher can encourage a student to think in terms of moving coherently from one idea to the next by making transitions between the two. If the shift from one thought to another is too abrupt, the student can be asked to provide a transitional paragraph. Provide lists of possible transitions and encourage students to have the list at hand when composing essays. These are good tools for nudging students to more mature writing styles.

Skill 11.13 Understand selection of appropriate details to support an argument or opinion

There are three main ways to support an argument or opinion: 1) experts; 2) facts; and 3) personal experience.

Using key words and phrases from your outline, research can lead to the facts and expert opinion. Expert opinion will have been evaluated by peers in the discipline. Facts will be repeatable from one source to another. (Facts are not arguable.)

Personal experience can both illustrate and support an argument or opinion. For example, if a student were arguing that "divorce is not that bad for kids," it is easy to see how a good personal experience of divorce could lead to that conclusion.

Skill 11.14 Demonstrate applications of technology in all phases of the writing process

Whether researching for your own purposes or teaching students to research, the best place to start research is usually at a library. Not only does it have numerous books, videos, and periodicals to use for references, the librarian is the researcher's "best friend." The librarian can help the student find necessary materials and can help to evaluate sources.

> Those who declared librarians obsolete when the Internet rage first appeared are now red-faced. We need them more than ever. The Internet is full of 'stuff' but its value and readability is often questionable. 'Stuff' doesn't give you a competitive edge, high-quality related information does.
> -Patricia Schroeder, President of the Association of American Publishers

Different libraries have different resources. A good rule to follow when researching is the 20-minute rule. If information can't be discovered in 20 minutes, it is time to consult the librarian for help.

The Internet is a multi-faceted goldmine of information, but students need to learn to discriminate between reliable and unreliable sources. It can be valuable to utilize sites that are associated with an academic institution, such as a university or a scholarly organization. Typical domain names will end in "edu" or "org." The search engine http://**scholar.google**.com/ assists in the effort for finding scholarly resources.

- There are multiple ways to obtain information. Finding an encyclopedia article about the topic to get a general overview is often a good way to begin. Note important names of people associated with the subject, time periods, and geographic areas. Make a list of keywords and their synonyms to use while searching for information. Articles in magazines and newspapers, and personal interviews with experts can be helpful.
- Record of any sources consulted during the research process.
- Avoid plagiarism.
- Summarize and paraphrase
- Cite anything that is not common knowledge. This includes direct quotes as well as ideas or statistics.

Skill 11.15 **Identify the distinguishing features of various forms of writing (reflective essay, autobiographical narrative, editorial, memorandum, summary/abstract, argument, résumé, play, short story, poem, newspaper or journalistic article).**

See Competency 7.0.

COMPETENCY 12.0   UNDERSTAND WRITTEN LANGUAGE CONVENTIONS

Skill 12.1   Display accurate use and effective application of written language conventions (sentence and paragraph construction, spelling, punctuation, usage, grammatical expression).

Correct Use of Coordination and Subordination

Connect independent clauses with the coordinating conjunctions—*and, but, or, for,* or *nor*—when their content is of equal importance. Use subordinating conjunctions—*although, because, before, if, since, though, until, when, whenever, where*—and relative pronouns—*that, who, whom, which*—introduce clauses that express ideas that are subordinate to main ideas expressed in independent clauses.

Be sure to place the conjunctions so that they express the proper relationship between ideas (cause/effect, condition, time, space).

Incorrect: Because mother scolded me, I was late.
Correct: Mother scolded me because I was late.

Incorrect: The sun rose after the fog lifted.
Correct: The fog lifted after the sun rose.

Notice that placement of the conjunction can completely change the meaning of the sentence. Main emphasis is shifted by the change.

Although Jenny was pleased, the teacher was disappointed.
Although the teacher was disappointed, Jenny was pleased.

The boys who had written the essay won the contest.
The boys who won the contest had written the essay.

While not syntactically incorrect, the second sentence makes it appear that the boys won the contest for something else before they wrote the essay.

Possessives

Make the possessives of singular nouns by adding an apostrophe followed by the letter *s* (*'s*).

baby's bottle, father's job, elephant's eye,
teacher's desk, sympathizer's protests, week's postponement

> Check out
> **The Tongue Untied**
> http://grammar.uoregon.edu/
> case/possnouns.html

Make the possessive of singular nouns ending in *s* by adding either an apostrophe or as (*'s*) depending upon common usage or sound. When making the possessive causes difficulty, use a prepositional phrase instead. Even with the sibilant ending, with a few exceptions, you should use the *'s* construction.

> dress's color, species' characteristics or characteristics of the species, James' hat or James's hat, Delores's shirt

Make the possessive of plural nouns ending in *s* by adding the apostrophe after the *s*.

> horses' coats, jockeys' times, four days' time

Make possessives of plural nouns that do not end in *s* the same as singular nouns by adding *'s*.

> children's shoes, deer's antlers, cattle's horns

Make possessives of compound nouns by adding the inflection at the end of the word or phrase.

> the mayor of Los Angeles' campaign, the mailman's new truck, the mailmen's new trucks, my father-in-law's first wife, the keepsakes' values, several daughters-in-law's husbands

Note: Because a gerund functions as a noun, any noun preceding it and operating as a possessive adjective must reflect the necessary inflection. However, if the gerund following the noun is a participle, no inflection is added.

> The general was perturbed by the private's sleeping on duty. (The word *sleeping* is a gerund, the object of the preposition *by*.

> *but*

> The general was perturbed to see the private sleeping on duty. (The word sleeping is a participle modifying private.)

Use of Pronouns

A pronoun used as a subject of predicate nominative is in nominative case.

> She was the drum majorette. The lead trombonists were Joe and <u>he</u>. The band director accepted <u>whoever</u> could march in step.

A pronoun used as a direct object, indirect object of object of a preposition is in objective case.

The teacher praised <u>him</u>. She gave <u>him</u> an A on the test. Her praise of <u>him</u> was appreciated. The students <u>whom</u> she did not praise will work harder next time.

Common pronoun errors occur from misuse of reflexive pronouns:

Singular:	*myself, yourself, herself, himself, itself*
Plural:	*ourselves, yourselves, themselves.*

Incorrect:	Jack cut hisself shaving.
Correct:	Jack cut himself shaving.

Incorrect:	They backed theirselves into a corner.
Correct:	They backed themselves into a corner.

Use of Adjectives

An adjective should agree with its antecedent in number.

<u>Those apples</u> are rotten. <u>This one</u> is ripe. <u>These peaches</u> are hard.

Comparative adjectives end in *-er* and superlatives in *-est*, with some exceptions like *worse* and *worst*. *More* and *most* precede some adjectives that cannot easily make comparative inflections.

Mrs. Carmichael is the better of the two basketball coaches.

That is the hastiest excuse you have ever contrived.

Candy is the most beautiful baby.

Avoid double superlatives.

Incorrect:	This is the worstest headache I ever had.
Correct:	This is the worst headache I ever had.

When comparing one thing to others in a group, exclude the thing under comparison from the rest of the group.

Incorrect:	Joey is larger than any baby I have ever seen. (Since you have seen him, he cannot be larger than himself.)
Correct:	Joey is larger than <u>any other</u> baby I have ever seen.

Include all necessary words to make a comparison clear in meaning.

> I am as tall as my mother. I am as tall as she (is).
> My cats are better behaved than those of my neighbor.

Subject-Verb Agreement

A verb agrees in number with its subject. Making them agree relies on the ability to properly identify the subject.

> <u>One</u> of the boys *was playing* too rough.

> <u>No one</u> in the class, not the teacher nor the students, <u>was listening</u> to the message from the intercom.

> The <u>candidates</u>, including a grandmother and a teenager, <u>are debating</u> some controversial issues.

If two singular subjects are connected by *and* the verb must be plural.

> A *man* and his *dog* were jogging on the beach.

If two singular subjects are connected by *or,* or *nor*, a singular verb is required.

> Neither <u>Dot</u> nor <u>Joyce</u> <u>has</u> missed a day of school this year.
> Either <u>Fran</u> or <u>Paul</u> <u>is</u> missing.

If one singular subject and one plural subject are connected by *or,* or *nor*, the verb agrees with the subject nearest to the verb.

> Neither the <u>coach</u> nor the <u>players</u> <u>were</u> able to sleep on the bus.

If the subject is a collective noun, its sense of number in the sentence determines the verb: singular if the noun represents a group or unit and plural if the noun represents individuals.

> The <u>House of Representatives</u> <u>has adjourned</u> for the holidays.
> The House of Representatives have failed to reach agreement on the subject of adjournment.

Use of Verbs (Tense)

Present tense is used to express that which is currently happening or is always true.

> Randy is playing the piano.

> Randy plays the piano like a pro.

Past tense is used to express action that occurred in a past time.

> Randy learned to play the piano when he was six years old.

Future tense is used to express action or a condition of future time.

> Randy will probably earn a music scholarship.

Present perfect tense is used to express action or a condition that started in the past and is continued to or completed in the present.

> Randy has practiced piano every day for the last ten years.

> Randy has never been bored with practice.

Past perfect tense expresses action or a condition that occurred as a precedent to some other past action or condition.

> Randy had considered playing clarinet before he discovered the piano.

Future perfect tense expresses action that started in the past or the present and will conclude at some time in the future.

> By the time he goes to college, Randy will have been an accomplished pianist for more than half of his life.

Use of Verbs (Mood)

Indicative mood is used to make unconditional statements; **subjunctive** mood is used for conditional clauses or wish statements that pose conditions that are untrue. Verbs in subjunctive mood are plural with both singular and plural subjects.

> If I <u>were</u> a bird, I would fly.

> I wish I <u>were</u> as rich as Donald Trump.

Verb Conjugation

The conjugation of verbs follows the patterns used in the discussion of tense above. However, the most frequent problems in verb use stem from the improper formation of past and past participial forms.

Regular verb: believe, believed, (have) believed

Irregular verbs: run, ran, run; sit, sat, sat; teach, taught, taught

Other problems stem from the use of verbs that are the same in some tenses but have different forms and different meanings in other tenses.

I lie on the ground. I lay on the ground yesterday. I have lain down. I lay the blanket on the bed. I laid the blanket there yesterday. I have laid the blanket down every night.

The sun rises. The sun rose. The sun has risen.

He raises the flag. He raised the flag. He had raised the flag.

I sit on the porch. I sat on the porch. I have sat in the porch swing.

I set the plate on the table. I set the plate there yesterday. I had set the table before dinner.

Two other verb problems stem from misusing the preposition *of* for the verb auxiliary *have* and misusing the verb *ought* (now rare).

Incorrect: I should of gone to bed.
Correct: I should have gone to bed.

Incorrect: He hadn't ought to get so angry.
Correct: He ought not get so angry.

Resources

Here is a brief list of basic teaching texts used by teachers at large and found to be most helpful in teaching structure, grammar, and composition:

English Journal. Urbana, IL: National Council of Teachers of English.

Hixon, Mamie W. *The Essentials of English Language*. Piscataway, New Jersey: Research and Education Association, 1995.

Oshima, Alice and Ann Hogue. *Writing Academic English* (Longman Series) A Writing and Sentence Structure Handbook. Reading, MA: Addison-Wesley Publications Co., 1991.

Warriner's Composition and Grammar. Fourth - First Course and Complete Course, Orlando, FL: Harcourt, Brace, Jovanovich.
Intermediate to advanced college-bound students and international-ESOL students

Teachers will find numerous other published local resources in the school library or district resource centers.

Punctuation

A basic way to show relationship of ideas in sentences is to use punctuation correctly and effectively. Be aware of the proper rules and conventions of punctuation, capitalization, and spelling. Competency exams will generally test the ability to apply the more advanced skills; thus, a limited number of more frustrating rules are presented here. Rules should be applied according to the American style of English, i.e. spelling *theater* instead of *theatre* and placing terminal marks of punctuation almost exclusively within other marks of punctuation.

Quotation Marks

The more troublesome punctuation marks involve the use of quotations.

Using Terminal Punctuation in Relation to Quotation Marks: In a quoted statement that is either declarative or imperative, place the period inside the closing quotation marks.

> "The airplane crashed on the runway during takeoff."

If the quotation is followed by other words in the sentence, place a comma inside the closing quotations marks and a period at the end of the sentence.

> "The airplane crashed on the runway during takeoff," said the announcer.

In most instances in which a quoted title or expression occurs at the end of a sentence, the period is placed before either the single or double quotation marks.

> The educator worried, "The middle school readers were unprepared to understand Bryant's poem 'Thanatopsis.'"

> Early book-length adventure stories like *Don Quixote* and *The Three Musketeers* are known as "picaresque novels."

There is an instance in which the final quotation mark would precede the period - if the content of the sentence were about a speech or quote so that the understanding of the meaning would be confused by the placement of the period.

The first thing out of his mouth was "Hi, I'm home." *but*
The first line of his speech began "I arrived home to an empty house".

In sentences that are interrogatory or exclamatory, the question mark or exclamation point should be positioned outside the closing quotation marks if the quote itself is a statement or command or cited title.

Who decided to lead us in the recitation of the "Pledge of Allegiance"?

Why was Tillie shaking as she began her recitation, "Once upon a midnight dreary..."?

I was embarrassed when Mrs. White said, "Your slip is showing"!

In sentences that are declarative but the quotation is a question or an exclamation, place the question mark or exclamation point inside the quotation marks.

The hall monitor yelled, "Fire! Fire!"

"Fire! Fire!" yelled the hall monitor.

Cory shrieked, "Is there a mouse in the room?" (In this instance, the question supersedes the exclamation.)

Using Double Quotation Marks with Other Punctuation: Quotations—whether words, phrases, or clauses—should be punctuated according to the rules of the grammatical function they serve in the sentence.

The works of Shakespeare, "the bard of Avon," have been contested as originating with other authors.

"You'll get my money," the old man warned, "when 'Hell freezes over'."

Sheila cited the passage that began "Four score and seven years ago . . . ." (Note the ellipsis followed by an enclosed period.)

"Old Ironsides" inspired the preservation of the *U.S.S. Constitution.*

Use quotation marks to enclose the titles of shorter works: songs, short poems, short stories, essays, and chapters of books. (See "Using Italics" for punctuating longer titles.)

"The Tell-Tale Heart" - short story
"Casey at the Bat" - poem
"America the Beautiful" - song

Using Commas

Separate two or more coordinate adjectives modifying the same word and three or more nouns, phrases, or clauses in a list.

Maggie's hair was dull, dirty, and lice-ridden.

Dickens portrayed the Artful Dodger as skillful pickpocket, loyal follower of Fagin, and defendant of Oliver Twist.

Ellen daydreamed about getting out of the rain, taking a shower, and eating a hot dinner.

In Elizabethan England, Ben Jonson wrote comedy, Christopher Marlowe wrote tragedies, and William Shakespeare composed both.

Use commas to separate antithetical or complimentary expressions from the rest of the sentence.

The veterinarian, not his assistant, would perform the delicate surgery.

The more he knew about her, the less he wished he had known.

Randy hopes to, and probably will, get an appointment to the Naval Academy.

His thorough, though esoteric, scientific research could not be easily understood by high school students.

Using Semicolons

Use semicolons to separate independent clauses when the second clause is introduced by a transitional adverb. (These clauses may also be written as separate sentences, preferably by placing the adverb within the second sentence.)

> The Elizabethans modified the rhyme scheme of the sonnet; thus, it was called the English sonnet.
>
> *or*
>
> The Elizabethans modified the rhyme scheme of the sonnet. It thus was called the English sonnet.

Use semicolons to separate items in a series that are long and complex or have internal punctuation.

> The Italian Renaissance produced masters in the fine arts: Dante Alighieri, author of the *Divine Comedy;* Leonardo da Vinci, painter of *The Last Supper;* and Donatello, sculptor of the *Quattro Coronati*, the four saints.

> The leading scorers in the WNBA were Haizhaw Zheng, averaging 23.9 points per game; Lisa Leslie, 22; and Cynthia Cooper, 19.5.

Using Colons

Place a colon at the beginning of a list of items. (Note its use in the sentence about Renaissance Italians previously.)

> The teacher directed us to compare Faulkner's three symbolic novels: *Absalom, Absalom; As I Lay Dying;* and *Light in August.*

Do **not** use a comma if the list is preceded by a verb.

> Three of Faulkner's symbolic novels are *Absalom, Absalom; As I Lay Dying*, and *Light in August.*

Using Dashes

Place dashes (called an "em" dash) to denote sudden breaks in thought.

> Some periods in literature—the Romantic Age, for example—spanned different time periods in different countries.

Use dashes instead of commas if commas are already used elsewhere in the sentence for amplification or explanation.

> The Fireside Poets included three Brahmans—James Russell Lowell, Henry David Wadsworth, Oliver Wendell Holmes—and John Greenleaf Whittier.

Using Italics

Use italics to punctuate the titles of long works of literature, names of periodical publications, musical scores, works of art and motion picture television, and radio programs. (When unable to write in italics, you can instruct students to underline in their own writing where italics would be appropriate.)

The Idylls of the King	*Hiawatha*	*The Sound and the Fury*
Mary Poppins	*Newsweek*	*The Nutcracker Suite*

Skill 12.2   Identify techniques for editing written texts to achieve conformity with conventions of standard English usage (revising sentences and passages to maintain parallel form; revising sentences to eliminate misplaced modifiers; editing written texts to eliminate errors in spelling and punctuation).

Types of Clauses

Clauses are connected word groups that are composed of *at least* one subject and one verb. (A subject is the doer of an action or the element that is being joined. A verb conveys either the action or the link.)

> <u>Students</u> <u>are waiting</u> for the start of the assembly.
> Subject   Verb

> At the end of the play, <u>students</u> <u>wait</u> for the curtain to come down.
>   Subject   Verb

Clauses can be independent or dependent. Independent clauses can stand alone or can be joined to other clauses.

Comma and coordinating conjunction

Independent clause	, for	Independent clause
	, and	Independent clause
	, nor	Independent clause
	, but	Independent clause
	, or	Independent clause
	, yet	Independent clause
	, so	Independent clause

Semicolon

Independent clause	;	Independent clause

Subordinating conjunction, dependent clause, and comma

Dependent clause	,	Independent clause

Independent clause followed by a subordinating conjunction that introduces a dependent clause

Independent clause	Dependent clause

Dependent clauses, by definition, contain at least one subject and one verb. However, they cannot stand alone as a complete sentence. They are structurally dependent on the main clause.

There are two types of dependent clauses: (1) those with a subordinating conjunction, and (2) those with a relative pronoun.

Sample subordinating conjunctions

Although   When   If   Unless   Because

Unless a cure is discovered, many more people will die of the disease.
Dependent clause   +   Independent clause

Sample relative pronouns

Who   Whom   Which   That

The White House has an official website, which contains press releases, news updates, and biographies of the President and Vice President.
(Independent clause + relative pronoun + relative dependent clause)

Misplaced and Dangling Modifiers

Particular phrases that are not placed near the one word they modify often result in misplaced modifiers. Particular phrases that do not relate to the subject being modified result in dangling modifiers.

Error: Weighing the options carefully, a decision was made regarding the punishment of the convicted murderer.

Problem: Who is weighing the options? No one capable of weighing is named in the sentence; thus, the participle phrase weighing the options carefully dangles. This problem can be corrected by adding a subject of the sentence capable of doing the action.

Correction: Weighing the options carefully, the judge made a decision regarding the punishment of the convicted murderer.

Error: Returning to my favorite watering hole brought back many fond memories.

Problem: The person who returned is never indicated, and the participle phrase dangles. This problem can be corrected by creating a dependent clause from the modifying phrase.

Correction: When I returned to my favorite watering hole, many fond memories came back to me.

Error: One damaged house stood only to remind townspeople of the hurricane.

Problem: The placement of the misplaced modifier only suggests that the sole reason the house remained was to serve as a reminder. The faulty modifier creates ambiguity.

Correction: Only one damaged house stood, reminding townspeople of the hurricane.

Sentence Completeness

Avoid fragments and run-on sentences. Recognize the sentence elements necessary to make a complete thought and use independent and dependent clauses properly. Proper punctuation will correct such errors.

Sentence Structure

Recognize simple, compound, complex, and compound-complex sentences. Use dependent (subordinate) and independent clauses correctly to create these sentence structures.

Simple	Joyce wrote a letter.
Compound	Joyce wrote a letter, and Dot drew a picture.

Complex	While Joyce wrote a letter, Dot drew a picture.
Compound/Complex	When Mother asked the girls to demonstrate their new-found skills, Joyce wrote a letter, and Dot drew a picture.

Note: Do **not** confuse compound sentence elements with compound sentences.

Simple sentence with compound subject
<u>Joyce</u> and <u>Dot</u> wrote letters.
The <u>girl</u> in row three and the <u>boy</u> next to her were passing notes across the aisle.

Simple sentence with compound predicate
Joyce <u>wrote letters</u> and <u>drew pictures</u>.
The captain of the high school debate team <u>graduated with honors</u> and <u>studied broadcast journalism in college</u>.

Simple sentence with compound object of preposition
Coleen graded the students' essays for <u>style</u> and <u>mechanical accuracy</u>.

Parallelism

Recognize parallel structures using phrases (prepositional, gerund, participial, and infinitive) and omissions from sentences that create the lack of parallelism. Parallelism provides balance to the grammar and the ideas.

> Learn more about
> **Parallel Structure vs.**
> **Faulty Parallelism**
> http://jerz.setonhill.edu/writing/grammar/parallel.html

Prepositional phrase/single modifier
Incorrect: Coleen ate the ice cream with enthusiasm and hurriedly.
Correct: Coleen ate the ice cream with enthusiasm and in a hurry.
Correct: Coleen ate the ice cream enthusiastically and hurriedly.

Participial phrase/infinitive phrase
Incorrect: After hiking for hours and to sweat profusely, Joe sat down to rest and drinking water.
Correct: After hiking for hours and sweating profusely, Joe sat down to rest and drink water.

Recognition of Syntactical Redundancy or Omission

These errors occur when superfluous words have been added to a sentence or key words have been omitted from a sentence.

Redundancy

Incorrect: Joyce made sure that when her plane arrived that she retrieved all of her luggage.

Correct: Joyce made sure that when her plane arrived she retrieved all of her luggage.

Incorrect: He was a mere skeleton of his former self.

Correct: He was a skeleton of his former self.

Omission

Incorrect: Dot opened her book, recited her textbook, and answered the teacher's subsequent question.

Correct: Dot opened her book, recited from the textbook, and answered the teacher's subsequent question.

Avoidance of Double Negatives

This error occurs from positioning two negatives that, in fact, cancel each other in meaning.

Incorrect: Harold couldn't care less whether he passes this class.

Correct: Harold could care less whether he passes this class.

Incorrect: Dot didn't have no double negatives in her paper.

Correct: Dot didn't have any double negatives in her paper.

NCTE Beliefs about the Teaching of Writing

by the Writing Study Group of the NCTE Executive Committee
November 2004

1. *Everyone has the capacity to write, writing can be taught, and teachers can help students become better writers.*

2. *People learn to write by writing.*

3. *Writing is a process.*

4. *Writing is a tool for thinking.*

5. *Writing grows out of many different purposes.*

6. *Conventions of finished and edited texts are important to readers and therefore to writers.*

7. *Writing and reading are related.*

8. *Writing has a complex relationship to talk.*

9. *Literate practices are embedded in complicated social relationships.*

10. *Composing occurs in different modalities and technologies.*

11. *Assessment of writing*

Skill 12.3   Identify strategies for effective proofreading

When assessing and responding to student writing, teachers should follow these guidelines.

Responding to Non-graded Writing (Formative)

- Avoid using a red pen. Whenever possible use a #2 pencil.
- Explain the criteria that will be used for assessment in advance.
- Read the writing once while asking the question, "Is the student's response appropriate for the assignment?"
- Reread and make note at the end whether the student met the objective of the writing task.
- Responses should be non-critical and use supportive and encouraging language.
- Resist writing on or over the student's writing.
- Highlight the ideas you wish to emphasize, question, or verify.
- Encourage your students to take risks.

Responding to and Evaluating Graded Writing (Summative)

- Ask students to submit prewriting and rough-draft materials including all revisions with their final draft.
- For the first reading, use a holistic method, examining the work as a whole.
- When reading the draft for the second time, assess it using the standards previously established.
- Write your responses in the margin and use supportive language.
- Make sure you address the process as well as the product. It is important that students value the learning process as well as the final product.
- After scanning the piece a third time, write final comments at the end of the draft.

DOMAIN III.   **READING THEORY, RESEARCH, AND INSTRUCTION**

COMPTENCY 13.0   **UNDERSTAND LANGUAGE ACQUISITION, READING PROCESSES, AND RESEARCH-BASED THEORIES RELATING TO READING**

Skill 13.1   **Understand basic processes of first- and second-language acquisition and use**

Considerations for teaching to English Language Learners (ELL) include recognition by the teacher that what works for the English-language speaking student from an English-language speaking family, does not necessarily work in other languages.

> Visit **Dave's ESL Café**
> http://www.eslcafe.com/

Students who are raised in homes where English is not the first language and/or where standard English is not spoken may have difficulty with hearing the difference between similar sounding words like "send" and "sent." Any student who is not in an environment where English phonology operates may have difficulty perceiving and demonstrating the differences between English language phonemes. If students cannot hear the difference between words that "sound the same" such as "grow" and "glow," they will be confused when these words appear in a print context. This confusion will of course, impact their comprehension.

Research recommends that ELL students learn to read initially in their first language. Further, it has been found that a priority for ELL should be learning to speak English before being taught to read English. Research supports oral language development since it lays the foundation for phonological awareness.

Skill 13.2   **Identify strategies to research word origins and analyze word formation to understand meanings, derivations, and spellings.**

Just as countries and families have histories, so do words. Knowing and understanding the origin of a word, where and how it has been used through the years, and the history of its meaning as it has changed are important components of the writing and language teacher's tool kit.

Never in the history of the English language or any other language for that matter have the forms and meanings of words changed so rapidly. When America was settled originally, immigration from many countries made it a "melting pot." Immigration accelerated rapidly within the first hundred years, resulting in pockets of language throughout the country.

> Check out the
> **Learning Resources of the OED**
> hhttp://www.oed.com/learning/

When trains began to make transportation available and affordable, individuals from those various pockets came in contact with each other, shared vocabularies, and attempted to converse. From that time forward, every generation brought the introduction of a technology that made language interchange not only more possible but more important.

In the past, the Oxford English Dictionary has been the most reliable source for etymologies. Some of the collegiate dictionaries are also useful. *Merriam-Webster's 3rd Unabridged Dictionary* is useful in tracing the sources of words in American English. *Merriam-Webster's Unabridged Dictionary* may be out of date, so a teacher should also have a *Merriam-Webster's Collegiate Dictionary*, which is updated regularly.

In addition to etymologies, knowing how and when to label a usage "jargon" or "colloquial" is important. The teacher must be aware of the possibility that it's a word that is now accepted as standard. To be on top of this, the teacher must continually keep up with the etymological aids that are available, particularly online.

If you "google" "etymology," for instance, or even the word you're unsure of, you can find a multitude of sources. The information should be validated by at least three sources. Wikipedia is very useful, but it can be changed by anyone who chooses, so any information on it should be backed up by other sources. If you go to http://www.etymonline.com/sources.php, you will find a long list of resources on etymology.

Spelling in English is complicated because it is not phonetic—that is, it is not based on the one-sound/one letter formula used by many other languages. It is based on the Latin alphabet, which originally had twenty letters, consisting of the present English alphabet minus J, K, V, W, Y, and Z. The Romans added K to be used in abbreviations and Y and Z in words that came from the Greek. This 23-letter alphabet was adopted by the English, who developed W as a ligatured doubling of U and later J and V as consonantal variants of I and U. The result was our alphabet of 26 letters with upper case (capital) and lower case forms.

Spelling is based primarily on fifteenth-century English. The problem is that pronunciation has changed drastically since then, especially long vowels and diphthongs. This Great Vowel Shift affected the seven long vowels.

For a long time, spelling was erratic—there were no standards. As long as the meaning was clear, spelling was not considered very important. Samuel Johnson tackled this problem, and his *Dictionary of the English Language* (1755) brought standards to spelling, so important once printing presses were invented. There have been some changes, of course, through the years, but spelling is still not strictly phonetic.

Despite many attempts to nudge the spelling into a more phonetic representation of the sounds, all have failed for the most part. A good example is Noah Webster's *Spelling Book* (1783), which was a precursor to the first edition (1828) of his *American Dictionary of the English Language*. While there are rules for spelling, and it's important that students learn the rules, there are also many exceptions; and memorizing exceptions and giving plenty of opportunities for practicing them seems the only solution for the teacher of English.

Skill 13.3   Identify relationships among words (homonyms, synonyms, antonyms) and issues related to word choice (denotative and connotative meanings, multiple-meaning words).

Students frequently encounter problems with **homonyms**—words that are spelled and pronounced the same as another but that have different meanings such as *mean*, a verb, "to intend"; *mean* an adjective, "unkind"; and *mean* a noun or adjective, "average." These words are actually both homonyms and homographs (written the same way).

A similar phenomenon that causes trouble is **heteronyms** (also sometimes called heterophones), words that are spelled the same but have different pronunciations and meanings (in other words, they are homographs that differ in pronunciation or, technically, homographs that are not homophones). For example, the homographs *desert* (abandon) and *desert* (arid region) are heteronyms (pronounced differently); but *mean* (intend) and *mean* (average) are not. They are pronounced the same, or are homonyms.

Another similar occurrence in English is the **capitonym**, a word that is spelled the same but has different meanings when it is capitalized and may or may not have different pronunciations. Example: *polish* (to make shiny) and *Polish* (from Poland).

Some of the most troubling homonyms are those that are spelled differently but sound the same. Examples: *its* (third-person singular neuter pronoun) and *it's* (the contraction for "it is"); *there*, *their* (third-person plural pronoun) and *they're* ("they are"). Others: *to, too, two;*

Find more troublesome words at
An English Homophone Dictionary
http://www.earlham.edu/~peters/writing/homofone.htm

Some homonyms/homographs are particularly complicated. Fluke, for instance is a fish, a flatworm, the end parts of an anchor, the fins on a whale's tail, and a stroke of luck.

Common Troublesome Words to Student Writers

accept: tolerate; *except*: everything but.

add: put together with; *ad*: short for advertisement.

allowed: permitted; *aloud*: audibly.

allot: to distribute, allocate; *a lot* (often "*alot*"): much, many (a lot of).

allusion: indirect reference; *illusion*: a distortion of sensory perception.

bare: naked, exposed or very little (bare necessities); *bear*: as a noun, a large mammal and as a verb, to carry.

boy: a male adolescent or child; *buoy*: a floating marker in the sea.

bridal: pertaining to a bride (bridal gown, bridal suite); *bridle*: part of a horse's tack.

capital: punishable by death; with an upper-case letter, principal town or city, or wealth and money; *Capitol*: the home of the Congress of the United States or within each state—the capitol building.

chord: group of musical notes; *cord*: rope, long electrical line.

compliment: a praising or flattering remark; *complement*: something that completes.

discreet: tactful or diplomatic; *discrete*: separate or distinct.

dyeing: artificially coloring; *dying*: passing away.

effect: outcome; *affect*: have an effect upon.

gorilla: the largest of the great apes; *guerrilla*: a small combat group.

hair: an outgrowth of the epidermis in mammals; *hare*: rabbit; *heir*-the person who inherits

hoard: to accumulate and store up; *horde*: large group of warriors, mob.

lam: U.S. slang "on the lam" means "on the run"; *lamb*: a young sheep.

lead: pronounced to rhyme with "seed," to guide or serve as the head of; *lead*: pronounced to rhyme with "head," a heavy metal; *led*: the past tense of "lead."

medal: an award to be strung around the neck; *meddle*: stick one's nose into others' affairs; *metal*: shiny, malleable element or alloy like silver or gold; *mettle*: toughness, guts.

morning: the time between midnight and midday; *mourning*: period of grieving after a death.

past: time before now (past, present and future); *passed*: past tense of "to pass."

piece: portion; *peace*: opposite of war.

peak: tip, height, to reach its highest point; *peek*: to take a brief look; *pique*: fit of anger; to incite (pique one's interest).

Here are a few strategies to help students conquer these demons:

- Practice using them in sentences.
- Determine context to help understand the difference.
- Drill if necessary to overcome the misuses.

Skill 13.4   Identify research-based theories relating to the reading process.

Our eyes look at the different letters that make up a word and combine them in to syllables, then into words, and the process ultimately results in understanding meaning. *"The art of reading is a process of becoming conscious,"* said Wolfgang Iser.

The one word that best characterizes students is *change*. Not only are they changing physically, but they are undergoing rapid cognitive development which, in turn, brings about personality and behavioral changes. The parts of the brain that affect emotions (the limbic system) are growing faster than the cerebral cortex. For this reason, emotions are erratic.

As students grow, their thinking is advanced compared to only a short time ago. They develop the ability to think abstractly and ponder such things as art and beauty. They become able to retain instructions and ideas in their memories and retrieve them more rapidly. They are also more aware of their learning abilities and limitations and are more likely to be able to assume more responsibility for assignments.

Adolescent thinking tends to include only two poles—black and white, perfect or worthless, right or wrong. They are not inclined to make nuanced judgments and are judgmental regarding others as well as themselves. On the positive side, they are now able to have passionate feelings even about expressive literature.

How does this translate into classroom planning for the teacher of literature or composition—reading or writing? Remember that for Piaget, the end result of the stages of development should be autonomy, and the teacher of reading and composition has an excellent opportunity to assist students to grow toward that stage. Helping them claim responsibility for their own thoughts, whether private, spoken, or written, should be the ultimate goal of the English curriculum.

Communication should flow back and forth from student to teacher as much as possible. Introducing a poet and feeding relevant information about his/her life and times, then turning students loose to find their own meanings in specific poems can be a very successful exercise for adolescents.

Giving them opportunities to share their own feelings about the poetry with each other, either in a classroom setting or in study/discussion groups sometimes leads a student to a lifetime of poetry reading. Stories about adolescents are useful. The role of the English teacher in cognitive development is to encourage the students, provide the information they are not able to obtain on their own, and validate their efforts. They come into the classroom fearful that they will be forced into a situation where everyone will be watching them and they will be embarrassed. The teacher must develop a level of trust that relieves that fear. The opportunity to express freely their own emotional and cognitive response to literature will help them to grow cognitively into responsible adults.

Free writing in the composition classroom can be very useful in introducing students to more structured forms. With some encouragement, students can learn to use free writing to explore their own feelings and convictions. The teacher needs to be aware that writing is a process that occurs in stages that are recursive.

The first stage, discovery, can be achieved by building on the free writing that students have already become comfortable with, to move on to more formalized research to find new information and ideas and explore their own thoughts and feelings about topics or positions. The development of a thesis based on what they have done in the first stage gives them an opportunity to claim responsibility for their convictions.

Once they have settled on a tentative thesis, they are ready to begin to think about development and organization. If they feel free to move backward as well as forward, they will not only feel more comfortable in establishing a conviction about a topic but also will be willing to move forward toward a final essay that makes a point they feel strongly about and are willing to defend. Cognitively, this is an appropriate progression that taps into their stage (or stages) of development and helps them to move toward Piaget's goal of autonomy.

Skill 13.5   Identify word analysis skills and strategies (phonics, syllabication, structural analysis)

Phonics

Beginning phonics focuses on simple one-letter graphemes representing consonants (b, c, d, f, g, h, and so on) and vowels (a, e, i, o, u) and blending them together to make simple words (sat, met, and so on). While phonics instruction, viewed narrowly, is restricted to teaching grapheme-phoneme (letter-sound) correspondences, word analysis instruction may also include other methods that students can use to figure out words. One of these, sight word recognition, is taught along with phonics. Common and irregularly spelled words (was, want, to) are taught to be recognized on sight as whole words rather than being analyzed into graphemes and phonemes and then blended.

Syllabication

Syllabication is the breaking down of words into each uninterrupted unit of spoken language. Readers generally use sounds to determine syllable division. Students who need to use syllabication to decode words must be taught syllabication rules holistically. When they apply basic rules in steps, they begin to recognize patterns and break down unknown words. Initially, the rules are applied to two-syllable rules.

Once students learn the patterns, the same rules are used to break down longer words. Even those students who read words with ease in context generally improve spelling accuracy if they become more cognizant of word structure and syllabication patterns.

Step 1: Assure that students have prerequisite phonics skills

Students should possess certain prerequisite skills and concepts before being taught the syllabication rules. Frequently, it is necessary to review short and long vowels as well as prefixes/root words/suffixes, before proceeding with syllabication. You will see why as you review the following foundation concepts.

- Each syllable must contain a sounded vowel. It can be a single vowel sound (i•de•a) or used with one or more consonant sounds (be•gin).
- There are two kinds of syllables: open and closed. A closed syllable ends with a consonant and the vowel is usually short (or a schwa). An open syllable ends with a vowel that is generally long (clo•ver, e•vent). The vowel may be a y pronounced as /e/ (fun•ny) or occasionally /i/ (my•self).
- Since the first rule deals with dividing between root words and affixes, students must be familiar with prefixes, suffixes, and root words.
- Digraphs, or two consonants that make a single sound (ch, sh, th, wh, ng, nk, ng, ck, ...), cannot be divided (buck•le, noth•ing, cash•ier, bush•el, fur•ther).
- In some cases, blends are not divided (se•cret, mi•grate, ze•bra). Do not prêt each since students discover this when identifying open vs. closed syllables.

Step 2: Teach syllabication rules and apply in order.

- Check the word for prefixes and suffixes. The first step is to divide between affixes and the root word because this rule overrides the others.
- Check for multiple consonants between vowels. Divide between consonants.
- If the word has one consonant between vowels, decide whether the vowel before the consonant is short or long. If vowel is long, divide after the vowel leaving an open syllable. Otherwise, divide after the consonant leaving a closed syllable.

See also Skill 9.1

Skill 13.6   Demonstrate use of semantic and syntactic cues to verify word meanings

Advocates of the Whole Language movement support the Three Cueing System model that utilizes: 1) semantics or context; 2) syntax; and 3) letter-sounds. In other words, the reader would first guess the meaning of an unrecognized word by context; then guess meaning based on syntax (verb, noun, adjective); then attempt to sound out the word (grapho-phonemic).

In the alternative model, semantics and syntax are important for comprehension of the text, but are not primary for identifying words. Grapho-phonemic information is the first step for decoding an unfamiliar word. Then the semantic and syntaxic modes are used for comprehension.

Spelling to speech requires understanding the phonemic structure of the spoken language; learning about letter-sound correspondences; and learning the conventions in spelling.

Theory says that as the readers become more proficient, less attention is needed for sounding out words and more for comprehension of the text, thus the syntax and the context. By the time students are in middle school, junior high, or high school, students' focus will first be upon the semantics and syntax rather than grapho-phonemic information (which will be attended to for pronunciation of the unfamiliar word). In Massachusetts, it is important to teach children to how to understand and use phonics.

Skill 13.7 Know the role of vocabulary skills and strategies in the development of reading proficiency.

Children who learn to read on schedule and who are avid readers have been seen to have superior vocabularies compared to nonreaders in their age group. Learning vocabulary through visual, auditory, kinesthetic, and tactical experiences in a systematic order will enhance the learning process.

> Learn more about
> **Re-establishing Reading and Writing Workshops**
> http://curriculum.dpsk12.org/ Planning_guides/ Literacy/7/7_Addenda.pdf

A planned, effective vocabulary program is not an "extra" but an across-the-curriculum necessity. In this four-step process you should accomplish the following:

1. Evaluate to determine what the students know.

2. Devise a plan to teach the students what they must learn as part of continuum.

3. Determine if students have heard the words to be studied and in what context.

4. Teach vocabulary for mastery.

To reach mastery, set clear objectives and maintain an appropriate pacing since some students will need more practice than others. Building in time for practice, review, and testing is an integral component of a successful program.

Re-teaching words missed on tests or misused in writing is essential until mastery is achieved. The teacher may construct crossword puzzles using terms from their literature or language lessons. Another good exercise for developing vocabulary is the crossword puzzle. The ability to think in terms of analogy is a step upward toward mature language understanding and use. Providing exercises for development of vocabularies is useful, including exercises where the vocabulary learning is based on context. Putting words into context requires different thinking and learning than simply looking up the definitions of words.

Poetry is also useful for developing vocabulary exercises, especially rhymed poetry, where the pronunciation of a term may be deduced by what the poet intended for it to rhyme with. In some poetry of earlier periods, the teacher may need to intervene because words that would have rhymed when the poem was written do not rhyme in today's English. Even so, this is a good opportunity to help students understand some of the important principles about their changing language.

Methods of presentation for a well-balanced program at all levels include

- Recognizing and using words in context
- Giving attention to varying definitions of the same word
- Studying word families (synonyms, antonyms, and homonyms)
- Locating etymologies (word origins)
- Analyzing word parts (roots, prefixes, suffixes)
- Locating phonetic spellings and identifying correct pronunciation
- Spelling words properly
- Using words semantically

Countless enrichment materials are available and include computer software, CD-ROM, board games, flashcards, puzzles, and so on. The more varied the experience, the more easily and quickly students will commit the words to memory and achieve mastery.

The Shostak Vocabulary Series that spans middle school through grade 13, including SAT/ACT preparation is recommended by the authors for use in grades 9-12.

Within the literature series, vocabulary lists and practices are included. Classroom teachers should also review content area texts to add technical and specialized words to the weekly vocabulary study.

Skill 13.8 Application of literal, inferential, and evaluative comprehension skills

To *interpret* means essentially to read with understanding and appreciation. It is not as daunting as it is made out to be. Simple techniques for interpreting literature follow.

Context

Context includes the author's feelings, beliefs, past experiences, goals, needs, and physical environment. Incorporate an understanding of how these elements may have affected the writing to enrich an interpretation of it.

Symbols

Also referred to as a sign, a symbol designates something which stands for something else. In most cases, it is standing for something that has a deeper meaning than its literal denotation. Symbols can have personal, cultural, or universal associations. Use an understanding of symbols to unearth a meaning the author might have intended but not expressed, or even something the author never intended at all.

Inferential Comprehension Skills

Inferential comprehension skills involve the reader highlighting information—whether on the page or in the mind—to link concepts without having to refer back to the text. Inferential comprehension skills also involve making hypotheses, observing pronouns, and noticing verb tenses in the text. Inferential skills involve recognizing the literal meaning (who, what, where?); observing syntax that reveals relationships, time, or specificity; and incorporating real world knowledge.

The reader will access prior knowledge to make relevant connections, will create interpretations, clarify thinking, and draw conclusions. Inferential comprehension skills will enable determining cause/effect relationships and making predictions about what will happen in the text.

Deductive and Inductive Reasoning

Deductive reasoning works from the generalization to the more specific. Inductive reasoning moves from specific observations to broader generalizations and theories. Inductive reasoning is more open-ended and exploratory that deductive reasoning which involves testing and/or confirming hypotheses.

Skill 13.9   Apply the use of metacognitive techniques to monitor reading comprehension.

Metacognition is essentially defined as "thinking about thinking." Metacognitive techniques for monitoring reading comprehension involve having students 1) identify what they know; 2) identify what they do not know; 3) discuss their thinking about the reading materials; 4) keep a journal about the readings; 5) think again through their thinking process concerning what they've read; 6) provide a self-evaluation over the ideas they've developed about the reading.

In middle and secondary schools, the emphasis of reading instruction spans the range of comprehension skills: literal, inferential, and critical. Most instruction in grades five and six is based on the skills delineated in basal readers adopted for those grade levels. Reading instruction in grades seven through nine is usually part of the general language arts class instead of being a distinct subject in the curriculum, unless the instruction is remedial. Reading in tenth through twelfth grades is part of the literature curriculum—World, American, and British.

Teachers have many techniques to assure that students understand the text, and these techniques will vary with student age and ability.

Reading Emphasis in Middle School

Reading for comprehension of factual material—content area textbooks, reference books, and newspapers—is closely related to study strategies in the middle/junior high.

Organized study models teach students to locate main ideas and supporting details, to recognize sequential order, to distinguish fact from opinion, and to determine cause/effect relationships. One such model is the **SQ3R method**, a technique that enables students to learn the content of even large amounts of text (Survey, Question, Read, Recite, and Review Studying),

Strategies

Teacher-guided activities that require students to organize and to summarize information based on the author's explicit intent are pertinent strategies in middle grades. Evaluation techniques include oral and written responses to standardized or teacher-made worksheets.

Teachers can identify the skills to be studied, choose the appropriate reading resources, and develop activities to guide students' reading for meaning. To monitor the progress of acquiring these comprehension skills, teachers have at their disposal a variety of printed materials as well as individualized computer software programs.

Older middle school students should be given opportunities for more student-centered activities, such as the individual and collaborative selection of reading choices based on student interest, small group discussions of selected works, and greater written expression. Evaluation techniques include teacher monitoring and observation of discussions and written work samples from individuals and from groups.

Students may begin some fundamental critical interpretation. Some approaches may be seeking to recognize fallacious reasoning in news media, examining the accuracy of both news reports and advertising, or explaining preference for one author's writing over another's.

> Learn more about
> **Monitoring Comprehension**
> http://www.indiana.edu/~l517/
> monitoring.html

A learning-centered approach may be when the teacher identifies a number of objectives and suggested resources from which the student may choose a course of study. Teachers can stress self-evaluation through a reading diary, or they can encourage teacher and peer evaluation of creative projects resulting from such study.

Teachers should encourage one-on-one tutoring or peer-assisted reading when necessary.

Reading Emphasis in High School

Students in high school literature classes should focus on interpretive and critical reading. The Herringbone Pattern can help students visually organize text details by answering six questions

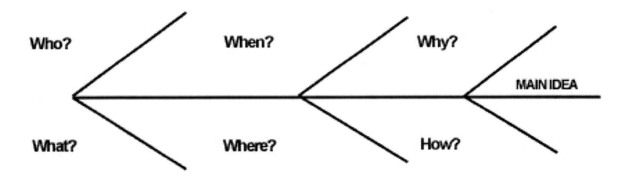

Teachers will guide the study of the elements of interpretive reading—drawing conclusions, predicting outcomes, and recognizing examples of specific genre characteristics. Students can be guided toward developing critical reading to judge the quality of the writer's work against recognized standards. Small group discussion can be extremely helpful, and projects can be assigned to determine comprehension.

Additionally, vocabulary words should continue to be mastered and reading speed to increase. At this level students should understand the skills of language and reading, but that doesn't mean the teacher cannot help to enhance student skills, no matter where each student ranks.

Skill 13.10   Application of strategies before, during, and after reading to promote comprehension of expository texts (previewing and predicting, self-questioning, writing and discussing)

To assess student comprehension of reading materials, teachers employ a wide variety of diagnostic tools.

Skills to Evaluate

- Ability to understand what is happening in a story.
- Ability to use more than one example or piece of information when responding to the reading.
- Ability to ask questions regarding the reading to show analytical thinking.
- Ability to make predictions based on information from the story or from personal experiences that are similar to events in the story.
- Ability to make clear and understandable connections between the literature and personal experiences as well as other literature the student has read.

Methods of Evaluation:

- Have students keep reading journals that document their reactions to the literature they are reading.
- Assign free writing exercises to respond to any element of the story, and prompt-driven responses to a specified topic you assign. Make sure the prompts are created to get the students thinking deeply about the reading. An example might be, "Write about the main conflict in the story. Explain why it is so important, and how it is solved."
- Ask that students back up any assertions or assumptions they make with evidence from the text. This clearly demonstrates their mental comprehension processes.

Skill 13.11   Know the role of oral reading fluency in facilitating comprehension of texts.

Use oral reading to assess reading skills and comprehension. Pay attention to word recognition skills rather than the reader's ability to communicate the author's message. Strong oral reading sounds like natural speech, uses phrasing and pace that match the meaning of the text, and uses pitch and tone to interpret the text. This ability to read prosodically is important for word recognition and comprehension.

Students who experience comprehension difficulties when reading silently can improve their comprehension by reading the same material out loud, And with paired reading, assisted reading, and echo reading.

Skill 13.12 **Know ways in which text characteristics and purposes for reading determine the selection of reading strategies**

Students approaching new texts can use various reading strategies to enhance their comprehension.

- Providing a guide regarding the concepts that will be encountered in the test
- Annotating either individually or collaboratively
- Conversations about common topics in other places and times
- Questioning
- Making inferences
- Keeping notebook
- Activating comprehension strategies: predicting, questioning, clarifying, summarizing and reciprocal teaching utilizing these strategies
- Synthesizing key concepts
- Paying attention to writer's voice or characters' voices
- Utilizing "Question Answer Relationship "(QAR) strategy – Questions that are: 1)Text-based: "Right There" and "Think & Search"; 2) Knowledge-based: "Author & You" and "On My Own"
- Analyzing metaphor
- Writing "Role, Audience, Format, Topic" (RAFT) responses
- Creating art items or a play to illustrate the text content, including conflict

One way is to ask a series of questions. What is my objective? What do I want to achieve from this reading? How will I use the information from this reading? Do I need to grasp only the gist of the piece? Do I need to know the line of reasoning—not only the thesis but the sub-points? Will I be reporting important and significant details orally or in a written document?

> Check out different
> **Reading Strategies**
> http://www.greece.k12.ny.us
> /instruction/ela/6-12/
> Reading/Reading%20Strategies/
> reading%20strategies%20index.htm

A written document can be expected to have a thesis—either expressed or derived. To discover the thesis, readers need to ask what point the writer intended to make. The writing can also be expected to be organized in some logical way and to have sub-points that support or establish that the thesis is valid.

Readers can reasonably expect details or examples to support the sub-points. Knowing this, they can decide which reading techniques are required to exemplify the purpose.

If readers need to know only the gist of a written document, they may use speed-reading skimming techniques by using the forefinger, moving the eyes down the page, picking up the important statements in each paragraph and deducing mentally that this piece is about such-and-such. If readers need a better grasp of how the writer achieved the purpose in the document, they can give a quick and cursory glance—a skimming—of each paragraph which will yield 1) sub-points; 2) topic sentences of the paragraphs; 3) thesis development; and 4) greater understanding of the author's purpose and method of development.

If readers need to scrutinize each phrase or sentence with care, they can look first for the thesis and then look for topic sentences in the paragraphs that provide the development of the thesis. They can also look for connections, such as transitional devices, that provide clues to the direction of the reasoning.

From the first reading, the student can create a map of each chapter to accompany the rereading or second reading. The map will provide a summary or other notes—or even drawings--that inspire memory.

Some new understandings may occur in a rereading, and the "map" from the first reading will need to be adjusted. If this rereading is for the purpose of writing an analysis or using material for a report, encourage students to either highlight or take notes.

COMPETENCY 14.0   UNDERSTAND EFFECTIVE, RESEARCH-BASED READING INSTRUCTION AND THE ROLE OF CHILDREN'S LITERATURE AND YOUNG ADULT LITERATURE IN PROMOTING READING PROFICIENCY

Skill 14.1   Evaluate research-based theories and practices relating to reading instruction.

Many theories have been posited and much research has been done to determine reading proficiency. *Lenses on Reading: An Introduction to Theories and Models* by Diane H. Tracey and Lesley Mandel Monroe is one text that helps to provide evaluation of the theories and practices relating to reading instruction.

Research shows that students find performing such activities as designing websites, creating magazines, and developing and playing reading games are activities that help to engage them in reading. Mentoring younger students in reading improves reading skills for both the mentor and the mentored. Teachers at times may forget, but research also shows that rewards motivate and encourage students to engage in reading. Many students today enjoy blogs and reading news online instead of on paper. Research has also been done about *where* students most like to read. Home comes in first.

Teachers should provide ample opportunities for oral interpretation of literature, special projects in creative dramatics, writing for publication in school literary magazines or newspapers, and speech/debate activities. A student portfolio provides for teacher and peer evaluation.

The National Institute for Literacy reports:

> By age 17, only about 1 in 17 seventeen-year-olds can read and gain information from specialized text, for example the science section in the local newspaper. This includes:

- 1 in 12 White 17 year olds,
- 1 in 50 Latino 17 year olds, and
- 1 in 100 African American 17 year olds. (Haycock, 5)

Skill 14.2   Identify methods for planning, managing, and differentiating reading instruction to support students' reading development

Encourage students to react honestly to literature. Allow them to choose their reading selections; if the choice is their own, their reactions can be more spontaneous and comfortable. With middle school/junior high students, keeping a reading diary may be as much as they can handle. High school students can be encouraged to write analytical reviews but try to keep them informal. Encourage students to read book reviews in current periodicals to see how critics express their responses.

Encourage students to attempt to write in certain genres. Have middle school students compose their own myths. High school students can try their hands at poems, short stories, and one-act plays. By attempting to write in a particular form, the student will gain a greater appreciation of the author's task.

Remember that teaching for appreciation and the encouragement of life-long reading means that instruction must be student-centered. If you ever sat through a lecture in a college literature survey class, you can identify with the problems students have with lecturing in secondary schools. Teach the elements of literature and the process of learning through lecture, but avoid lecturing on the meaning of the literature at all costs. If you really want to inspire your students, perform the Lady Macbeth soliloquy or give your own book review--gratis.

Read and write when they do and share your creativity with them. High school students are especially appreciative of teachers who would never ask them to do something the teachers themselves cannot or will not do.

Skill 14.3   Understand the role of children's literature and young adult literature in promoting reading proficiency and motivating students to read independently.

Prior to twentieth-century research on child development and child/adolescent literature's relationship to that development, books for adolescents were primarily didactic. They were designed to address history, manners, and morals.

Middle Ages

As early as the eleventh century, Anselm, the Archbishop of Canterbury, wrote an encyclopedia designed to instill in children the beliefs and principles of conduct acceptable to adults in medieval society. Early monastic translations of the Bible and other religious writings were written in Latin for the edification of the upper class.

Fifteenth-century hornbooks were designed to teach reading and religious lessons. William Claxton printed English versions of *Aesop's Fables*, Mallory's *Le Morte d'Arthur,* and stories from Greek and Roman mythology. Though printed for adults, tales of adventures of Odysseus and the Arthurian knights were also popular with literate adolescents.

Renaissance

The Renaissance saw the introduction of the inexpensive chapbooks, 16-64 pages in length. Chapbooks were condensed versions of mythology and fairytales. Designed for the common people, chapbooks were imperfect grammatically but were immensely popular because of their adventurous contents. Though most of the serious, educated adults frowned on the sometimes vulgar little books, they received praise from Richard Steele of *Tattler* fame for inspiring his grandson's interest in reading and in pursuing his other studies.

Meanwhile, the Puritans' three most popular reads were the Bible, John Foe's *Book of Martyrs*, and John Bunyan's *Pilgrim's Progress*. Though venerating religious martyrs and preaching the moral propriety which was to lead to eternal happiness, the stories of the *Book of Martyrs* were often lurid in their descriptions of the fate of the damned. In contrast, *Pilgrim's Progress*, not written for children and difficult reading even for adults, was as attractive to adolescents for its adventurous plot as for its moral outcome.

In Puritan America, the *New England Primer* set forth the prayers, catechisms, Bible verses, and illustrations meant to instruct children in the Puritan ethic. The seventeenth-century French used fables and fairytales to entertain adults, but children found them enjoyable as well.

"I never use it, but I've found it to be a great deterrent."

Seventeenth Century

The late seventeenth century brought the first concern with providing literature that specifically targeted the young. Pierre Peril's *Fairy tales*, Jean de la Fontaine's retellings of famous fables, Mme. d'Aulnoy's novels based on old folktales, and Mme. de Beaumont's "Beauty and the Beast" were written to delight as well as instruct young people.

In England, publisher John Newbury was the first to publish a line for children. These included a translation of Perrault's *Tales of Mother Goose; A Little Pretty Pocket-Book*, "intended for instruction and amusement" but decidedly moralistic and bland in comparison to the previous century's chapbooks; and *The Renowned History of Little Goody Two Shoes*, allegedly written by Oliver Goldsmith for a juvenile audience.

Eighteenth Century

Eighteenth-century adolescents found reading pleasure in adult books: Daniel Defoe's *Robinson Crusoe*, Jonathan Swift's *Gulliver's Travels*, and Johann Wyss's *Swiss Family Robinson*. More books were being written for children, and moral didacticism, though less religious, was nevertheless ever-present.

The short stories of Maria Edgeworth, the four-volume *The History of Sandford and Merton* by Thomas Day, and Martha Farquharson's twenty-six volume *Elsie Dinsmore* series dealt with pious protagonists who learned restraint, repentance, and rehabilitation from sin.

Two bright spots in this period of didacticism were Jean Jacques Rousseau's *Emile* and *The Tales of Shakespeare*, and Charles and Mary Lamb's simplified versions of Shakespeare's plays. Rousseau believed that a child's abilities were enhanced by a free, happy life, and the Lambs subscribed to the notion that children were entitled to entertaining literature written in language comprehensible to them.

Nineteenth Century

Child/adolescent literature truly began its modern rise in nineteenth-century Europe. Hans Christian Andersen's *Fairy Tales* were fanciful adaptations of the somber revisions of the Grimm brothers in the previous century. Andrew Lang's series of colorful fairy books contain the folklores of many nations and are still part of the collections of many modern libraries. Clement Moore's "A Visit from St. Nicholas" is a cheery, non-threatening view of the night before Christmas. The humor of Lewis Carroll's books about Alice's adventures, Edward Lear's poems with caricatures, and Lucretia Nole's stories of the Philadelphia Peterkin family are full of fancy and not a smidgen of morality.

Other popular Victorian novels introduced the modern fantasy and science fiction genres: William Makepeace Thackeray's *The Rose and the Ring*, Charles Dickens' *The Magic Fishbone*, and Jules Verne's *Twenty Thousand Leagues Under the Sea*. Adventure to exotic places became a popular topic: Rudyard Kipling's *Jungle Books*, Verne's *Around the World in Eighty Days*, and Robert Louis Stevenson's *Treasure Island* and *Kidnapped*. In 1884, the first English translation of Johanna Spyri's *Heidi* appeared.

North America was also finding its voices for adolescent readers. American Louisa May Alcott's *Little Women* and Canadian L.M. Montgomery's *Anne of Green Gables* ushered in the modern age of realistic fiction. American youth were enjoying the adventures of Tom Sawyer and Huckleberry Finn. For the first time, children were able to read books about real people just like themselves.

Twentieth Century

The literature of the twentieth century is extensive and diverse, and, as in previous centuries, much influenced by the adults who write, edit, and select books for youth consumption. In the first third of the century, suitable

> For more information, read
> **Introductory Lecture on Children's & Adolescent Literature**
> http://homepages.wmich.edu/~tarboxg/
> Introductory_Lecture_on_Children's_&_Adol_Lit.html

adolescent literature dealt with children from good homes with large families. These books projected an image of a peaceful, rural existence.

Though the characters and plots were more realistic, the stories maintained focus on topics that were considered emotionally and intellectually proper. Popular at this time were Laura Ingalls Wilder's *Little House on the Prairie* series and Carl Sandburg's biography *Abe Lincoln Grows Up*. English author J.R.R. Tolkien's fantasy, *The Hobbit*, prefaced modern adolescent readers' fascination with the works of Piers Antony, Madeleine L'Engle, and Anne McCaffery.

Of course, the most popular recent bestsellers among youth since 1997 have been the Harry Potter books written by J. K. Rowling.

Adolescent Development

The social changes of post-World War II significantly affected adolescent literature. The Civil Rights movement, feminism, the protest of the Vietnam conflict, and issues surrounding homelessness, neglect, teen pregnancy, drugs, and violence have bred a new vein of contemporary fiction that helps adolescents understand and cope with the world they live in.

Popular books for preadolescents deal with establishing relationships with members of the opposite sex (Sweet Valley High series) and learning to cope with their changing bodies, personalities, or life situations, as in Judy Blume's *Are You There, God? It's Me, Margaret.* Adolescents are still interested in the fantasy and science fiction genres as well as popular juvenile fiction. Middle school students still read the Little House on the Prairie series and the mysteries of the Hardy Boys and Nancy Drew.

Teens value the works of Emily and Charlotte Brontë, Willa Cather, Jack London, William Shakespeare, and Mark Twain as much as those of Piers Anthony, S.E. Hinton, Madeleine L'Engle, Stephen King, and J.R.R. Tolkien because they're fun to read whatever their underlying worth may be.

Older adolescents enjoy the writers in these genres.

Fantasy: Piers Anthony, Ursula LeGuin, Ann McCaffrey

Horror: V.C. Andrews, Stephen King

Juvenile Fiction: Judy Blume, Robert Cormier, Rosa Guy, Virginia Hamilton, S.E. Hinton, M.E. Kerr, Harry Mazer, Norma Fox Mazer, Richard Newton Peck, Cynthia Voigt, and Paul Zindel.

Science Fiction: Isaac Asimov, Ray Bradbury, Arthur C. Clarke, Frank Herbert, Larry Niven, H.G. Wells.

Child Development Theories Influence on Literature

The studies by behaviorists and developmental psychologists in the late nineteenth and early twentieth centuries affected the manner in which the education community and parents approached the selection of literature for children.

The cognitive development studies of Piaget, the epigenetic view of personality development by Erik Erikson, the formulation of Abraham Maslow's hierarchy of basic needs, and the social learning theory of behaviorists like Albert Bandura contributed to a greater understanding of child/adolescent development--even as these theorists contradicted each others' findings.

Though few educators today subscribe to Piaget's inflexible stages of mental development, his principles of both qualitative and quantitative mental capacity, his generalizations about the parallels between physical growth and thinking capacity, and his support of the adolescent's heightened moral perspective are still used as measures to evaluate child/adolescent literature.

Piaget's Four Stages of Mental Development:

Sensimotor intelligence (birth to age two) deals with the pre-language period of development. The child is most concerned with coordinating movement and action. Words begin to represent people and things.

Preoperational thought is the period spanning ages 2-12. It is broken into several substages.

- Preconceptual (2-4) phase - most behavior is based on subjective judgment.

- Intuitive (4-7) phase - children use language to verbalize their experiences and mental processes.

Concrete operations (7-11) occur when children begin to apply logic to concrete things and experiences. They can combine performance and reasoning to solve problems.

Formal operations (12-15) occur when adolescents begin to think beyond the immediate and to theorize. They apply formal logic to interpreting abstract constructions and to recognizing experiences that are contrary to fact.

Though Piaget presented these stages as progressing sequentially, a child might enter any period earlier or later than most children. Furthermore, a child might perform at different levels in different situations. Thus, a fourteen-year-old female might be able to function at the formal operations stage in a literature class but function at a concrete operations level in mathematical concepts.

> Learn more about
> **Piaget's Cognitive Development**
> http://courses.dsu.edu/epsy330/
> theorists/cognitive.htm

Piaget's Theories Influence Literature

Most middle school students have reached the concrete operations level. By this time they have left behind their egocentrism for a need to understand the physical and social world around them. They become more interested in ways to relate to other people. Their favorite stories become those about real people rather than animals or fairy tale characters. The conflicts in their literature are internal as well as external.

Books like Paula Fox's *The Stone-Faced Boy*, Betsy Byars' *The Midnight Fox*, and Lois Lenski's *Strawberry Girl* deal with a child's loneliness, confusion about identity or loyalty, and poverty. Pre-adolescents are becoming more aware of and interested in the past, thus their love of adventure stories about national heroes like Davy Crockett, Daniel Boone, and Abe Lincoln and biographies and autobiographies of real life heroes, like Jackie Robinson and César Chávez. At this level, children also become interested in the future--thus, their love of both fantasy (most medieval in spirit) and science fiction.

The seven- to eleven-year-olds also internalize moral values. They are concerned with their sense of self and are willing to question rules and adult authority. In books such as Beverly Cleary's *Henry Huggins* and *Mitch and Amy*, the protagonists are children pursuing their own desires with the same frustrations as other children. When these books were written in the 1960s, returning a found pet or overcoming a reading disability were common problems.

From twelve to fifteen, adolescents advance beyond the concrete operations level to begin developing communication skills that enable them to articulate attitudes and opinions and exchange knowledge. They can recognize and contrast historical fiction from pure history and biography. They can identify the elements of literature and their relationships within a specific story. As their thinking becomes more complex, early adolescents become more sensitive to others' emotions and reactions. They become better able to suspend their disbelief and enter the world of literature, thus expanding their perceptions of the real world.

In discussing the adolescent's moral judgment, Piaget noted that after age eleven, children stopped viewing actions as either "right" or "wrong." The older child considers both the intent and the behavior in its context. A younger child would view an accidental destruction of property in terms of the amount of damage. The older child would find the accident less wrong than minor damage done with intended malice.

Kohlberg's Theories of Moral Development

Expanding on Piaget's thinking, Lawrence Kohlberg developed a hierarchy of values. Though progressive, the stages of Kohlberg's hierarchy are not clearly aligned to chronological age. The six stages of development correlate to three levels of moral judgment.

Level I. Moral values reside in external acts rather than in persons or standards.

Stage 0. Premoral. No association of actions or needs with sense of right or wrong.

Stage 1. Obedience and punishment orientation. Child defers to adult authority. Child's actions are motivated by a desire to stay out of trouble.

Stage 2. Right action/self-interest orientation. Performance of right deeds results in needing satisfaction.

Level II. Moral values reside in maintaining conventions of right behavior.

Stage 3. Good person orientation. The child performs right actions to receive approval from others, conforming to the same standards.

Stage 4. Law and order orientation. Doing one's duty and showing respect for authority contributes to maintaining social order.

Level III. Moral values reside in principles separate in association from the persons or agencies that enforce these principles.

Stage 5. Legalistic orientation. The rules of society are accepted as correct but alterable. Privileges and duties are derived from social contact. Obedience to society's rules protects the rights of self and others.

Stage 6. Conscience orientation. Ethical standards, such as justice, equality, and respect for others, guide moral conduct more than legal rules.

Though these stages represent a natural progression of values to actions relationships, persons may regress to an earlier stage in certain situations. An adolescent already operating at Stage 5 may regress to Stage 3 in a classroom where consequences of non-conformity are met with disapproval or punishment. An adult operating at Stage 6 may regress to Stage 4 when obligated by military training or confronted with a conflict between self-preservation and the protection of others.

Values clarification education based on Piaget's and Kohlberg's theories imply that development is inherent in human socialization. Becoming a decent person is a natural result of human development.

Social Learning Theory

Much of traditional learning theory resulted from the work of early behaviorists, including B. F. Skinner. Theory has been refined by modern theorists such as Albert Bandura.

Behaviorists believe that intellectual--and therefore behavioral-- development cannot be divided into specific stages. They believe that behavior is the result of conditioning experiences, a continuum of rewards and punishments.

Environmental conditions are viewed as greater stimuli than inherent qualities. Thus in social learning theory the consequences of behavior-- that is, the rewards or punishments-- are more significant in social development than are the motivations for the behavior.

Bandura proposed that a child learns *vicariously* through observing the behavior of others. The developmental psychologists, however, presumed that children developed through the *actual* self-experience.

The Humanistic Theory of Development

No discussion of child development would be complete without a review of Abraham Maslow's hierarchy of needs, from basic physiological needs to the need for self-actualization. The following list represents those needs from the hierarchy that most affect children.

- **Need for Physical Wellbeing**. In young children the provisions for shelter, food, clothing, and protection by significant adults satisfy this need. In older children, this satisfaction of physical comforts translates to a need for material security and may manifest itself in struggles to overcome poverty and maintain the integrity of home and family.

- **Need for Love**. The presumption is that every human being needs to love and be loved. With young children, this reciprocal need is directed at and received from parents and other family members, pets, and friends. In older children and adolescents, this need for love forms the basis for romance and peer acceptance.

- **Need to Belong**. Beyond the need for one-on-one relationships, a child needs the security of being an accepted member of a group. Young children identify with family, friends, and schoolmates. They are concerned with having happy experiences and being accepted by people they love and respect. Later, they associate with community, country, and perhaps world groups. Adolescents become more aware of a larger world order and thus develop concerns about issues facing society, such as political or social unrest, wars, discrimination, and environmental issues.

They seek to establish themselves with groups who accept and share their values. They become more team oriented.

- **Need to Achieve Competence.** A human's need to interact satisfactorily with his environment begins with the infant's exploration of the immediate surroundings. Visual and tactile identification of objects and persons provides confidence to perform further explorations. To become well adjusted, the child must achieve competence to feel satisfaction. Physical and intellectual achievements become measures of acceptance. Frustrations resulting from physical or mental handicaps are viewed as hurtles to be overcome if satisfaction is to be achieved. Older children view the courage-overcome obstacles as part of the maturing process.

- **Need to Know.** Curiosity is the basis of intelligence. The need to learn is persistent. To maintain intellectual security, children must be able to find answers to their questions in order to stimulate further exploration of information to satisfy that persistent curiosity.

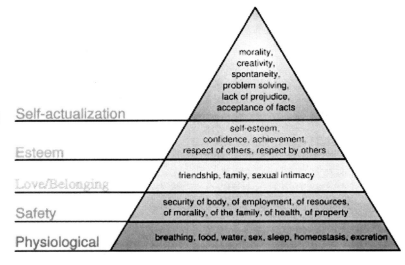

- **Need for Beauty and Order.** Aesthetic satisfaction is as important as the need for factual information. Intellectual stimulation comes from satisfying curiosity about the fine arts, as well as the practical arts. Acceptance for one's accomplishments in dance, music, drawing, writing, performing, or appreciating any of the arts leads to a sense of accomplishment and self-actualization.

Theory of Psychosocial Development

Erik Erikson, a follower of Sigmund Freud, presented the theory that human development consists of maturation through a series of psychosocial crisis. The struggle to resolve these crises helps a person achieve individuality as the person learns to function in society.

Maturation occurs as the individual moves through a progression of increasingly complex stages. The movement from one stage to the next hinges on the successful resolution of the conflicts encountered in each stage, and each of the stages represents a step in identity formation. Stage 1 (trust versus distrust), Stage 2 (achieving autonomy), and Stage 3 (developing initiative) relate to infants and young/middle children. Stages 4 and 5 relate to late childhood through adolescents.

Stage 4—**Becoming Industrious**. Late childhood, according to Erikson, occurs between seven and eleven. Children have already mastered conflicts that helped them overcome mistrust of unfamiliar persons, places, and things. Now they are more independent in caring for themselves and their possessions. Their sense of guilt at behavior that creates opposition with others is overcome. Now children are ready to assert themselves in suppressing feelings of inferiority. Children at this stage learn to master independent tasks as well as to work cooperatively with other children. They increasingly measure their own competence by comparing themselves to their peers.

Stage 5—**Establishing Identity**. From age eleven through the teen years, a person's conflicts arise from the search for identity, as an individual and a member of society. Because internal demands for independence and peer acceptance sometimes oppose external demands for conformity to rules and standards, friction with family, school, and society in general occur during these years. The adolescent must resolve issues such as the amount of control to concede to family and other rule-enforcing adults as the teen searches for other acceptance models. In the quest for self-identity, the teen experiments with adult behavior and attitudes. At the end of the teen years, this person should have a well-established sense of identity.

Theory of Multiple Intelligences

Howard Gardner's research in the 1980s has been recently influential in helping teachers understand that human beings process information differently and, therefore, communicate their knowledge through different modes of operation.

It is important to present language and literature in visual, auditory, tactile, and kinesthetic ways to allow every child to develop good skills through that child's own mode of learning. Then, the child alone must be allowed to perform through the strength of intelligence. The movement toward learning academies in the practical and fine arts and in the sciences is a result of our growing understanding of all aspects of child development.

Modern Society's Role in Child Development

Despite their differences, there are many similarities in the theories of child development. However, most of these theories were developed prior to the social unrest of the 1970s. In industrialized Western society, children are increasingly excluded from the activities of work and play with adults, and education has become their main occupation. This exclusion tends to prolong childhood and adolescents and thus inhibit development as visualized by theorists.

For adolescents in America, this prolongs results in slower social and intellectual maturation contrasted to increasing physical maturity. Adolescents today deal with drugs, violence, communicable diseases, and a host of social problems that were of minimal concern thirty years ago. Even pre-adolescent children are dealing with poverty, disease, broken homes, abuse, and drugs.

Influence of Theories on Literature

All of these development theories and existing social conditions influence the literature created and selected for and by child/adolescent readers.

Child/adolescent literature has always been to some degree didactic, whether nonfiction or fiction. Until the twentieth century, "kiddie lit" was also morally prescriptive. Written by adults who determined either what they believed children needed or liked or what they *should* need or like, most books, stories, poems, and essays dealt with experiences or issues that would make children into better adults.

The fables, fairy tales, and epics of old set the moral and social standards of their times while entertaining the child in every reader/listener. These tales are still popular because they have a universal appeal. Except for the rare exceptions discussed earlier in this section, most books were written for literate adults. Educated children found their pleasure in the literature that was available.

Benefits of Research

One benefit of the child development and learning theory research is that they provide guidelines for writers, publishers, and educators to follow in the creation, marketing, and selection of good reading materials. MacMillan introduced children's literature as a separate publishing market in 1918. By the 1930s, most major publishers had a children's department. Though arguments have existed throughout this century about quality versus quantity, there is no doubt that children's literature is a significant piece of the publishing market.

Another influence is that children's books are a reflection of both developmental theories and social changes. Reading provides children with the opportunity to become more aware of societal differences, to measure their behavior against the behavior of realistic fictional characters or the subjects of biographies, to become informed about events of the past and present that will affect their futures, and to acquire a genuine appreciation of literature.

Furthermore, adults are obligated to provide instruction and entertainment that all children in our democratic society can use. Parents and educators have a further obligation to guide children in the selection of books that are appropriate to their reading ability and interest levels. Of course, there is a fine line between guidance and censorship. As with discipline, parents learn that to make forbidden is to make more desirable. To publish a list of banned books is to make them suddenly attractive. Most children and adolescents, left to their own selections, will choose books on topics that interest them and are written in language they can understand.

Impact of Research on Teachers

Adolescent literature, because of the age range of readers, is extremely diverse. Fiction for the middle group, usually ages ten/eleven to fourteen/fifteen, deals with issues of coping with internal and external changes in their lives. Because children's writers in the twentieth century have produced increasingly realistic fiction, adolescents can now find problems dealt with honestly in novels.

Teachers of middle/junior high school students see the greatest change in interests and reading abilities as students move toward adolescence.

Ninth-graders are either the upper tier in junior high school or the underlings in high school. They definitely view themselves as teenagers. Their literature choices will often be governed more by interest than by ability--thus, a wealth of high-interest, low-readability books has flooded the market in recent years. Tenth- through twelfth-graders will still select high-interest books for pleasure reading but are also easily encouraged to stretch their literature muscles by reading more classics.

Because of the rapid social changes, topics that once did not interest young people until they reached their teens—suicide, gangs, and homosexuality—are now subjects of books for even younger readers. The plethora of high-interest books reveals how the market has adapted.

No matter how tastefully written however, some contents are inappropriate for younger readers. The task is encouraging them toward books whose content is appropriate to younger students' levels of cognitive and social development. A fifth-grader may be able to read V.C. Andrews book *Flowers in the Attic* but not possess the social or moral development to handle the deviant behavior of the characters.

At the same time, because of the complex changes affecting adolescents, the teacher must be well-versed in learning theory and child development as well as competent to teach the subject matter of language and literature.

Skill 14.4   Know instructional strategies to promote development of particular reading skills (e.g., word analysis, vocabulary, comprehension).

See Skills 13.5, 13.7 and 14.1.

Skill 14.5   Gauge the adjustment of reading instruction based on ongoing assessment.

Skills to Evaluate

- Ability to use syntactic cues when encountering an unknown word. A good reader will expect the word to fit the syntax he/she is familiar with. A poor reader may substitute a word that does not fit the syntax, and will not correct themselves.
- Ability to use semantic cues to determine the meaning of an unknown word. A good reader will consider the meanings of all the known words in the sentence. A poor reader may read one word at a time with no regard for the other words.
- Ability to use schematic cues to connect words read with prior knowledge. A good reader will incorporate what he/she knows with what the text says or implies. A poor reader may think only of the word he/she is reading without associating it with prior knowledge.
- Ability to use phonics cues to improve ease and efficiency in reading. A good reader will apply letter and sound associations almost subconsciously. A poor reader may have one of two kinds of problems. S/he may have underdeveloped phonics/skills, and use only an initial clue without analyzing vowel patterns before quickly guessing the word. Or s/he may use phonics skills in isolation, becoming so absorbed in the word "noises" that s/he ignores or forgets the message of the text.
- Ability to process information from text. A student should be able to get information from the text as well as store, retrieve, and integrate it for later use.

- Ability to use interpretive thinking to make logical predictions and inferences.
- Ability to use critical thinking to make decisions and insights about the text.
- Ability to use appreciative thinking to respond to the text, whether emotionally, mentally, or ideologically

Methods of Evaluation

- Assess students at the beginning of each year to determine grouping for instruction.
- Judge whether a student recognizes when a word does not make sense.
- Monitor whether the student corrects him/herself, if they know when to ignore and read on or when to reread a sentence.
- Looks for skill such as recognizing cause and effect, finding main ideas, and using comparison and contrast techniques.
- Keep dated records to follow individual progress. Focus on a few students each day. Grade them on a scale of 1-5 according to how well they perform certain reading abilities (e.g., logically predicts coming events). Also include informal observations, such as "Ed was able to determine the meaning of the word 'immigrant' by examining the other words in the sentence."
- Standardized tests are a formal method of measuring reading skills.
- Remember that evaluation is important, but enjoyment of reading is the most important thing to emphasize. Keep reading a pressure-free, fun activity so students do not become intimidated by reading. Even if the students are not meeting excellent standards, if they continue wanting to read each day that is a success!

Skill 14.6   Identify strategies to promote independent reading

Reading for enjoyment enables us to go to places in the world we will never be able to visit; we can learn about the enchantments of a particular place, so we will set a goal of going there someday. When *Under the Tuscan Sun* by Frances Mayes was published, it became a best seller. It also increased tourism to Italy. Many of the readers of that book visited Italy for the first time in their lives.

In fiction, we can live through experiences that we will never encounter. We delve into feelings that are similar to our own or are so far removed from our own that we are filled with wonder and curiosity. In fact, we read because we're curious—curious to visit, experience, and know new and different things.

http://www.neabigread.org/
communities.php

The reader lives with a crowd of people and a vast landscape. The reading is constantly enriching life, and the mind is constantly expanding. To read is to grow. Sometimes the experience of reading a particular book or story is so delicious that we go back and read it again and again. We keep track of what is truly happening in the world when we read current best-sellers because not only do they reflect what everyone else is interested in right now, but they can influence trends. We can know in-depth what television news cannot cram in by reading news publications—for example, *Time* or *Newsweek*.

How do we model this wonderful gift for our students? We can bring interesting stories into our classrooms and share the excitement we feel when we discover them. We can relate stories that make us laugh so students may see the humor and laugh with us. We can vary the established curriculum to include something we are reading that we want to share. The tendency of students nowadays is to receive all of their information from television or the Internet. It's important for the teacher to help students understand that television and the Internet are not substitutes for reading. They should be an accessory, an extension, and a springboard for reading.

Another way teachers can inspire students to become readers is to assign am unread book read along with them, chapter by chapter. Run a contest and the winner gets to pick a book that you and the class will read chapter by chapter. If you are excited about it and experience satisfaction from the reading, the excitement will be contagious. Just be sure that the discussion sessions allow for students to relate what *they* are thinking and feeling about what the class is reading. Lively discussions and the opportunity to express students' own feelings lead to more spontaneous reading.

You can also hand out a reading list of your favorite books and spend some time telling the students what you liked about each. Make sure the list is diverse, and include nonfiction along with fiction. Don't forget that a good biography or autobiography may encourage students to read beyond thrillers and detective stories.

When the class is discussing the latest movie, whether formally or informally, if the movie is based on a book, it is a good opportunity to demonstrate how much more can be derived from the reading than from the watching. --Or how the two combined make the experience more satisfying and worthwhile. What incidents or characters are missing from the Harry Potter movies? How does Keira Knightley in *Pride and Prejudice* match Austen's description of Elizabeth Bentley?

Share with your students the excitement you have for reading. Successful writers are usually good readers. The two go hand-in-hand.

Skill 14.7   Identify strategies for selecting and using meaningful reading materials at appropriate levels of difficulty for all students

For Fifth and Sixth Grades

These classic and contemporary works combine the characteristics of multiple theories. Functioning at the concrete operations stage (Piaget), being of the "good person" orientation (Kohlberg), still highly dependent on external rewards (Bandura), and exhibiting all five needs previously discussed from Maslow's hierarchy,

> Check out these
> **Online Resources for K-12 Teachers: Children's and Adolescent Literature**
> http://www.indiana.edu/~reading/ieo/digests/d149.html

eleven- to twelve-year-olds should appreciate the following titles, grouped by reading level. These titles are also cited for interest at that grade level and do not reflect high-interest titles for older readers who do not read at grade level. Some high-interest titles are listed below.

Reading Level 6.0 to 6.9
Barrett, William. *Lilies of the Field*
Cormier, Robert. *Other Bells for Us to Ring*
Dahl, Roald. *Danny, Champion of the World; Charlie and the Chocolate Factory*
Lindgren, Astrid. *Pippi Longstocking*
Lindbergh, Anne. *Three Lives to Live*
Lowry, Lois. *Rabble Starkey*
Naylor, Phyllis. *The Year of the Gopher, Reluctantly Alice*
Peck, Robert Newton. *Arly*
Speare, Elizabeth. *The Witch of Blackbird Pond*
Sleator, William. *The Boy Who Reversed Himself*

For Seventh and Eighth Grades

Most seventh- and eighth-grade students, according to learning theory, are still functioning cognitively, psychologically, and morally as sixth-graders. As these are not inflexible standards, some twelve- and thirteen-year-olds are much more mature socially, intellectually, and physically than the younger children who share the same school. The mature students are becoming concerned with establishing individual and peer group identities, and that presents conflicts--breaking from authority and rigidity of rules. Some at this age are still tied firmly to the family and its expectations while others identify more with those their own age or older.

Enrichment reading for this group must help them cope with life's rapid changes or provide escape and thus must be either realistic or fantastic depending on the child's needs. Adventures and mysteries (the Hardy Boys and Nancy Drew series) are still popular today. These preteens also become more interested in biographies of contemporary figures rather than legendary figures of the past.

Reading Level 7.0 to 7.9
Armstrong, William. *Sounder*
Bagnold, Enid. *National Velvet*
Barrie, James. *Peter Pan*
London, Jack. *White Fang, Call of the Wild*
Lowry, Lois. *Taking Care of Terrific*
McCaffrey, Anne. *The Dragonsinger* series
Montgomery, L. M. *Anne of Green Gables* and sequels
Steinbeck, John. *The Pearl*
Tolkien, J. R. R. *The Hobbit*
Zindel, Paul. *The Pigman*

Reading Level 8.0 to 8.9
Cormier, Robert. *I Am the Cheese*
McCullers, Carson. *The Member of the Wedding*
North, Sterling. *Rascal*
Twain, Mark. *The Adventures of Tom Sawyer*
Zindel, Paul. *My Darling, My Hamburger*

For Ninth Grade
Depending upon the school environment, much of ninth-graders' social development--and thus their reading interests--becomes motivated by peer associations. They are adolescents at the early stages of formal operations in cognitive development. Their perceptions of their own identities are becoming well-defined, and they are fully aware of the ethics required by society. Ninth-graders are more receptive to the challenges of classic literature but still enjoy popular teen novels.

Reading level 9.0 to 9.9
Brown, Dee. *Bury My Heart at Wounded Knee*
Defoe, Daniel. *Robinson Crusoe*
Dickens, Charles. *David Copperfield*
Greenberg, Joanne. *I Never Promised You a Rose Garden*
Kipling, Rudyard. *Captains Courageous*
Mathabane, Mark. *Kaffir Boy*
Nordhoff, Charles. *Mutiny on the Bounty*
Shelley, Mary. *Frankenstein*
Washington, Booker T. *Up From Slavery*

For Tenth to Twelfth Grades

High school sophomores, juniors, and seniors can handle almost all other literature except for a few of the most difficult titles such as *Moby Dick* or *Vanity Fair*. However, since many high school students do not progress to the eleventh or twelfth grade reading level, they will still have their favorites among authors whose writings they can understand. Many will struggle with assigned novels but still read high-interest books for pleasure. A few high-interest titles are listed below without reading level designations, though most are 6.0 to 7.9.

> Bauer, Joan. *Squashed*
> Borland, Hal. *When the Legends Die*
> Danzinger, Paula. *Remember Me to Harold Square*
> Duncan, Lois. *Stranger with My Face*
> Hamilton, Virginia. *The Planet of Junior Brown*
> Hinton, S. E. *The Outsiders*
> Paterson, Katherine. *The Great Gilly Hopkins*

Teachers of students at all levels must be familiar with the materials offered by the libraries in their own schools. Only then can they guide their students into appropriate selections for their social age and reading level development.

Skill 14.8   Apply uses of instructional technologies to promote students' reading development.

See Skill 11.4.

DOMAIN IV.   INTEGRATION OF KNOWLEDGE AND UNDERSTANDING

In addition to answering multiple-choice items, candidates will prepare written responses to questions addressing content from the preceding objectives, which are summarized in the objective and descriptive statement below.

COMPETENCY 15.0   PREPARE AN ORGANIZED, DEVELOPED ANALYSIS ON A TOPIC RELATED TO ONE OR MORE OF THE FOLLOWING: LITERATURE AND LANGUAGE; RHETORIC AND COMPOSITION; READING THEORY, RESEARCH, AND INSTRUCTION

Skill 15.1   Identify the characteristics of various genres and types of literature; major authors, works, and movements in the literature of the United States, Great Britain, and the world; the historical, social, and cultural contexts from which ancient and modern literature emerged; literary theory and criticism; the structure and development of the English language; principles of rhetoric as they apply to various forms and purposes of communication; the composition process and conventions of writing; reading skills and comprehension; language acquisition; and theories and methods of reading instruction.

RESOURCES

Abrams, M. H. ed. *The Norton Anthology of English Literature.* 6th ed. 2 vols.
New York: Norton, 1979.
A comprehensive reference for English literature, containing selected works from Beowulf through the twentieth century and information about literary criticism.

Beach, Richard. "Strategic Teaching in Literature." *Strategic Teaching and Learning: Cognitive Instruction in the Content Areas.* Edited by Beau Fly Jones and others. ASCD Publications, 1987: 135-159.
A chapter dealing with a definition of and strategic teaching strategies for literature studies.

Brown, A. C. and others. *Grammar and Composition* 3rd Course. Boston:
Houghton Mifflin, 1984.
A standard ninth-grade grammar text covering spelling, vocabulary, reading, listening, and writing skills.

Burmeister, L. E. *Reading Strategies for Middle and Secondary School Teachers.*
Reading, MA: Addison-Wesley, 1978.
A resource for developing classroom strategies for reading and content area classes, using library references, and adapting reading materials to all levels of students.

Carrier, W. and B. Neumann, eds. *Literature from the World.* New York: Scribner,
1981.
A comprehensive world literature text for high school students, with a section on mythology and folklore.

Cline, R. K. J. and W. G. McBride. *A Guide to Literature for Young Adults: Background, Selection, and Use.* Glenview, IL: Scott Foresman, 1983.
A literature reference containing sample readings and an overview of adolescent literature and the developmental changes that affect reading.

Coater, R.B., Jr., ed. "Reading Research and Instruction." *Journal of the College Research Association.* Pittsburgh, PA: 1995.
A reference tool for reading and language arts teachers, covering the latest research and instructional techniques.

Corcoran, B. and E. Evans, eds. *Readers, Texts, Teachers.* Upper Montclair, NJ:
Boynton/Cook, 1987.
A collection of essays concerning reader response theory, including activities that help students interpret literature and help the teacher integrate literature into the course study.

Cutting, Brian. *Moving on in Whole Language: The Complete Guide for Every Teacher.* Bothell, WA: Wright Group, 1992.
A resource of practical knowledge in whole language instruction.

Damrosch, L. et al. *Adventures in English Literature.* Orlando, FL: Harcourt, Brace, Jovanovich, 1985.
One of many standard high school English literature textbooks with a solid section on the development of the English language.

Davidson, A. *Literacy 2000 Teacher's Resource. Emergent Stages 1 & 2.*1990.

Devine, T. G. *Teaching Study Skills: A Guide for Teachers.* Boston: Allyn and Bacon, 1981.

Duffy, G. G. and others. *Comprehension Instruction: Perspectives and Suggestions.* New York: Longman, 1984.
Written by researchers at the Institute of Research on Teaching and the Center for the Study of Reading, this reference includes a variety of instructional techniques for different levels.

Fleming, M. ed. *Teaching the Epic.* Urbana, IL: NCTE, 1974.
Methods, materials, and projects for the teaching of epics with examples of Greek, religious, national, and American epics.

Flood, J. Ed. *Understanding Reading Comprehension: Cognition, Language, and the Structure of Prose.* Newark, DE: IRA, 1984.
Essays by preeminent scholars dealing with comprehension for learners of all levels and abilities.

Fry, E. B. and others. *The Reading Teacher's Book of Lists.* Edgewood Cliffs, NJ: Prentice-Hall, 1984.
A comprehensive list of book lists for students of various reading levels.

Garnica, Olga K. and Martha L. King. *Language, Children, and Society.* New York: Pergamon Press, 1981.

Gere, A. R. and E. Smith. *Attitude, Language and Change.* Urbana, IL: NCTE, 1979.
A discussion of the relationship between standard English and grammar and the vernacular usage, including various approaches to language instruction.

Haycock, Kati and Sandra Huang, *Are Today's High School Graduates Ready?*, Thinking K-16, Vol. 5, Issue 1, The Education Trust. Washington, DC, 2001.

Hayakawa, S. I. *Language in Thought and Action.* 4th ed. Orlando, Fl: Harcourt, Brace, Jovanovich, 1979.

Hook, J. N. et al. *What Every English Teacher Should Know.* Champaign, IL: NCTE, 1970.
Research-based text that summarizes methodologies and specific application for use with students.

Johnson, D. D. and P. D. Pearson. *Teaching Reading Vocabulary.* 2nd ed. New York: Holt, Rinehart, and Winston, 1984.
A student text that stresses using vocabulary study in improving reading comprehension, with chapters on instructional components in the reading and content areas.

Kaywell, I. F. Ed. *Adolescent Literature as a Complement to the Classics.* Norwood, MA: Christopher-Gordon Pub., 1993.
A correlation of modern adolescent literature to classics of similar themes.

Mack, M. Ed. *World Masterpieces.* 3rd ed. 2 vols. New York: Norton, 1973.
A standard world literature survey, with useful introductory material on a critical approach to literature study.

McLuhan, M. *Understanding Media: The Extensions of Man.* New York: Signet, 1964.
The most classic work on the effect media has on the public and the power of the media to influence thinking.

McMichael, G. ed. *Concise Anthology of American Literature.* New York: Macmillan, 1974.
A standard survey of American literature.

Moffett, J. *Teaching the Universe of Discourse.* Boston: Houghton Mifflin, 1983.
A significant reference text that proposes the outline for a total language arts program, emphasizing the reinforcement of each element of the language arts curriculum to the other elements.

Moffett, James and Betty Jane Wagner. *Student-Centered Language Arts K-12.* 4th ed. Boston: Houghton Mifflin, 1992.

Nelms, B. F., ed. *Literature in the Classroom: Readers, Texts, and Contexts.* Urbana, IL: NCTE, 1988.
Essays on adolescent and multicultural literature, social aspects of literature, and approaches to literature interpretation.

Nilsen, A. P. and K. L. Donelson. *Literature for Today's Young Adults.* 2nd ed. Glenview, IL: Scott, Foresman, and Co., 1985.
An excellent overview of young adult literature - its history, terminologies, bibliographies, and book reviews.

Perrine, L. *Literature: Structure, Sound, and Sense.* 5th ed. Orlando, FL: Harcourt, Brace, Jovanovich, 1988.
A much revised text for teaching literature elements, genres, and interpretation.

Piercey, Dorothy. *Reading Activities in Content Areas: An Ideabook for Middle and Secondary Schools.* 2nd ed. Boston: Allyn and Bacon, 1982.

Pooley, R. C. *The Teaching of English Usage.* Urbana, IL: NCTE, 1974.
A revision of the important 1946 text, which discusses the attitudes toward English usage through history and recommends specific techniques for usage instruction.

Probst, R. E. *Response and Analysis: Teaching Literature in Junior and Senior High School.* Upper Montclair, NJ: Boynton/Cook, 1988.
A resource that explores reader response theory and discusses student-centered methods for interpreting literature. Contains a section on the progress of adolescent literature.

Pyles, T. and J. Alges. *The Origin and Development of the English Language.* 3rd ed. Orlando, FL: Harcourt, Brace, Jovanovich, 1982.
A history of the English language; sections on social, personal, historical, and geographical influences on language usage.

Readence, J. E. and others. *Content Area Reading: An Integrated Approach.* 2nd ed. Dubuque, IA: Kendall/Hunt, 1985.
A practical instruction guide for teaching reading in the content areas.

Robinson, H. Alan. *Teaching Reading and Study Strategies: The Content Areas.* Boston: Allyn and Bacon, 1978.

Roe, B. D. and others. *Secondary School Reading Instruction: The Content Areas.* 3rd ed. Boston: Houghton Mifflin, 1987.
A resource of strategies for the teaching of reading for language arts teachers with little reading instruction background.

Rosenberg, D. *World Mythology: An Anthology of the Great Myths and Epics.* Lincolnwood, IL: National Textbook, 1986.
Presents selections of main myths from which literary allusions are drawn. Thorough literary analysis of each selection.

Rosenblatt, L. M. *The Reader, the Text, the Poem. The Transactional Theory of the Literary Work.* Southern Illinois University Press, 1978.
A discussion of reader-response theory and reader-centered methods for analyzing literature.

Santeusanio, Richard P. *A Practical Approach to Content Area Reading.* Reading, MA.: Addison-Wesley Publishing Co., 1983.

Strickland, D. S. and others. *Using Computers in the Teaching of Reading.* New York: Teachers College Press, 1987.
Resource for strategies for teaching and learning language and reading with computers and recommendations for software for all grades.

Sutherland, Zena and others. *Children and Books.* 6th ed. Glenview, IL: Scott, Foresman, and Co., 1981.
Thorough study of children's literature, with sections on language development theory and chapters on specific genres with synopses of specific classic works for child/adolescent readers.

Tchudi, S. and D. Mitchell. *Explorations in the Teaching of English.* 3rd ed. New York: Harper Row, 1989.
A thorough source of strategies for creating a more student-centered involvement in learning.

Tompkins, Gail E. *Teaching Writing: Balancing Process and Product.* 2nd ed. New York: Macmillan, 1994.
A tool to aid teachers in integrating research and theory about the writing process, writing reading connections, collaborative learning, and writing across the curriculum with practices in the fourth- through eighth-grade classrooms.

Warriners, J. E. *English Composition and Grammar.* Benchmark ed. Orlando, FL: Harcourt, Brace, Jovanovich, 1988.
Standard grammar and composition textbook, with a six-book series for seventh through twelfth grades; includes vocabulary study, language history, and diverse approaches to writing process.

Sample Test

Section I: Essay Test

You will respond to several prompts intended to gauge your competence in a variety of writing skills. In most testing situations, you will have 30 minutes to respond to these prompts. Some tests may allow 60 minutes for the essay in order to incorporate more than one question or to allow for greater preparation and editing time. Read the directions carefully and organize your time wisely.

Section II: Multiple-choice Test

This section contains 125 questions. In most testing situations, you would be expected to answer 35-40 questions in about 30 minutes. If you time yourself on the entire battery, try to finish it in about 90 minutes.

Section III: Answer Key

Section I: Essay Prompts

Prompt A

Write an expository essay discussing effective teaching strategies for helping a heterogeneous class of ninth-graders to appreciate literature. Select any appropriate piece(s) of world literature to use as examples in the discussion.

Prompt B

After reading the following passage from Aldous Huxley's *Brave New World,* discuss the types of reader responses possible with a group of eighth-graders.

> He hated them all--all the men who came to visit Linda. One afternoon, when he had been playing with the other children--it was cold, he remembered, and there was snow on the mountains--he came back to the house and heard angry voices in the bedroom. They were women's voices, and they were words he didn't understand; but he knew they were dreadful words. Then suddenly, crash! something was upset; he heard people moving about quickly, and there was another crash and then a noise like hitting a mule, only not so bony; then Linda screamed. 'Oh, don't, don't, don't!' she said. He ran in. There were three women in dark blankets. Linda was on the bed. One of the women was holding her wrists. Another was lying across her legs, so she couldn't kick. The third was hitting her with a whip. Once, twice, three times; and each time Linda screamed.

Prompt C

Write a persuasive letter to the editor on any contemporary topic of special interest. Employ whatever forms of discourse, stylistic devices, and audience-appeal techniques that seem appropriate to the topic.

Section II: Writing and Language Skills

Part A

Directions: Each underlined portion of sentences 1-10 contains one or more errors in grammar, usage, mechanics, or sentence structure. Circle the choice which best corrects the error without changing the meaning of the original sentence.

Explanation of Rigor

Easy: The majority of test takers would get this question correct. It is a simple understanding of the facts and/or the subject matter is part of the basics of an education for teaching English.

Average Rigor: This question represents a test item that most people would pass. It requires a level of analysis or reasoning and/or the subject matter exceeds the basics of an education for teaching English.

Rigor: The majority of test takers would have difficulty answering this question. It involves critical thinking skills such as a very high level of abstract thought, analysis or reasoning, and it would require a very deep and broad education for teaching English.

Each underlined portion of sentences 1-10 contains one or more errors in grammar, usage, mechanics, or sentence structure. Circle the choice which best corrects the error without changing the meaning of the original sentence.

1. There were <u>fewer pieces</u> of evidence presented during the second trial (Skill 12.1, Easy)

   A. fewer peaces

   B. less peaces

   C. less pieces

   D. fewer pieces

2. The teacher <u>implied</u> from our angry words that there was conflict <u>between you and me</u>. (Skill 12.1, Average Rigor)

   A. Implied… between you and I

   B. Inferred… between you and I

   C. Inferred… between you and me

   D. Implied… between you and me

3. Wally said with a <u>groan, "Why</u> do I have to do an oral interpretation <u>of "The Raven."</u> (Skill 12.1, Average Rigor)

   A. groan, "Why… of 'The Raven'?"

   B. groan "Why… of "The Raven"?

   C. groan ", Why… of "The Raven?"

   D. groan, "Why… of "The Raven."

4. The Taj Mahal <u>has been designated</u> one of the Seven Wonders of the World, and people <u>know it</u> for its unique architecture. (Skill 12.1, Rigorous)

A. The Taj Mahal has been designated one of the Seven Wonders of the World, and it is known for its unique architecture.

B. People know the Taj Mahal for its unique architecture, and it has been designated one of the Seven Wonders of the World.

C. People have known the Taj Mahal for its unique architecture, and it has been designated of the Seven Wonders of the World.

D. The Taj Mahal has designated itself one of the Seven Wonders of the World.

5. A teacher must know <u>not only her subject matter but also</u> the strategies of content teaching. (Skill 12.1, Rigorous)

A. must not only know her subject matter but also the strategies of content teaching

B. not only must know her subject matter but also the strategies of content teaching

C. must not know only her subject matter but also the strategies of content teaching

D. must know not only her subject matter but also the strategies of content teaching

6. **The coach offered her <u>assistance but the athletes</u> wanted to practice on their own. (Skill 12.1, Rigorous)**

   A. The coach offered her assistance, however, the athletes wanted to practice on their own.

   B. The coach offered her assistance: furthermore, the athletes wanted to practice on their own.

   C. Having offered her assistance, the athletes wanted to practice on their own.

   D. The coach offered her assistance; however, the athletes wanted to practice on their own.

   E. The coach offered her assistance, and the athletes wanted to practice on their own.

7. **Joe <u>didn't hardly know</u> his cousin Fred who'd had a rhinoplasty. (Skill 12.2, Easy)**

   A. hardly did know his cousin Fred

   B. didn't know his cousin Fred hardly

   C. hardly knew his cousin Fred

   D. didn't know his cousin Fred

   E. didn't hardly know his cousin Fred

8. **<u>Mixing the batter for cookies,</u> the cat licked the Crisco from the cookie sheet. (Skill 12.2, Average Rigor)**

   A. While mixing the batter for cookies

   B. While the batter for cookies was mixing

   C. While I mixed the batter for cookies

   D. While I mixed the cookies

   E. Mixing the batter for cookies

9. Mr. Smith <u>respectfully submitted his resignation and had</u> a new job. (Skill 12.2, Average Rigor)

A. respectfully submitted his resignation and has

B. respectfully submitted his resignation before accepting

C. respectfully submitted his resignation because of

D. respectfully submitted his resignation and had

10. Walt Whitman was famous for his composition, *Leaves of Grass*, serving as a nurse during the Civil War, and a devoted son (Skill 12.2, Rigorous)

A. *Leaves of Grass*, his service as a nurse during the Civil War, and a devoted son

B. composing *Leaves of Grass*, serving as a nurse during the Civil War, and being a devoted son

C. his composition, *Leaves of Grass*, his nursing during the Civil War, and his devotion as a son

D. his composition, *Leaves of Grass*, serving as a nurse during the Civil War, and a devoted son

E. his composition, *Leaves of Grass*, serving as a nurse during the Civil War, and a devoted son

Part B

Directions: Select the best answer in each group of multiple choices.

11. **The tendency to emphasize and value the qualities and peculiarities of life in a particular geographic area exemplifies (Skill 1.1, Easy)**

    A. pragmatism.

    B. regionalism.

    C. pantheism.

    D. abstractionism.

12. **Which poet was a major figure in the Harlem Renaissance? (Skill 1.1, Easy)**

    A. e. e. Cummings

    B. Rita Dove

    C. Margaret Atwood

    D. Langston Hughes

13. **Which of the following writers did not win a Nobel Prize for literature? (Skill 1.1, Average Rigor)**

    A. Gabriel Garcia-Marquez of Colombia

    B. Nadine Gordimer of South Africa

    C. Pablo Neruda of Chile

    D. Alice Walker of the United States

14. **What were two major characteristics of the first American literature? (Skill 1.1, Rigorous)**

    A. Vengefulness and arrogance

    B. Bellicosity and derision

    C. Oral delivery and reverence for the land

    D. Maudlin and self-pitying egocentricism

15. **Which of the following titles is known for its scathingly condemning tone? (Skill 1.3, Average Rigor)**

    A. Boris Pasternak's *Dr Zhivago*

    B. Albert Camus' *The Stranger*

    C. Henry David Thoreau's "On the Duty of Civil Disobedience"

    D. Benjamin Franklin's "Rules by Which a Great Empire May Be Reduced to a Small One"

16. **American colonial writers were primarily (Skill 1.3, Average Rigor)**

    A. Romanticists.

    B. Naturalists.

    C. Realists.

    D. Neo-classicists.

17. **Which of the following is not a theme of Native American writing? (Skill 1.3, Average Rigor)**

    A. Emphasis on the hardiness of the human body and soul

    B. The strength of multi-cultural assimilation

    C. Contrition for the genocide of native peoples

    D. Remorse for the love of the Indian way of life

18. To explore the relationship of literature to modern life, which of these activities would not enable students to explore comparable themes? (Skill 2.2 Average Rigor)

A. After studying various world events, such as the Palestinian-Israeli conflict, students write an updated version of *Romeo and Juliet* using modern characters and settings.

B. Before studying *Romeo and Juliet*, students watch *West Side Story*.

C. Students research the major themes of *Romeo and Juliet* by studying news stories and finding modern counterparts for the story.

D. Students would explore compare the romantic themes of *Romeo and Juliet* and *The Taming of the Shrew*.

19. The students in Mrs. Cline's seventh grade language arts class were invited to attend a performance of *Romeo and Juliet* presented by the drama class at the high school. To best prepare, they should (Skill 2.2, Average Rigor)

A. read the play as a homework exercise.

B. read a synopsis of the plot and a biographical sketch of the author.

C. examine a few main selections from the play to become familiar with the language and style of the author.

D. read a condensed version of the story and practice attentive listening skills.

20. Mr. Phillips is creating a unit to study *To Kill a Mockingbird* and wants to familiarize his high school freshmen with the attitudes and issues of the historical period. Which activity would familiarize students with the attitudes and issues of the Depression-era South? (Skill 2.2, Rigorous)

    A. Create a detailed timeline of 15-20 social, cultural, and political events that focus on race relations in the 1930s.

    B. Research and report on the life of its author Harper Lee. Compare her background with the events in the book.

    C. Watch the movie version and note language and dress.

    D. Write a research report on the stock market crash of 1929 and its effects.

21. In preparing a unit on twentieth-century immigration, you prepare a list of books for students to read. Which book would not be appropriate for this topic? (Skill 2.4, Easy)

    A. *Fox in Sox* by Dr. Seuss

    B. *Exodus* by Leon Uris

    C. *The Joy Luck Club* by Amy Tan

    D. *Tortilla Flat* by John Steinbeck

22. Arthur Miller wrote *The Crucible* as a parallel to what twentieth century event? (Skill 2.4, Average Rigor)

    A. Senator McCarthy's House Un-American Activities Committee Hearing

    B. The Cold War

    C. The fall of the Berlin Wall

    D. The Persian Gulf War

23. **Which of the writers below is a renowned black poet? (Skill 2.4, Average Rigor)**

    A. Maya Angelou

    B. Sandra Cisneros

    C. Richard Wilbur

    D. Richard Wright

24. **What is considered the first work of English literature because it was written in the vernacular of the day? (Skill 3.1, Easy)**

    A. *Beowulf*

    B. *Le Morte d'Arthur*

    C. *The Faerie Queene*

    D. *Canterbury Tales*

25. **An extended metaphor comparing two very dissimilar things (one lofty one lowly) is a definition of a/an (Skill 3.1, Average)**

    A. antithesis.

    B. aphorism.

    C. apostrophe.

    D. conceit.

26. **"Everyone must pass through Vanity Fair to get to the celestial city" is an allusion from a (Skill 3.1, Rigorous)**

    A. Chinese folk tale.

    B. Norse saga.

    C. British allegory.

    D. German fairy tale.

27. **Which sonnet form describes the following? (Skill 3.1, Rigorous)**

My galley charg'd with
   forgetfulness,
Through sharp seas, in
   winter night doth pass
'Tween rock and rock; and
   eke mine enemy, alas,
That is my lord steereth with
   cruelness.
And every oar a thought with
   readiness,
As though that death were
   light in such a case.
An endless wind doth tear
   the sail apace
Or forc'ed sighs and trusty
   fearfulness.
A rain of tears, a cloud of dark
   disdain,
Hath done the wearied
   cords great hinderance,
Wreathed with error and eke
   with ignorance.
The stars be hid that led me
   to this pain
Drowned is reason that
   should me consort,
And I remain despairing
   of the poet

  A. Petrarchan or Italian sonnet

  B. Shakespearian or
     Elizabethan sonnet

  C. Romantic sonnet

  D. Spenserian sonnet

28. **Which of the following was not an effect of the Industrial Revolution in England during the nineteenth century? (Skill 3.3, Average)**

  A. Development of a middle class of industrialists and businessmen and a decline in the landed class of nobility and gentry

  B. Enormous shift from hand-produced goods to machine-produced ones and the loss of jobs

  C. The separation of husband and wife; gender roles began to be defined by the new configuration of labor in this new world order

  D. Naturalism, the literary, intellectual, and artistic movement occurred along with the Industrial Movement in response to the increasing mechanization of society

29. **Charles Dickens, Robert Browning, and Robert Louis Stevenson were (Skill 4.1, Easy Rigor)**

  A. Victorians.

  B. Medievalists.

  C. Elizabethans.

  D. Absurdists.

30. **The following lines from Robert Browning's poem "My Last Duchess" come from an example of what form of dramatic literature? (Skill 4.1, Rigorous)**

    That's my last Duchess painted on the wall,
    Looking as if she were alive. I call
    That piece a wonder, now: Frà Pandolf's hands
    Worked busily a day, and there she stands.
    Will 't please you sit and look at her?

    A. Tragedy

    B. Comic opera

    C. Dramatis personae

    D. Dramatic monologue

31. **Which choice below best defines naturalism? (Skill 4.3, Rigorous)**

    A. A belief that the writer or artist should apply scientific objectivity in his/her observation and treatment of life without imposing value judgments.

    B. The doctrine that teaches that the existing world is the best to be hoped for.

    C. The doctrine which teaches that God is not a personality, but that all laws, forces and manifestations of the universe are God-related.

    D. A philosophical doctrine which professes that the truth of all knowledge must always be in question.

32. **Which of the following is not one of the novels by the Brontë sisters? (Skill 4.4, Easy)**

    A. *Jane Eyre*

    B. *Wuthering Heights*

    C. *Agnes Gray*

    D. *Pride and Prejudice*

33. **What is the salient literary feature of this excerpt from an epic? (Skill 5.1, Rigorous)**

Hither the heroes and the
    nymphs resorts,
To taste awhile the pleasures
of a court;
In various talk th'instructive
hours they passed,
Who gave the ball, or paid the
visit last;
One speaks the glory of the
English Queen,
And another describes a
charming Indian screen;
A third interprets motion, looks
    and eyes;
At every word a reputation dies.

A. Sprung rhythm

B. Onomatopoeia

C. Heroic couplets

D. Motif

34. **Which events contributed to the invention of writing, thus making possible the emergence of literature as well as the development of human civilization? (Skill 5.2, Average)**

A. Domestication of animals, the development of agriculture, and the establishment of an agricultural surplus.

B. Development of the printing press and the subsequent growth of literacy in the ruling classes.

C. The travels of the nomadic tribes who spread tales through oral tradition and the development of papyrus.

D. Growth of towns and cities, religious education, and development of local government.

35. **Which of the following statements is not true about Greek drama? (Skill 5.3, Rigorous)**

    A. Greek plays were performed as part of a religious festival honoring Dionysus.

    B. The chorus was a group of men in masks who would sing, dance, and often interact with the actors in the play.

    C. Many of the plots were based on ancient myths although dramatists were known to exercise creativity.

    D. Greek plays were categorized as comedies, tragedies, or satires.

36. **Who was Dante's guide through the Inferno in *The Divine Comedy*? (Skill 5.4, Easy)**

    A. The poetic muse Beatrice

    B. Jesus of Nazareth

    C. The Latin poet Virgil

    D. The Greek philosopher Socrates

37. **A traditional, anonymous story, ostensibly having a historical basis, usually explaining some phenomenon of nature or aspect of creation, defines a (Skill 5.5, Easy)**

    A. proverb.

    B. idyll.

    C. myth.

    D. epic.

38. Hoping to take advantage of the popularity of the Harry Potter series, a teacher develops a unit on mythology comparing the story and characters of Greek and Roman myths with the story and characters of the Harry Potter books. Which of these is a commonality that would link classical literature to popular fiction? (Skill 5.5, Rigorous)

A. The characters are gods in human form with human-like characteristics.

B. The settings are realistic places in the world where the characters interact as humans would.

C. The themes center on the universal truths of love and hate and fear.

D. The heroes in the stories are young males and only they can overcome the opposing forces.

39. Considered one of the first feminist plays, this Ibsen drama ends with a gunshot symbolizing the lead character's emancipation from traditional societal norms. (Skill 6.1, Easy)

A. *The Wild Duck*

B. *Hedda Gabler*

C. *Ghosts*

D. *The Doll's House*

40. The writing of Russian naturalists is (Skill 6.1, Average Rigor)

A. optimistic.

B. pessimistic.

C. satirical.

D. whimsical.

41. **Which of the following is the best definition of existentialism? (Skill 6.1, Rigorous)**

    A. The philosophical doctrine that matter is the only reality and that everything in the world, including thought, will and feeling can be explained only in terms of matter.

    B. Philosophy which views things as they should be or as one would wish them to be.

    C. A philosophical and literary movement, variously religious and atheistic, stemming from Kierkegaard and represented by Sartre.

    D. The belief that all events are determined by fate and are hence inevitable.

42. **Latin words that entered the English language during the Elizabethan Age include (Skill 6.2, Average Rigor)**

    A. allusion, education, and esteem

    B. vogue and mustache

    C. canoe and cannibal

    D. alligator, cocoa, and armadillo

43. **Which is an untrue statement about a theme in literature? (Skill 7.2, Average Rigor)**

    A. The theme is always stated directly somewhere in the text.

    B. The theme is the central idea in a literary work.

    C. All parts of the work (plot, setting, and mood) should contribute to the theme in some way.

    D. By analyzing the various elements of the work, the reader should be able to arrive at an indirectly stated theme.

44. **Which of the following is not a characteristic of a fable? (Skill 7.4, Easy)**

    A. Animals that feel and talk like humans.

    B. Happy solutions to human dilemmas.

    C. Teaches a moral or standard for behavior.

    D. Illustrates specific people or groups without directly naming them.

45. **What is not a characteristic of an effective editorial cartoon? (Skill 7.5, Easy)**

   A. It presents a message or point of view concerning people, events, or situations using caricature and symbolism to convey the cartoonist's ideas

   B. It will have wit and humor, which is usually obtained by exaggeration that is slick and not used merely for comic effect.

   C. It will also have a foundation in truth; that is, the characters must be recognizable to the viewer and the point of the drawing must have some basis in fact even if it has a philosophical bias.

   D. It will seek to reflect the editorial opinion of the newspaper that carries it.

46. **In classic tragedy, a protagonist's defeat is brought about by a tragic flaw which is called (Skill 7.6 Rigorous)**

   A. hubris

   B. hamartia

   C. catharsis

   D. the skene

47. **Which poem is typified as a villanelle? (Skill 7.8, Rigorous)**

   A. "Do not go gentle into that good night"

   B. "Dover Beach"

   C. Sir Gawain and the Green Knight

   D. Pilgrim's Progress

48. **The technique of starting a narrative at a significant point in the action and then developing the story through flashbacks is called (Skill 7.7, Rigorous)**

   A. in medias res

   B. octava rima

   C. irony

   D. suspension of willing disbelief

49. **Which is the best definition of free verse, or *vers libre*? (Skill 7.9, Average Rigor)**

A. Poetry which consists of an unaccented syllable followed by an unaccented sound.

B. Short lyrical poetry written to entertain but with an instructive purpose.

C. Poetry which does not have a uniform pattern of rhythm.

D. A poem which tells the story and has a plot

50. **Which of the following is a characteristic of blank verse? (Skill 7.9, Average Rigor)**

A. Meter in iambic pentameter

B. Clearly specified rhyme scheme

C. Lack of figurative language

D. Unspecified rhythm

51. **The substitution of "went to his rest" for "died" is an example of a/an (Skill 7.10, Easy)**

A. bowdlerism.

B. jargon.

C. euphemism.

D. malapropism.

52. **The literary device of personification is used in which example below? (Skill 7.10, Average Rigor)**

A. "Beg me no beggary by soul or parents, whining dog!"

B. "Happiness sped through the halls cajoling as it went."

C. "O wind thy horn, thou proud fellow."

D. "And that one talent which is death to hide."

53. **What syntactic device is most evident from Abraham Lincoln's "Gettysburg Address"? (Skill 7.10, Rigorous)**

> It is rather for us to be here dedicated to the great task remaining before us -- that from these honored dead we take increased devotion to that cause for which they gave the last full measure of devotion -- that we here highly resolve that these dead shall not have died in vain -- that this nation, under God, shall have a new birth of freedom -- and that government of the people, by the people, for the people, shall not perish from the earth.

A. Affective connotation

B. Informative denotations

C. Allusion

D. Parallelism

TEACHER CERTIFICATION STUDY GUIDE

54. **How will literature help students in a science class understand the following passage? (Skill 7.10, Rigorous)**

> Just as was the case more than three decades ago, we are still sailing between the Scylla of deferring surgery for too long and risking irreversible left ventricular damage and sudden death, and the Charibdas of operating too early and subjecting the patient to the early risks of operation and the later risks resulting from prosthetic valves.
> --E. Braunwald, *European Heart Journal*, July 2000

A. They will recognize the allusion to Scylla and Charibdas from Greek mythology and understand that the medical community has to select one of two unfavorable choices.

B. They will recognize the allusion to sailing and understand its analogy to doctors as sailors navigating unknown waters.

C. They will recognize that the allusion to Scylla and Charybdas refers to the two islands in Norse mythology where sailors would find themselves shipwrecked and understand how the doctors feel isolated by their choices.

D. They will recognize the metaphor of the heart and relate it to Eros, the character in Greek mythology who represents love. Eros was the love child of Scylla and Charybdas.

55. **Which is not a Biblical allusion? (Skill 7.10, Rigorous)**

A. The patience of Job

B. Thirty pieces of silver

C. "Man proposes; God disposes"

D. "Suffer not yourself to be betrayed by a kiss"

56. **Using the selection below from Edgar Alan Poe's "The Tell-Tale Heart," what form of literary criticism would you introduce to high school students? (Skill 8.1, Average)**

"And have I not told you that what you mistake for madness is but over-acuteness of the sense? -- now, I say, there came to my ears a low, dull, quick sound, such as a watch makes when enveloped in cotton. I knew that sound well, too. It was the beating of the old man's heart. It increased my fury, as the beating of a drum stimulates the soldier into courage."

A. Marxist

B. Feminist

C. Psychoanalytic

D. Classic

57. **In the following poem, what literary movement is reflected? (Skill 8.3, Rigorous)**

"My Heart Leaps Up" by William Wordsworth

My heart leaps up when I behold
   A rainbow in the sky:
So was it when my life began;
So is it now I am a man;
So be it when I shall grow old,
   Or let me die!
The Child is father of the Man;
And I could wish my days to be
Bound each to each by natural piety

A. Neo-classicism

B. Victorian literature

C. Romanticism

D. Naturalism

58. What is the best course of action when a child refuses to complete a reading/ literature assignment on the grounds that it is morally objectionable? (Skill 8.4, Average Rigor)

A. Speak with the parents and explain the necessity of studying this work

B. Encourage the child to sample some of the text before making a judgment

C. Place the child in another teacher's class where that class is studying an acceptable work

D. Provide the student with alternative selections that cover the same performance standards that the rest of the class is learning.

59. Students have been asked to write a research paper on automobiles and have brainstormed a number of questions they will answer based on their research findings. Which of the following is not an interpretive question to guide research? (Skill 8.4, Rigorous)

A. Who were the first ten automotive manufacturers in the United States?

B. What types of vehicles will be used fifty years from now?

C. How do automobiles manufactured in the United States compare and contrast with each other?

D. What do you think is the best solution for the fuel shortage?

60. Recognizing empathy in literature is mostly a/an (Skill 8.4, Rigorous)

A. emotional response.

B. interpretive response.

C. critical response.

D. evaluative response.

61. **Which sentence below best minimizes the impact of bad news? (Skill 9.1, Rigorous)**

    A. We have denied you permission to attend the event.

    B. Although permission to attend the event cannot be given, you are encouraged to buy the video.

    C. Although you cannot attend the event, we encourage you to buy the video.

    D. Although attending the event is not possible, watching the video is an option.

62. **Which word in the following sentence is a bound morpheme: "The quick brown fox jumped over the lazy dog"? (Skill 9.1, Rigorous)**

    A. The

    B. fox

    C. lazy

    D. jumped

63. **The Elizabethans wrote in (Skill 9.2, Easy)**

    A. Celtic

    B. Old English

    C. Middle English

    D. Modern English

64. **the synonyms *gyro*, *hero*, and *submarine* reflect which influence on language usage? (Skill 9.2, Average Rigor)**

    A. Social

    B. Geographical

    C. Historical

    D. Personal

65. **Overcrowded classes prevent the individual attention needed to facilitate language development. This drawback can be best overcome by (Skill 9.2, Average Rigor)**

    A. dividing the class into independent study groups.

    B. assigning more study time at home.

    C. using more drill practice in class.

    D. team teaching.

66. **Which of the following is not true about the English language? (Skill 9.2, Average Rigor)**

    A. English is the easiest language to learn.

    B. English is the least inflected language.

    C. English has the most extensive vocabulary of any language.

    D. English originated as a Germanic tongue.

67. **What was responsible for the standardizing of dialects across America in the twentieth century? (Skill 9.2, Rigorous)**

    A. With the immigrant influx, American became a melting pot of languages and cultures.

    B. Trains enabled people to meet other people of different languages and cultures.

    C. Radio, and later, television, used actors and announcers who spoke without pronounced dialects.

    D. Newspapers and libraries developed programs to teach people to speak English with an agreed-upon common dialect.

68. **Which event triggered the beginning of Modern English? (Skill 9.3, Average Rigor)**

    A. Conquest of England by the Normans in 1066

    B. Introduction of the printing press to the British Isles

    C. Publication of Samuel Johnson's lexicon.

    D. American Revolution

69. **Which of the following is the least effective procedure for promoting consciousness of audience? (Skill 9.4, Average Rigor)**

    A. Pairing students during the writing process

    B. Reading all rough drafts before the students writes the final copies

    C. Having students compose stories or articles for publication in school literary magazines or newspapers

    D. Writing letters to friends or relatives

English

70. In literature, evoking feelings of pity or compassion is to create (Skill 10.1, Average Rigor)

    A. colloquy.

    B. irony.

    C. pathos.

    D. paradox

71. Identify the type of appeal used by Molly Ivins in this excerpt from her essay "Get a Knife, Get a Dog, But Get Rid of Guns." (Skill 10.1, Rigorous)

    As a civil libertarian, I, of course, support the Second Amendment. And I believe it means exactly what it says:

    A well regulated militia being necessary to the security of a free state, the right of the people to keep and bear arms shall not be infringed.

    A. Ethical

    B. Emotional

    C. Rational

    D. Literary

72. Which part of a classical argument is illustrated in this excerpt from the essay "What Should Be Done About Rock Lyrics?" (Skill 10.3, Rigorous)

    But violence against women is greeted by silence. It shouldn't be.
    This does not mean censorship, or book (or record) burning. In a society that protects free expression, we understand a lot of stuff will float up out of the sewer. Usually, we recognize the ugly stuff that advocates violence against any group as the garbage it is, and we consider its purveyors as moral lepers. We hold our nose and tolerate it, but we speak out against the values it proffers.
    --"What Should Be Done About Rock Lyrics?" Caryl Rivers

    A. Narration

    B. Confirmation

    C. Refutation and concession

    D. Summation

73. **In preparing students for their oral presentations, the instructor provided all of these guidelines, except one. Which is not an effective guideline? (Skill 10.5, Average Rigor)**

    A. Even if you are using a lectern, feel free to move about. This will connect you to the audience.

    B. Your posture should be natural, not stiff. Keep your shoulders toward the audience.

    C. Gestures can help communicate as long as you don't overuse them or make them distracting.

    D. You can avoid eye contact if you focus on your notes. This will make you appear more knowledgeable.

74. **The arrangement and relationship of words in sentences or sentence structures best describes (Skill 10.6, Rigorous)**

    A. style.

    B. discourse.

    C. thesis.

    D. syntax.

75. **Which of the following sentences contains a capitalization error? (Skill 10.7, Average Rigor)**

    A. The commander of the English navy was Admiral Nelson

    B. Napoleon was the president of the French First Republic

    C. Queen Elizabeth II is the Monarch of the British Empire

    D. William the Conqueror led the Normans to victory over the British

76. **In a class of non-native speakers of English, which type of activity will help students the most? (Skill 10.9, Rigorous)**

    A. Have students make oral presentations so that they can develop a phonological awareness of sounds.

    B. Provide students more writing opportunities to develop their written communication skills.

    C. Encourage students to listen to the new language on television and radio.

    D. Provide a variety of methods to develop speaking, writing, and reading skills.

77. **Oral debate is most closely associated with which form of discourse? (Skill 10.10, Average Rigor)**

    A. Description

    B. Exposition

    C. Narration

    D. Persuasion

78. **Which of the following type of question will not stimulate higher-level critical thinking? (Skill 10.10, Rigorous)**

    A. A hypothetical question

    B. An open-ended question

    C. A close-ended question

    D. A judgment question

79. **In presenting a report to peers about the effects of Hurricane Katrina on New Orleans, the students wanted to use various media in their argument to persuade their peers that more needed to be done. Which of these would be the most effective? Skill 10.11, Rigorous)**

    A. A PowerPoint presentation showing the blueprints of the levees before the flood and redesigned now for current construction.

    B. A collection of music clips made by the street performers in the French Quarter before and after the flood.

    C. A recent video showing the areas devastated by the floods and the current state of rebuilding.

    D. A collection of recordings of interviews made by the various government officials and local citizens affected by the flooding.

80. **Mr. Ledbetter has instructed his students to prepare a slide presentation that illustrates an event in history. Students are to include pictures, graphics, media clips and links to resources. What competencies will students exhibit at the completion of this project? Skill 10.11, Rigorous)**

A. Analyze the impact of society on media.

B. Recognize the media's strategies to inform and persuade.

C. Demonstrate strategies and creative techniques to prepare presentations using a variety of media.

D. Identify the aesthetic effects of a media presentation.

81. **What is the common advertising technique used by these advertising slogans? (Skill 10.11, Rigorous)**

"It's everywhere you want to be." Visa
"Have it your way." - Burger King
"When you care enough to send the very best" - Hallmark
"Be all you can be" – U.S. Army

A. Peer Approval

B. Rebel

C. Individuality

D. Escape

82. **Which of the following is most true of expository writing? (Skill 11.1, Easy)**

A. It is mutually exclusive of other forms of discourse.

B. It can incorporate other forms of discourse in the process of providing supporting details.

B. It should never employ informal expression.

D. It should only be scored with a summative evaluation.

83. **Explanatory or informative discourse is (Skill 11.1, Average Rigor)**

    A. exposition.

    B. narration.

    C. persuasion.

    D. description.

84. **Which of the following is not one of the four forms of discourse? (Skill 11.1, Average Rigor)**

    A. Exposition

    B. Description

    C. Rhetoric

    D. Persuasion

85. **Middle and high school students are more receptive to studying grammar and syntax (Skill 11.2, Average Rigor)**

    A. through worksheets and end of lessons practices in textbooks.

    B. through independent, homework assignment.

    C. through analytical examination of the writings of famous authors.

    D. through application to their own writing.

86. In general, the most serious drawback of using a computer in writing is (Skill 11.2, Average Rigor)

    A. the copy looks so good that students tend to overlook major mistakes.

    B. the spell check and grammar programs discourage students from learning proper spelling and mechanics.

    C. the speed with which corrections can be made detracts from the exploration and contemplation of composing.

    D. the writer loses focus by concentrating on the final product rather than the details.

87. Modeling is a practice that requires students to (Skill 11.2, Average Rigor)

    A. create a style unique to their own language capabilities.

    B. emulate the writing of professionals.

    C. paraphrase passages from good literature.

    D. peer evaluate the writings of other students.

88. In preparing a report about William Shakespeare, students are asked to develop a set of interpretive questions to guide their research. Which of the following would not be classified as an interpretive question? (Skill 11.2, Rigorous)

A. What would be different today if Shakespeare had not written his plays?

B. How will the plays of Shakespeare affect future generations?

C. How does the Shakespeare view nature in *A Midsummer's Night Dream* and *Much Ado About Nothing*?

D. During the Elizabethan age, what roles did young boys take in dramatizing Shakespeare's plays?

89. In this paragraph from a student essay, identify the sentence that provides a detail. (Skill 11.3 Rigorous)

(1) The poem concerns two different personality types and the human relation between them. (2) Their approach to life is totally different. (3) The neighbor is a very conservative person who follows routines. (4) He follows the traditional wisdom of his father and his father's father. (5) The purpose in fixing the wall and keeping their relationship separate is only because it is all he knows.

A. Sentence 1

B. Sentence 3

C. Sentence 4

D. Sentence 5

90. If a student uses slang and expletives, what is the best course of action to take in order to improve the student's formal communication skills? (Skill 11.4, Average Rigor)

A. Ask the student to paraphrase writing, that is, translate it into language appropriate for the school principal to read.

B. Refuse to read the student's papers until s/he conforms to a more literate style.

C. Ask the student to read his/her work aloud to the class for peer evaluation.

D. Rewrite the flagrant passages to show the student the right form of expression.

91. Which of the following should not be included in the opening paragraph of an informative essay? (Skill 11.6, Easy)

A. Thesis sentence

B. Details and examples supporting the main idea

C. Broad general introduction to the topic

D. A style and tone that grabs the reader's attention

92. The following passage is written from which point of view? (Skill 11.8, Easy)

As she mused the pitiful vision of her mother's life laid its spell on the very quick of her being —that life of commonplace sacrifices closing in final craziness. She trembled as she heard again her mother's voice saying constantly with foolish insistence: *Derevaun Seraun! Derevaun Seraun!**
* "The end of pleasure is pain!" (Gaelic)

A. First person, narrator

B. Second person, direct address

C. Third person, omniscient

D. First person, omniscient

English 237

93. In the phrase "The Cabinet conferred with the President," Cabinet is an example of a/an (Skill 11.9, Rigorous)

    A. metonym

    B. synecdoche

    C. metaphor

    D. allusion

94. Which of the following is not a fallacy in logic? (Skill 11.10, Rigorous)

    A. --All students in Ms. Suarez's fourth period class are bilingual.
       --Beth is in Ms. Suarez's fourth period.
       --Beth is bilingual.

    B. --All bilingual students are in Ms. Suarez's class.
       --Beth is in Ms. Suarez's fourth period.
       --Beth is bilingual.

    C. --Beth is bilingual.
       --Beth is in Ms. Suarez's fourth period.
       --All students in Ms. Suarez's fourth period are bilingual.

    D. --If Beth is bilingual, then she speaks Spanish.
       --Beth speaks French.
       --Beth is not bilingual.

95. **Which transition word would show contrast between these two ideas? (Skill 11.12, Average Rigor)**

We are confident in our skills to teach English. We welcome new ideas on this subject.

A. We are confident in our skills to teach English, and we welcome new ideas on this subject.

B. Because we are confident in our skills to teach English, we welcome new ideas on the subject.

C. When we are confident in our skills to teach English, we welcome new ideas on the subject.

D. We are confident in our skills to teach English; however, we welcome new ideas on the subject.

96. **In preparing your high school freshmen to write a research paper about a social problem, what recommendation can you make so they can determine the credibility of their information? (Skill 11.13, Easy)**

A. Assure them that information on the Internet has been peer-reviewed and verified for accuracy.

B. Find one solid source and use that exclusively.

C. Use only primary sources.

D. Cross check your information with another credible source.

97. **To determine the credibility of information, researchers should do all of the following except (Skill 11.14, Rigorous)**

A. Establish the authority of the document.

B. Disregard documents with bias.

C. Evaluate the currency and reputation of the source.

D. Use a variety of research sources and methods.

98. **Which of the following situations is not an ethical violation of intellectual property? (Skill 11.14, Rigorous)**

A. A student visits ten different websites and writes a report to compare the costs of downloading music. He uses the names of the websites without their permission.

B. A student copies and pastes a chart verbatim from the Internet but does not document it because it is available on a public site.

C. From an online article found in a subscription database, a student paraphrases a section on the problems of music piracy. She includes the source in her Works Cited but does not provide an in-text citation.

D. A student uses a comment from M. Night Shyamalan without attribution claiming the information is common knowledge.

99. **For their research paper on the effects of the Civil War on American literature, students have brainstormed a list of potential online sources and are seeking your authorization. Which of these represent the strongest source? (Skill 11.14, Rigorous)**

A. http://www.wikipedia.org/

B. http://www.google.com

C. http://www.nytimes.com

D. http://docsouth.unc.edu /southlit/civilwar.html

100. **A punctuation mark indicating omission, interrupted thought, or an incomplete statement is a/an (Skill 12.1, Easy)**

A. ellipsis.

B. anachronism.

C. colloquy.

D. idiom.

101. **Which of the following sentences is properly punctuated? (Skill 12.1, Easy)**

    A. The more you eat; the more you want.

    B. The authors—John Steinbeck, Ernest Hemingway, and William Faulkner—are staples of modern writing in American literature textbooks.

    C. Handling a wild horse, takes a great deal of skill and patience.

    D. The man, who replaced our teacher, is a comedian.

102. **Which of the following sentences contains a subject-verb agreement error? (Skill 12.1, Average Rigor)**

    A. Both mother and her two sisters were married in a triple ceremony.

    B. Neither the hen nor the rooster is likely to be served for dinner.

    C. My boss, as well as the company's two personnel directors, have been to Spain.

    D. Amanda and the twins are late again.

103. In preparing a speech for a contest, your student has encountered problems with gender specific language. Not wishing to offend either women or men, he seeks your guidance. Which of the following is not an effective strategy? (Skill 12.3, Rigorous)

A. Use the generic "he" and explain that people will understand and accept the male pronoun as all-inclusive.

B. Switch to plural nouns and use "they" as the gender neutral pronoun.

C. Use passive voice so that the subject is not required.

D. Use male pronouns for one part of the speech and then use female pronouns for the other part of the speech.

104. Which aspect of language is innate? (Skill13.1, Rigorous)

A. Biological capability to articulate sounds understood by other humans

B. Cognitive ability to create syntactical structures

C. Capacity for using semantics to convey meaning in a social environment

D. Ability to vary inflections and accents

105. To understand the origins of a word, one must study the (Skill 13.2, Easy)

A. synonyms

B. inflections

C. phonetics

D. etymology

106. Which of the following would be the most significant factor in teaching Homer's Iliad and Odyssey to any particular group of students? (Skill 13.2, Average Rigor)

A. Identifying a translation on the appropriate reading level

B. Determining the students' interest level

C. Selecting an appropriate evaluative technique

D. Determining the scope and delivery methods of background study

107. Writing ideas quickly without interruption of the flow of thoughts or attention to conventions is called (Skill 13.4, Easy)

A. brainstorming.

B. mapping.

C. listing.

D. free writing.

108. If a student has a poor vocabulary, the teacher should recommend that first (Skill 13.7, Average Rigor)

A. the student read newspapers, magazines and books on a regular basis.

B. the student enroll in a Latin class.

C. the student write the words repetitively after looking them up in the dictionary.

D. the student use a thesaurus to locate synonyms and incorporate them into his/her vocabulary

109. Which of the following responses to literature typically give middle school students the most problems? (Skill 13.8, Average Rigor)

A. Interpretive

B. Evaluative

C. Critical

D. Emotional

110. What type of reasoning does Henry David Thoreau use in the following excerpt from "Civil Disobedience"? (Skill 13.8, Rigorous)

Unjust laws exist; shall we be content to obey them, or shall we endeavor to amend them, and obey them until we have succeeded, or shall we transgress them at once? Men generally, under such a government as this, think that they ought to wait until they have persuaded the majority to alter them. They think that, if they should resist, the remedy would be worse than the evil. But it is the fault of the government itself that the remedy *is* worse than the evil. … Why does it always crucify Christ, and excommunicate Copernicus and Luther, and pronounce Washington and Franklin rebels?

   "Civil Disobedience" by Henry David Thoreau

A. Ethical reasoning

B. Inductive reasoning

C. Deductive reasoning

D. Intellectual reasoning

111. Which of the following is an example of the post hoc fallacy? (Skill 13.8, Rigorous)

A. When the new principal was hired, student reading scores improved; therefore, the principal caused the increase in scores.

B. Why are we spending money on the space program when our students don't have current textbooks?

C. You can't give your class a 10-minute break. Once you do that, we'll all have to give our students a 10-minute break.

D. You can never believe anything he says because he's not from the same country as we are.

112. The new teaching intern is developing a unit on creative writing and is trying to encourage her freshman high school students to write poetry. Which of the following would not be an effective technique? (Skill 13.9, Average Rigor)

A. In groups, students will draw pictures to illustrate "The Love Song of J. Alfred Prufrock" by T.S. Eliot.

B. Either individually or in groups, students will compose a song, writing lyrics that try to use poetic devices.

C. Students will bring to class the lyrics of a popular song and discuss the imagery and figurative language.

D. Students will read aloud their favorite poems and share their opinions of and responses to the poems.

113. Which teaching method would best engage underachievers in the required senior English class? (Skill 13.9, Average Rigor)

A. Assign use of glossary work and extensively footnoted excerpts of great works.

B. Have students take turns reading aloud the anthology selection

C. Let students choose which readings they'll study and write about.

D. Use a chronologically arranged, traditional text, but assigning group work, panel presentations, and portfolio management

114. In the paragraph below, which sentence does not contribute to the overall task of supporting the main idea? (Skill 13.12 Easy)

1) The Springfield City Council met Friday to discuss new zoning restrictions for the land to be developed south of the city. 2) Residents who opposed the new restrictions were granted 15 minutes to present their case. 3) Their argument focused on the dangers that increased traffic would bring to the area. 4) It seemed to me that the Mayor Simpson listened intently. 5) The council agreed to table the new zoning until studies would be performed.

A. Sentence 2

B. Sentence 3

C. Sentence 4

D. Sentence 5

115. **For students to prepare for a their roles in a dramatic performance, (Skill 14.1, Rigorous)**

    A. they should analyze their characters to develop a deeper understanding of the character's attitudes and motivations.

    B. they should attend local plays to study settings and stage design

    C. they should read articles and books on acting methodology.

    D. they should practice the way other actors have performed in these roles.

116. **Among junior-high school students of low-to-average readability levels, which work would most likely stir reading interest? (Skill 14.3, Easy)**

    A. *Elmer Gantry*, Sinclair Lewis

    B. *Smiley's People*, John Le Carre

    C. *The Outsiders*, S.E. Hinton

    D. *And Then There Were None*, Agatha Christie.

117. **Most children's literature prior to the development of popular literature was intended to be didactic. Which of the following would not be considered didactic? (Skill 14.3, Average Rigor)**

    A. "A Visit from St. Nicholas" by Clement Moore

    B. McGuffy's Reader

    C. Any version of Cinderella

    D. Parables from the Bible

118. **Children's literature became established in the (Skill 14.3, Average Rigor)**

    A. seventeenth century

    B. eighteenth century

    C. nineteenth century

    D. twentieth century

119. **Which author did not write satire? (Skill 14.3, Rigorous)**

    A. Joseph Addison

    B. Richard Steele

    C. Alexander Pope

    D. John Bunyan

120. The most significant drawback to applying learning theory research to classroom practice is that (Skill 14.3, Rigorous)

A. today's students do not acquire reading skills with the same alacrity as when greater emphasis was placed on reading classical literature.

B. development rates are complicated by geography and culture. In analyzing literature and in looking for ways to bring a work to life for an audience, the use of comparable themes and ideas from other pieces of literature and from one's own life experiences, including from reading the daily newspaper, is important and useful.

C. homogeneous grouping has contributed to faster development of some age groups.

D. social and environmental conditions have contributed to an escalated maturity level than research done twenty or more years ago would seem to indicate.

121. After watching a movie of a train derailment, a child exclaims, "Wow, look how many cars fell off the tracks. There's junk everywhere. The engineer must have really been asleep." Using the facts that the child is impressed by the wreckage and assigns blame to the engineer, a follower of Piaget's theories would estimate the child to be about (Skill 14.3, Rigorous)

A. ten years old.

B. twelve years old.

C. fourteen years old.

D. sixteen years old.

122. Which of the following is a formal reading-level assessment? (Skill 14.5, Average Rigor)

A. A standardized reading test

B. A teacher-made reading test

C. An interview

D. A reading diary

123. Based on the excerpt below from Kate Chopin's short story "The Story of an Hour," what can students infer about the main character? (Skill 14.5, Rigorous)

She did not stop to ask if it were or were not a monstrous joy that held her. A clear and exalted perception enabled her to dismiss the suggestion as trivial. She knew that she would weep again when she saw the kind, tender hands folded in death; the face that had never looked save with love upon her, fixed and gray and dead. But she saw beyond that bitter moment a long procession of years to come that would belong to her absolutely. And she opened and spread her arms out to them in welcome.

A. She dreaded her life as a widow.

B. Although she loved her husband, she was glad that he was dead for he had never loved her.

C. She worried that she was too indifferent to her husband's death.

D. Although they had both loved each other, she was beginning to appreciate that opportunities had opened because of his death.

124. The English department is developing strategies to encourage all students to become a community of readers. From the list of suggestions below, which would be the least effective way for teachers to foster independent reading? (Skill 14.6, Average Rigor)

A. Each teacher will set aside a weekly 30-minute in-class reading session during which the teacher and students read a magazine or book for enjoyment.

B. Teacher and students develop a list of favorite books to share with each other.

C. The teacher assigns at least one book report each grading period to ensure that students are reading from the established class list.

D. The students gather books for a classroom library so that books may be shared with each other.

125. Written on the sixth grade reading level, most of S. E. Hinton's novels (for instance, *The Outsiders*) have the greatest reader appeal with (Skill 14.7, Average Rigor)

A. sixth-graders.

B. ninth-graders.

C. twelfth-graders.

D. adults.

Answer Key

1.	D	26.	C	51.	C	76.	A	101.	B
2.	C	27.	A	52.	B	77.	D	102.	C
3.	A	28.	D	53.	D	78.	C	103.	A
4.	A	29.	A	54.	A	79.	C	104.	A
5.	D	30.	D	55.	C	80.	B	105.	D
6.	D	31.	A	56.	C	81.	C	106.	A
7.	C	32.	D	57.	C	82.	B	107.	D
8.	C	33.	C	58.	D	83.	A	108.	A
9.	C	34.	A	59.	A	84.	C	109.	B
10.	B	35.	D	60.	C	85.	D	110.	C
11.	B	36.	C	61.	B	86.	C	111.	A
12.	D	37.	C	62.	D	87.	B	112.	A
13.	D	38.	C	63.	D	88.	D	113.	C
14.	D	39.	D	64.	B	89.	C	114.	C
15.	D	40.	B	65.	A	90.	A	115.	A
16.	D	41.	C	66.	A	91.	B	116.	C
17.	B	42.	A	67.	C	92.	C	117.	A
18.	D	43.	A	68.	B	93.	B	118.	A
19.	D	44.	D	69.	B	94.	A	119.	D
20.	A	45.	D	70.	C	95.	D	120.	D
21.	A	46.	B	71.	A	96.	D	121.	A
22.	A	47.	A	72.	C	97.	B	122.	A
23.	A	48.	A	73.	D	98.	A	123.	D
24.	D	49.	C	74.	D	99.	D	124.	C
25.	D	50.	A	75.	C	100.	A	125.	B

Rigor Table

	Easy 20%	Average Rigor 40%	Rigorous 40%
Question #	1, 7, 11, 12, 21, 24, 29, 32, 36, 37, 39, 44, 45, 51, 63, 82, 91, 92, 96, 100, 101, 105, 107, 114, 116	2, 3, 8, 9, 13, 15, 16, 17, 18, 19, 22, 23, 25, 28, 34, 40, 42, 43, 49, 50, 52, 56, 58, 64, 65, 66, 68, 69, 70, 73, 75, 77, 83, 84, 85, 86, 87, 90, 95, 102, 106, 108, 109, 112, 113, 117, 118, 122, 124, 125	4, 5, 6, 10, 14, 20, 26, 27, 30, 31, 33, 35, 38, 41, 46, 47, 48, 53, 54, 55, 57, 59, 60, 61, 62, 67, 71, 72, 74, 76, 78, 79, 80, 81, 88, 89, 93, 94, 97, 98, 99, 103, 104, 110, 111, 115, 119, 120, 121, 123

Rationales for Answers

Easy: The majority of test takers would get this question correct. It is a simple understanding of the facts and/or the subject matter is part of the basics of an education for teaching English.

Average Rigor: This question represents a test item that most people would pass. It requires a level of analysis or reasoning and/or the subject matter exceeds the basics of an education for teaching English.

Rigor: The majority of test takers would have difficulty answering this question. It involves critical thinking skills such as a very high level of abstract thought, analysis or reasoning, and it would require a very deep and broad education for teaching English.

Part A

Each underlined portion of sentences 1-10 contains one or more errors in grammar, usage, mechanics, or sentence structure. Circle the choice which best corrects the error without changing the meaning of the original sentence.

1. There were <u>fewer pieces</u> of evidence presented during the second trial (Skill 12.1, Easy)

       A. fewer peaces

       B. less peaces

       C. less pieces

       D. fewer pieces

The answer is D. Use "fewer" for countable items; use "less" for amounts and quantities, such as fewer minutes but less time "Peace" is the opposite of war, not a "piece" of evidence.

2.

  2 The teacher <u>implied</u> from our angry words that there was conflict <u>between you and me</u>. (Skill 12.1, Average Rigor)

       A. Implied… between you and I

       B. Inferred… between you and I

       C. Inferred… between you and me

       D. Implied… between you and me

The answer is C: the difference between the verb "to imply" and the verb "to infer" is that implying is directing an interpretation toward other people; to infer is to deduce an interpretation from someone else's discourse. Moreover, "between you and I" is grammatically incorrect: after the preposition "between," the object (or 'disjunctive' with this particular preposition) pronoun form, "me," is needed.

3. **Wally said with a <u>groan,</u> "<u>Why</u> do I have to do an oral interpretation <u>of</u> "The Raven."** (Skill 12.1, Average Rigor)

    A. groan, "Why... of 'The Raven'?"

    B. groan "Why... of "The Raven"?

    C. groan ", Why... of "The Raven?"

    D. groan, "Why... of "The Raven."

The answer is A. The question mark in a quotation that is an interrogation should be within the quotation marks. Also, when quoting a work of literature within another quotation, one should use single quotation marks ('...') for the title of this work, and they should close before the final quotation mark.

4. **The Taj Mahal <u>has been designated</u> one of the Seven Wonders of the World, and people <u>know it</u> for its unique architecture.** (Skill 12.1, Rigorous)

    A. The Taj Mahal has been designated one of the Seven Wonders of the World, and it is known for its unique architecture.

    B. People know the Taj Mahal for its unique architecture, and it has been designated one of the Seven Wonders of the World.

    C. People have known the Taj Mahal for its unique architecture, and it has been designated of the Seven Wonders of the World.

    D. The Taj Mahal has designated itself one of the Seven Wonders of the World.

The answer is A. In the original sentence, the first clause is passive voice and the second clause is active voice, causing a voice shift. B merely switches the clauses but does not correct the voice shift. In C, only the verb tense in the first clause has been changed but it still active voice. Sentence D changes the meaning. In A, both clauses are passive voice.

5.   **A teacher must know not only her subject matter but also the strategies of content teaching. (Skill 12.1, Rigorous)**

      A.   must not only know her subject matter but also the strategies of content teaching

      B.   not only must know her subject matter but also the strategies of content teaching

      C.   must not know only her subject matter but also the strategies of content teaching

      D.   must know not only her subject matter but also the strategies of content teaching

The answer is D: "not only" must come directly after "know" because the intent is to create the clearest meaning link with the "but also" predicate section later in the sentence.

6.   **The coach offered her assistance but the athletes wanted to practice on their own. (Skill 12.1, Rigorous)**

      A.   The coach offered her assistance, however, the athletes wanted to practice on their own.

      B.   The coach offered her assistance: furthermore, the athletes wanted to practice on their own.

      C.   Having offered her assistance, the athletes wanted to practice on their own.

      D.   The coach offered her assistance; however, the athletes wanted to practice on their own.

      E.   The coach offered her assistance, and the athletes wanted to practice on their own.

The answer is D. A semicolon precedes a transitional adverb that introduces an independent clause. A is a comma splice. In B, the colon is used incorrectly since the second clause does not explain the first. In C, the opening clause confuses the meaning of the sentence. In D, the conjunction "and" is weak since the two ideas show contrast rather than an additional thought.

7.   Joe <u>didn't hardly know</u> his cousin Fred who'd had a rhinoplasty. (Skill 12.2, Easy)

   A. hardly did know his cousin Fred

   B. didn't know his cousin Fred hardly

   C. hardly knew his cousin Fred

   D. didn't know his cousin Fred

   E. didn't hardly know his cousin Fred

The answer is C: using the adverb "hardly" to modify the verb creates a negative, and adding "not" creates the dreaded double negative.

8.   <u>Mixing the batter for cookies</u>, the cat licked the Crisco from the cookie sheet. (Skill 12.2, Average Rigor)

   A. While mixing the batter for cookies

   B. While the batter for cookies was mixing

   C. While I mixed the batter for cookies

   D. While I mixed the cookies

   E. Mixing the batter for cookies

The answer is C. A and E give the impression that the cat was mixing the batter (it is a "dangling modifier"), B that the batter was mixing itself, and D lacks precision: it is the batter that was being mixed, not the cookies themselves.

9. Mr. Smith <u>respectfully submitted his resignation and had</u> a new job.
    (Skill 12.2, Average Rigor)

    A. respectfully submitted his resignation and has

    B. respectfully submitted his resignation before accepting

    C. respectfully submitted his resignation because of

    D. respectfully submitted his resignation and had

The answer is C. A eliminates any relationship of causality between submitting the resignation and having the new job. B just changes the sentence and does not indicate the fact that Mr. Smith had a new job before submitting his resignation. D means that Mr. Smith first submitted his resignation, and then got a new job.

10. Walt Whitman was famous for his composition, *Leaves of Grass* , serving as a nurse during the Civil War, and a devoted son (Skill 12.2, Rigorous)

    A. *Leaves of Grass,* his service as a nurse during the Civil War, and a devoted son

    B. composing *Leaves of Grass*, serving as a nurse during the Civil War, and being a devoted son

    C. his composition, *Leaves of Grass*, his nursing during the Civil War, and his devotion as a son

    D. his composition, *Leaves of Grass*, serving as a nurse during the Civil War, and a devoted son

    E. his composition, *Leaves of Grass*, serving as a nurse during the Civil War, and a devoted son

The answer is B: In order to be parallel, the sentence needs three gerunds. The other sentences use both gerunds and nouns, which is a lack of parallelism.

Part B

Directions: Select the best answer in each group of multiple choices.

11.   **The tendency to emphasize and value the qualities and peculiarities of life in a particular geographic area exemplifies (Skill 1.1, Easy)**

A. pragmatism.

B. regionalism.

C. pantheism.

D. abstractionism.

The answer is B. Pragmatism is a philosophical doctrine according to which there is no absolute truth. All truths change their trueness as their practical utility increases or decreases. The main representative of this movement is William James who in 1907 published *Pragmatism: A New Way for Some Old Ways of Thinking*. Pantheism is a philosophy according to which God is omnipresent in the world, everything is God and God is everything. The great representative of this sensibility is Spinoza. Also, the works of writers such as Wordsworth, Shelly and Emerson illustrate this doctrine. Abstract Expressionism is one of the most important movements in American art. It began in the 1940's with artists such as Willem de Kooning, Mark Rothko and Arshile Gorky. The paintings are usually large and non representational.

12.   **Which poet was a major figure in the Harlem Renaissance? (Skill 1.1, Easy)**

A. E. E. Cummings

B. Rita Dove

C. Margaret Atwood

D. Langston Hughes

The answer is D. Hughes' collection of verse includes *The Weary Blues* (1926), *Shakespeare in Harlem* (1942), and *The Panther and the Lash* (1967). E. E. Cummings used the lower case in the spelling of his name until the 1930s. He is also a celebrated poet, but is not a part of the Harlem Renaissance. Rita Dove is a respected African American poet, but she was born in 1952 and was not a part of the Harlem Renaissance. Margaret Atwood is a Canadian novelist.

13. **Which of the following writers did not win a Nobel Prize for literature? (Skill 1.1, Average Rigor)**

    A. Gabriel Garcia-Marquez of Colombia

    B. Nadine Gordimer of South Africa

    C. Pablo Neruda of Chile

    D. Alice Walker of the United States

The answer is D. Even though Alice Walker received the Pulitzer Price and the American Book Award for her best-known novel, *The Color Purple*, and is the author of six novels and three collections of short stories that have received wide critical acclaim, she has not yet received the Nobel Prize.

14. **What were two major characteristics of the first American literature? (Skill 1.1, Rigorous)**

    A. Vengefulness and arrogance

    B. Bellicosity and derision

    C. Oral delivery and reverence for the land

    D. Maudlin and self-pitying egocentricism

The answer is D. This characteristic can be seen in Captain John Smith's work, as well as William Bradford's and Michael Wigglesworth's works.

15. **Which of the following titles is known for its scathingly condemning tone? (Skill 1.3, Average Rigor)**

    A. Boris Pasternak's *Dr Zhivago*

    B. Albert Camus' *The Stranger*

    C. Henry David Thoreau's "On the Duty of Civil Disobedience"

    D. Benjamin Franklin's "Rules by Which a Great Empire May Be Reduced to a Small One"

The answer is D. In this work, Benjamin Franklin adopts a scathingly ironic tone to warn the British about the probable outcome in their colonies if they persist with their policies. These are discussed one by one in the text, and the absurdity of each is condemned.

16. **American colonial writers were primarily (Skill 1.3, Average Rigor)**

> A. Romanticists.
>
> B. Naturalists.
>
> C. Realists.
>
> D. Neo-classicists.

The answer is D. The early colonists mostly had been schooled in England, and even though their writing became quite American in content, their emphasis on clarity and balance in their language remained British. This literature reflects the lives of the early colonists, such as William Bradford's excerpts from 'The Mayflower Compact," Anne Bradstreet's poetry, and William Byrd's journal, *A History of the Dividing Line.*

17. **Which of the following is not a theme of Native American writing? (Skill 1.3, Average Rigor)**

> A. Emphasis on the hardiness of the human body and soul
>
> B. The strength of multi-cultural assimilation
>
> C. Contrition for the genocide of native peoples
>
> D. Remorse for the love of the Indian way of life

The answer is B. Native American literature was first a vast body of oral traditions from as early as before the fifteenth century. The characteristics include reverence for and awe of nature and the interconnectedness of the elements in the life cycle. The themes often reflect the hardiness of body and soul, remorse for the destruction of the Native American way of life, and the genocide of many tribes by the encroaching settlements of European Americans. These themes are still present in today's contemporary Native American literature, such as in the works of Duane Niatum, Paula Gunn Allen, Louise Erdrich, and N. Scott Momaday.

18. **To explore the relationship of literature to modern life, which of these activities would not enable students to explore comparable themes? (Skill 2.2 Average Rigor)**

    A. After studying various world events, such as the Palestinian-Israeli conflict, students write an updated version of *Romeo and Juliet* using modern characters and settings.

    B. Before studying *Romeo and Juliet*, students watch *West Side Story*.

    C. Students research the major themes of *Romeo and Juliet* by studying news stories and finding modern counterparts for the story.

    D. Students would explore compare the romantic themes of *Romeo and Juliet* and *The Taming of the Shrew*.

The answer is D. By comparing the two plays by Shakespeare, students will be focusing on the culture of the period in which the plays were written, not the themes. In A, students should be able to recognize modern parallels with current culture clashes. By comparing the *Romeo and Juliet* to *West Side Story*, students can study how themes are similar in two completely different historical periods. In C, students can study local, national, and international news for comparable stories and themes.

19. **The students in Mrs. Cline's seventh grade language arts class were invited to attend a performance of *Romeo and Juliet* presented by the drama class at the high school. To best prepare, they should (Skill 2.2, Average Rigor)**

    A. read the play as a homework exercise.

    B. read a synopsis of the plot and a biographical sketch of the author.

    C. examine a few main selections from the play to become familiar with the language and style of the author.

    D. read a condensed version of the story and practice attentive listening skills.

The answer is D. By reading a condensed version of the story, students will know the plot and therefore be able to follow the play on stage. It is also important for them to practice listening techniques such as one one-to-one tutoring and peer-assisted reading.

20. **Mr. Phillips is creating a unit to study *To Kill a Mockingbird* and wants to familiarize his high school freshmen with the attitudes and issues of the historical period. Which activity would familiarize students with the attitudes and issues of the Depression-era South? (Skill 2.2, Rigorous)**

　　A. Create a detailed timeline of 15-20 social, cultural, and political events that focus on race relations in the 1930s.

　　B. Research and report on the life of its author Harper Lee. Compare her background with the events in the book.

　　C. Watch the movie version and note language and dress.

　　D. Write a research report on the stock market crash of 1929 and its effects.

The answer is A. By identifying the social, cultural, and political events of the 1930s, students will better understand the attitudes and values of America during the time of the novel. While researching the author's life could add depth to their understanding of the novel, it is unnecessary to the appreciation of the novel by itself. The movie version is an accurate depiction of the novel's setting but it focuses on the events in the novel, not the external factors that fostered the conflict. The stock market crash and the subsequent Great Depression would be important to note on the timeline but students would be distracted from themes of the book by narrowing their focus to only these two events.

21. **In preparing a unit on twentieth-century immigration, you prepare a list of books for students to read. Which book would not be appropriate for this topic? (Skill 2.4, Easy)**

　　A. *Fox in Sox* by Dr. Seuss

　　B. *Exodus* by Leon Uris

　　C. *The Joy Luck Club* by Amy Tan

　　D. *Tortilla Flat* by John Steinbeck

The answer is A. Dr. Seuss' book is for preschoolers. Uris' book details the founding of Israel after World War II. Tan's novel contrasts her family's life in China and in the United States. Steinbeck's novel illustrates the plight of Mexican migrant workers.

22. Arthur Miller wrote *The Crucible* as a parallel to what twentieth-century event? (Skill 2.4, Average Rigor)

   A. Senator McCarthy's House Un-American Activities Committee Hearing

   B. The Cold War

   C. The fall of the Berlin Wall

   D. The Persian Gulf War

The answer is A. The episode of the seventeenth-century witch hunt in Salem, MA, gave Miller a storyline comparable to what was happening to persons suspected of communist beliefs in the 1950s.

23. Which of the writers below is a renowned black poet? (Skill 2.4, Average Rigor)

   A. Maya Angelou

   B. Sandra Cisneros

   C. Richard Wilbur

   D. Richard Wright

The answer is A. Among Maya Angelou's most famous works are *I Know Why the Caged Bird Sings* (1970), *And Still I Rise* (1978), and *All God's Children Need Traveling Shoes* (1986). Richard Wilbur is a poet and a translator of French dramatists Racine and Moliere, but he is not African American. Richard Wright is the African American author of novels such as *Native Son* and *Black Boy*. However, he was not a poet. Sandra Cisneros is a Mexican-American poet and fiction writer.

24. **What is considered the first work of English literature because it was written in the vernacular of the day? (Skill 3.1, Easy)**

    A. *Beowulf*

    B. *Le Morte d'Arthur*

    C. *The Faerie Queene*

    D. *Canterbury Tales*

The answer is D. Chaucer wrote the *Canterbury Tales* in the street language of medieval England. *Beowulf* was written during the Anglo-Saxon period and is a Teutonic saga. *Le Morte d'Arthur*, by Thomas Malory was written after Chaucer. Sir Edmund Spencer's *The Faerie Queene* was written during the Renaissance under the reign of Queen Elizabeth I.

25. **An extended metaphor comparing two very dissimilar things (one lofty one lowly) is a definition of a/an (Skill 3.1, Average)**

    A. antithesis.

    B. aphorism.

    C. apostrophe.

    D. conceit.

The answer is D. A conceit is an unusually far-fetched metaphor in which an object, person or situation is presented in a parallel and simpler analogue between two apparently very different things or feelings, one very sophisticated and one very ordinary, usually taken either from nature or a well known every day concept, familiar to both reader and author alike. The conceit was first developed by Petrarch and spread to England in the sixteenth century.

26. **"Every one must pass through Vanity Fair to get to the celestial city" is an allusion from a (Skill 3.1, Rigorous)**

    A. Chinese folk tale.

    B. Norse saga.

    C. British allegory.

    D. German fairy tale.

The answer is C. This is a reference to John Bunyan's *Pilgrim's Progress* from This World to That Which Is to Come (Part I, 1678; Part II, 1684), in which the hero, Christian, flees the City of Destruction and must undergo different trials and tests to get to the Celestial City.

27.   **Which sonnet form describes the following?   (Skill 3.1, Rigorous)**

My galley chargèd with forgetfulness
Through sharp seas in winter nights doth pass
'Twene rock and rock; and eke mine enemy, alas,
That is my lord, steereth with cruelness.
And every oar a thought in readiness
As though that death were light in such a case;
An endless wind doth tear the sail apace
Of forcèd sighs and trusty fearfulness.
A rain of tears, a cloud of dark disdain
Hath done the wearied cords great hindrance,
Wreathèd with error and eke with ignorance.
The stars be hid that led me to this pain,
Drownèd is reason that should me comfort,
And I remain despairing of the port.

A. Petrarchan or Italian sonnet

B. Shakespearian or
Elizabethan sonnet

C. Romantic sonnet

D. Spenserian sonnet

The answer is A. The Petrarchan sonnet, also known as Italian sonnet, is named after the Italian poet Petrarch (1304-74). It is divided into an octave rhyming abba abba and a sestet normally rhyming cdecde.

28. **Which of the following was not an effect of the Industrial Revolution in England during the nineteenth century? (Skill 3.3, Average)**

    A. Development of a middle class of industrialists and businessmen and a decline in the landed class of nobility and gentry

    B. Enormous shift from hand-produced goods to machine-produced ones and the loss of jobs

    C. The separation of husband and wife; gender roles began to be defined by the new configuration of labor in this new world order

    D. Naturalism, the literary, intellectual, and artistic movement occurred along with the Industrial movement in response to the increasing mechanization of society

The answer is D. In opposition to the mechanization of society, Romanticism stressed the importance of nature in art and language in contrast to the monstrous machines and factories.

29. **Charles Dickens, Robert Browning, and Robert Louis Stevenson were (Skill 4.1, Easy Rigor)**

    A. Victorians.

    B. Medievalists.

    C. Elizabethans.

    D. Absurdists.

The answer is A. The Victorian Period is remarkable for the diversity and quality of its literature. Robert Browning wrote chilling monologues such as "My Last Duchess," and long poetic narratives such as The Pied Piper of Hamlin. Robert Louis Stevenson wrote his works partly for young adults, whose imaginations were quite taken by his *Treasure Island* and *The Case of Dr. Jekyll and Mr. Hyde*. Charles Dickens tells of the misery of the time and the complexities of Victorian society in novels such as *Oliver Twist* or *Great Expectations*.

30. **The following lines from Robert Browning's poem "My Last Duchess" come from an example of what form of dramatic literature? (Skill 4.1, Rigorous)**

> That's my last Duchess painted on the wall,
> Looking as if she were alive. I call
> That piece a wonder, now: Frà Pandolf's hands
> Worked busily a day, and there she stands.
> Will 't please you sit and look at her?

A. Tragedy

B. Comic opera

C. Dramatis personae

D. Dramatic monologue

The answer is D. A dramatic monologue is a speech given by a character or narrator that reveals characteristics of the character or narrator. This form was first made popular by Robert Browning, a Victorian poet. Tragedy is a form of literature in which the protagonist is overwhelmed by opposing forces. Comic opera is a form of sung music based on a light or happy plot. Dramatis personae is the Latin phrase for the cast of a play.

31. **Which choice below best defines naturalism? (Skill 4.3, Rigorous)**

    A. A belief that the writer or artist should apply scientific objectivity in his/her observation and treatment of life without imposing value judgments.

    B. The doctrine that teaches that the existing world is the best to be hoped for.

    C. The doctrine which teaches that God is not a personality, but that all laws, forces and manifestations of the universe are God-related.

    D. A philosophical doctrine which professes that the truth of all knowledge must always be in question.

The answer is A. Naturalism is a movement that was started by French writers Jules and Edmond de Goncourt with their novel *Germinie Lacerteux* (1865), but its real leader is Emile Zola, who wanted to bring "a slice of life" to his readers. His saga, *Les Rougon-Macquart*, consists of 22 novels depicting various aspects of social life. Authors writing in English representative of this movement include George Moore and George Gissing in England, but the most important naturalist novel in English is Theodore Dreiser's *Sister Carrie*.

32. **Which of the following is not one of the novels by the Brontë sisters? (Skill 4.4, Easy)**

    A. *Jane Eyre*

    B. *Wuthering Heights*

    C. *Agnes Gray*

    D. *Pride and Prejudice*

The answer is D. Jane Austen wrote *Pride and Prejudice*. Charlotte Brontë wrote *Jane Eyre*, Emily Brontë wrote *Wuthering Heights*, and Anne Brontë wrote *Agnes Gray*.

33. **What is the salient literary feature of this excerpt from an epic? (Skill 5.1, Rigorous)**

> Hither the heroes and the nymphs resort,
> To taste awhile the pleasures of a court;
> In various talk th' instructive hours they passed,
> Who gave the ball, or paid the visit last;
> One speaks the glory of the British Queen,
> And one describes a charming Indian screen;
> A third interprets motions, looks, and eyes;
> At every word a reputation dies.

A. Sprung rhythm

B. Onomatopoeia

C. Heroic couplets

D. Motif

The answer is C. A couplet is a pair of rhyming verse lines, usually of the same length. It is one of the most widely used verse-forms in European poetry. Chaucer established the use of couplets in English, notably in the *Canterbury Tales*, using rhymed iambic pentameters (a metrical unit of verse having one unstressed syllable followed by one stressed syllable) later known as heroic couplets. Other authors who used heroic couplets include Ben Jonson, Dryden, and especially Alexander Pope, who became the master of them.

34. **Which events contributed to the invention of writing, thus making possible the emergence of literature as well as the development of human civilization? (Skill 5.2, Average)**

   A. Domestication of animals, the development of agriculture, and the establishment of an agricultural surplus.

   B. Development of the printing press and the subsequent growth of literacy in the ruling classes.

   C. The travels of the nomadic tribes who spread tales through oral tradition and the development of papyrus.

   D. Growth of towns and cities, religious education, and development of local government.

The answer is A. Between 7000 B.C. and 3000 B.C., these three events allowed the roving groups of hunters and gatherers who had up until then existed in pockets all over the world to evolve into larger, stationary communities. These nomads settled along the Tigris and Euphrates rivers, and it was the Sumerians from this area who created the first written language.

35. **Which of the following statements is not true about Greek drama? (Skill 5.3, Rigorous)**

   A. Greek plays were performed as part of a religious festival honoring Dionysus.

   B. The chorus was a group of men in masks who would sing, dance, and often interact with the actors in the play.

   C. Many of the plots were based on ancient myths although dramatists were known to exercise creativity.

   D. Greek plays were categorized as comedies, tragedies, or satires.

The answer is D. Although the Greeks wrote satyr plays, these were not taken very seriously; satires became more popular as part of the Roman drama tradition. Greek plays were tragedies, where the protagonist, usually a god, hero or royalty, is defeated, and comedies, where the characters were common people who usually improved their situations.

36. **Who was Dante's guide through the Inferno in *The Divine Comedy*? (Skill 5.4, Easy)**

    A. The poetic muse Beatrice

    B. Jesus of Nazareth

    C. The Latin poet Virgil

    D. The Greek philosopher Socrates

The answer is C. Beatrice, Dante's ideal woman, guides him through Heaven. Virgil, condemned to Hell because he lived before Christianity, represents human reason and, while inept at times, he does assist Dante.

37. **A traditional, anonymous story, ostensibly having a historical basis, usually explaining some phenomenon of nature or aspect of creation, defines a (Skill 5.5, Easy)**

    A. proverb.

    B. idyll.

    C. myth.

    D. epic.

The answer is C. A myth is usually traditional and anonymous and e
plains natural and supernatural phenomena. Myths are usually about creation, divinity, the significance of life and death, and natural phenomena.

38.   Hoping to take advantage of the popularity of the Harry Potter series, a teacher develops a unit on mythology comparing the story and characters of Greek and Roman myths with the story and characters of the Harry Potter books. Which of these is a commonality that would link classical literature to popular fiction? (Skill 5.5, Rigorous)

A. The characters are gods in human form with human-like characteristics.

B. The settings are realistic places in the world where the characters interact as humans would.

C. The themes center on the universal truths of love and hate and fear.

D. The heroes in the stories are young males and only they can overcome the opposing forces.

The answer is C. Although the gods in Greek and Roman myths take human form, they are immortal as gods must be. The characters in Harry Potter may be wizards, but they are not immortal. Although the settings in these stories have familiar associations, their worlds are vastly different from those inhabited by mortals and Muggles. While male heroes may dominate the action, the females (Hera, Dianna, and Hermione) are powerful as well.

39.   Considered one of the first feminist plays, this Ibsen drama ends with a gunshot, symbolizing the lead character's emancipation from traditional societal norms. (Skill 6.1, Easy)

A. *The Wild Duck*

B. *Hedda Gabler*

C. *Ghosts*

D. *The Doll's House*

The answer is D. Nora in *The Doll's House* leaves her husband and her children when she realizes her husband is not the man she thought he was. Hedda Gabler, another feminist icon, shoots herself. *The Wild Duck* deals with the conflict between idealism and family secrets. *Ghosts*, considered one of Ibsen's most controversial plays, deals with many social ills, some of which include alcoholism, incest, and religious hypocrisy.

40. **The writing of Russian naturalists is (Skill 6.1, Average Rigor)**

     A. optimistic.

     B. pessimistic.

     C. satirical.

     D. whimsical.

The answer is B. Although the movement, which originated with the critic Vissarion Belinsky, was particularly strong in the 1840s, it can be said that the works of Dostoevsky, Tolstoy, Chekov, Turgenev and Pushkin owe much to it. These authors' works are among the best in international literature, yet are shrouded in stark pessimism. Tolstoy's *Anna Karenina* or Dostoevsky's *Crime and Punishment* are good examples of this dark outlook.

41. **Which of the following is the best definition of existentialism? (Skill 6.1, Rigorous)**

     A. The philosophical doctrine that matter is the only reality and that everything in the world, including thought, will and feeling, can be explained only in terms of matter.

     B. Philosophy which views things as they should be or as one would wish them to be.

     C. A philosophical and literary movement, variously religious and atheistic, stemming from Kierkegaard and represented by Sartre.

     D. The belief that all events are determined by fate and are hence inevitable.

The answer is C. Even though there are other very important thinkers in the movement known as Existentialism, such as Camus and Merleau-Ponty, Sartre remains the main figure in this movement.

42. **Latin words that entered the English language during the Elizabethan age include (Skill 6.2, Average Rigor)**

    A. allusion, education, and esteem

    B. vogue and mustache

    C. canoe and cannibal

    D. alligator, cocoa, and armadillo

The answer is A. These words reflect the Renaissance interest in the classical world and the study of ideas. The words in B are French derivation, and the words in C and D are more modern with younger etymologies.

43. **Which is an untrue statement about a theme in literature? (Skill 7.2, Average Rigor)**

    A. The theme is always stated directly somewhere in the text.

    B. The theme is the central idea in a literary work.

    C. All parts of the work (such as plot, setting, and mood) should contribute to the theme in some way.

    D. By analyzing the various elements of the work, the reader should be able to arrive at an indirectly stated theme.

The answer is A. The theme may be stated directly, but it can also be implicit in various aspects of the work, such as the interaction between characters, symbolism, or description.

44.   **Which of the following is not a characteristic of a fable? (Skill 7.4, Easy)**

A. Animals that feel and talk like humans.

B. Happy solutions to human dilemmas.

C. Teaches a moral or standard for behavior.

D. Illustrates specific people or groups without directly naming them.

The answer is D. A fable is a short tale with animals, humans, gods, or even inanimate objects as characters. Fables often conclude with a moral, delivered in the form of an epigram (a short, witty, and ingenious statement in verse). Fables are among the oldest forms of writing in human history: it appears in Egyptian papyri of c1500 BC. The most famous fables are those of Aesop, a Greek slave living in about 600 BC. In India, the *Panchatantra* appeared in the third century. The most famous modern fables are those of seventeenth century French poet Jean de La Fontaine.

45.   **What is not a characteristic of an effective editorial cartoon? (Skill 7.5, Easy)**

A. It presents a message or point of view concerning people, events, or situations using caricature and symbolism to convey the cartoonist's ideas

B. It will have wit and humor, which is usually obtained by exaggeration that is slick and not used merely for comic effect.

C. It will also have a foundation in truth; that is, the characters must be recognizable to the viewer and the point of the drawing must have some basis in fact even if it has a philosophical bias.

D. It will seek to reflect the editorial opinion of the newspaper that carries it.

The answer is D. Editorial cartoons do not necessarily reflect the opinions of the newspaper that publishes it.

46. In classic tragedy, a protagonist's defeat is brought about by a tragic flaw which is called (Skill 7.6 Rigorous)

    A. hubris

    B. hamartia

    C. catharsis

    D. the skene

The answer is B, *harmartia*. Hubris is excessive pride, a type of tragic flaw. Catharsis is an emotional purging the character feels. *Skene* is the Greek word for scene.

47. Which poem is typified as a villanelle? (Skill 7.8, Rigorous)

    A. "Do not go gentle into that good night"

    B. "Dover Beach"

    C. *Sir Gawain and the Green Knight*

    D. *Pilgrim's Progress*

The answer is A. This poem by Dylan Thomas typifies the villanelle because it was written as such. A villanelle is a form which was invented in France in the sixteenth century, and used mostly for pastoral songs. It has an uneven number (usually five) of tercets rhyming aba, with a final quatrain rhyming abaa. This poem is the most famous villanelle written in English. "Dover Beach" by Matthew Arnold is not a villanelle, while *Sir Gawain and the Green Knight* was written in alliterative verse by an unknown author usually referred to as The Pearl Poet around 1370. *The Pilgrim's Progress* is a prose allegory by John Bunyan.

48.   The technique of starting a narrative at a significant point in the action and then developing the story through flashbacks is called (Skill 7.4, Rigorous)

A. in medias res

B. octava rima

C. irony

D. suspension of willing disbelief

The answer is A, as its Latin translation suggests: in the middle of things. An octava rima is a specific eight-line stanza of poetry whose rhyme scheme is abab+abcc. Lord Byron's *Don Juan* is written in octava rima. Irony is an unexpected disparity between what is stated and what is really implied by the author. Benjamin Franklin's "Rules by Which A Great Empire May be Reduced to a Small One" and Voltaire's tales are texts which are written using irony. Drama is what Coleridge calls "the willing suspension of disbelief for the moment, which constitutes poetic faith."

49.   Which is the best definition of free verse, or *vers libre*? (Skill 7.9, Average Rigor)

A. Poetry which consists of an unaccented syllable followed by an unaccented sound.

B. Short lyrical poetry written to entertain but with an instructive purpose.

C. Poetry which does not have a uniform pattern of rhythm.

D. A poem which tells the story and has a plot

The answer is C. Free verse does not have a uniform pattern of rhythm

50. **Which of the following is a characteristic of blank verse? (Skill 7.9, Average Rigor)**

    A. Meter in iambic pentameter

    B. Clearly specified rhyme scheme

    C. Lack of figurative language

    D. Unspecified rhythm

The answer is A. An iamb is a metrical unit of verse having one unstressed syllable followed by one stressed syllable. This is the most commonly used metrical verse in English and American poetry. An iambic pentameter is a ten-syllable verse made of five of these metrical units, either rhymed as in sonnets, or unrhymed in blank verse.

51. **The substitution of "went to his rest" for "died" is an example of a/an (Skill 7.10, Easy)**

    A. bowdlerism.

    B. jargon.

    C. euphemism.

    D. malapropism.

The answer is C. A euphemism replaces an unpleasant or offensive word or expression by a more agreeable one. It also alludes to distasteful things in a pleasant manner, and it can even paraphrase offensive texts. Bowdlerism is named after Thomas Bowdler who excised from Shakespeare what he considered vulgar and offensive. Jargon is a specialized language used by a particular group, particularly in various professions. Named after Mrs. Malaprop, a character in a play by Richard Sheridan, a malapropism is a misuse of words, often to comical effect. Mrs. Malaprop once said ". . . she's as headstrong as an allegory on the banks of Nile" misusing "allegory" for "alligator."

52.   **The literary device of personification is used in which example below? (Skill 7.10, Average Rigor)**

A.   "Beg me no beggary by soul or parents, whining dog!"

B.   "Happiness sped through the halls cajoling as it went."

C.   "O wind thy horn, thou proud fellow."

D.   "And that one talent which is death to hide."

The answer is B. "Happiness," an abstract concept, is described as if it were a person.

53.   **What syntactic device is most evident from Abraham Lincoln's "Gettysburg Address"? (Skill 7.10, Rigorous)**

It is rather for us to be here dedicated to the great task remaining before us -- that from these honored dead we take increased devotion to that cause for which they gave the last full measure of devotion -- that we here highly resolve that these dead shall not have died in vain -- that this nation, under God, shall have a new birth of freedom -- and that government of the people, by the people, for the people, shall not perish from the earth.

A.   Affective connotation

B.   Informative denotations

C.   Allusion

D.   Parallelism

The answer is D. Parallelism is the repetition of grammatical structure. In speeches such as this one as well as speeches of Martin Luther King, Jr., parallel structure creates a rhythm and balance of related ideas. Lincoln's repetition of clauses beginning with "that" ties four examples back "to the great task." Connotation is the emotional attachment of words; denotation is the literal meaning of words. Allusion is a reference to a historic event, person, or place.

54. **How will literature help students in a science class understand the following passage? (Skill 7.10, Rigorous)**

> Just as was the case more than three decades ago, we are still sailing between the Scylla of deferring surgery for too long and risking irreversible left ventricular damage and sudden death, and the Charybdas of operating too early and subjecting the patient to the early risks of operation and the later risks resulting from prosthetic valves.
> --E. Braunwald, *European Heart Journal*, July 2000

A. They will recognize the allusion to Scylla and Charybdas from Greek mythology and understand that the medical community has to select one of two unfavorable choices.

B. They will recognize the allusion to sailing and understand its analogy to doctors as sailors navigating unknown waters.

C. They will recognize that the allusion to Scylla and Charybdas refers to the two islands in Norse mythology where sailors would find themselves shipwrecked and understand how the doctors feel isolated by their choices.

D. They will recognize the metaphor of the heart and relate it to Eros, the character in Greek mythology who represents love. Eros was the love child of Scylla and Charybdas.

The answer is A. Scylla and Charybdas were two sea monsters guarding a narrow channel of water. Sailors trying to elude one side would face danger by sailing too close to the other side. The allusion indicates two equally undesirable choices.

55. **Which is not a biblical allusion? (Skill 7.10, Rigorous)**

   A. The patience of Job

   B. Thirty pieces of silver

   C. "Man proposes; God disposes"

   D. "Suffer not yourself to be betrayed by a kiss"

The answer is C. This saying is attributed to Thomas à Kempis (1379-1471) in his *Imitation of Christ*, Book 1, Chapter 19. Anyone who exhibits the patience of Job is being compared to the Old Testament biblical figure who retained his faith despite being beset by a series of misfortunes. "Thirty pieces of silver" refers to the amount of money paid to Judas to identify Jesus. Used by Patrick Henry, the quote in D is a biblical reference to Judas' betrayal of Jesus by a kiss.

56. **Using the selection below from Edgar Alan Poe's "The Tell-Tale Heart," what form of literary criticism would you introduce to high school students? (Skill 8.1, Average)**

   "And have I not told you that what you mistake for madness is but over-acuteness of the sense? --now, I say, there came to my ears a low, dull, quick sound, such as a watch makes when enveloped in cotton. I knew that sound well, too. It was the beating of the old man's heart. It increased my fury, as the beating of a drum stimulates the soldier into courage."

   A. Marxist

   B. Feminist

   C. Psychoanalytic

   D. Classic

The answer is C. Poe's writings focus on the workings of the human mind and would provide a clear introduction of Freudian literary analysis. Marxist criticism focuses on class conflict and the exploitation of the workers, which is not evident in this short story. Feminist criticism focuses on gender roles, which is also not obvious in this short story. Classic criticism is not a recognized type of literary criticism; however, this story could be analyzed according to the New Criticism where the story would be studied as a work of literature.

57.   **In the following poem, what literary movement is reflected? (Skill 8.3, Rigorous)**

"My Heart Leaps Up" by William Wordsworth

My heart leaps up when I behold
  A rainbow in the sky:
So was it when my life began;
So is it now I am a man;
So be it when I shall grow old,
  Or let me die!
The Child is father of the Man;
And I could wish my days to be
Bound each to each by natural piety

A. Neo-classicism

B. Victorian literature

C. Romanticism

D. Naturalism

The answer is C. The Romantic period of the nineteenth century is known for its emphasis on feelings, emotions, and passions. William Wordsworth and William Blake were two notable poets from this period. In the neoclassicism of the previous period, the literature echoed the classical ideals of proportion, common sense, and reason over raw emotion and imagination, and the purpose was more didactic than celebratory. The Victorian period of the late nineteenth century exerted more restraint on emotions and feelings. In naturalistic writing, authors depict the world more harshly and more objectively.

58. **What is the best course of action when a child refuses to complete a reading/ literature assignment on the grounds that it is morally objectionable? (Skill 8.4, Average Rigor)**

    A. Speak with the parents and explain the necessity of studying this work

    B. Encourage the child to sample some of the text before making a judgment

    C. Place the child in another teacher's class where they are studying an acceptable work

    D. Provide the student with alternative selections that cover the same performance standards that the rest of the class is learning.

The answer is D. In the case of a student finding a reading offensive, it is the responsibility of the teacher to assign another title. As a general rule, it is always advisable to notify parents if a particularly sensitive piece is to be studied.

59. **Students have been asked to write a research paper on automobiles and have brainstormed a number of questions they will answer based on their research findings. Which of the following is not an interpretive question to guide research? (Skill 8.4, Rigorous)**

    A. Who were the first ten automotive manufacturers in the United States?

    B. What types of vehicles will be used fifty years from now?

    C. How do automobiles manufactured in the United States compare and contrast with each other?

    D. What do you think is the best solution for the fuel shortage?

The answer is A. The question asks for objective facts. B is a prediction that asks how something will look or be in the future, based on the way it is now. C asks for similarities and differences, which is a higher-level research activity that requires analysis. D is a judgment question that requires informed opinion.

60. **Recognizing empathy in literature is mostly a/an (Skill 8.4, Rigorous)**

    A. emotional response.

    B. interpretive response.

    C. critical response.

    D. evaluative response.

The answer is C. In critical responses, students make value judgments about the quality and atmosphere of a text. Through class discussion and written assignments, students react to and assimilate a writer's style and language.

61. **Which sentence below best minimizes the impact of bad news? (Skill 9.1, Rigorous)**

    A. We have denied you permission to attend the event.

    B. Although permission to attend the event cannot be given, you are encouraged to buy the video.

    C. Although you cannot attend the event, we encourage you to buy the video.

    D. Although attending the event is not possible, watching the video is an option.

The answer is B. Subordinating the bad news and using passive voice minimizes the impact of the bad news. In A, the sentence is active voice and thus too direct. The word "denied" sets a negative tone. In C, the bad news is subordinated but it is still active voice with negative wording. In D, the sentence is too unclear.

62. **Which word in the following sentence is a bound morpheme: "The quick brown fox jumped over the lazy dog"? (Skill 9.1, Rigorous)**

   A. The

   B. fox

   C. lazy

   D. jumped

The answer is D. The suffix *–ed* is an affix that cannot stand alone as a unit of meaning. Thus it is bound to the free morpheme "jump." "The" is always an unbound morpheme since no suffix or prefix can alter its meaning. As written, "fox" and "lazy" are unbound but their meaning is changed with affixes, such as "foxes" or "laziness."

63. **The Elizabethans wrote in (Skill 9.2, Easy)**

   A. Celtic

   B. Old English

   C. Middle English

   D. Modern English

The answer is D. There is no document written in Celtic in England, and a work such as *Beowulf* is representative of Old English in the eighth century. It is also the earliest Teutonic written document. Before the fourteenth century, little literature is known to have appeared in Middle English, which had absorbed many words from the Norman French spoken by the ruling class, but at the end of the fourteenth century, there appeared the works of Chaucer, John Gower, and the novel *Sir Gawain and the Green King*. The Elizabethans wrote in modern English; they imported the Petrarchan, or Italian, sonnet, which Sir Thomas Wyatt and Sir Philip Sydney illustrated in their works. Sir Edmund Spencer invented his own version of the Italian sonnet and wrote *The Faerie Queene*. Other literature of the time includes the hugely important works of Shakespeare and Marlowe.

64. **The synonyms *gyro*, *hero*, and *submarine* reflect which influence on language usage? (Skill 9.2, Average Rigor)**

    A. Social

    B. Geographical

    C. Historical

    D. Personal

The answer is B. They are interchangeable but their use depends on the region of the United States, not on the social class of the speaker. Nor is there any historical context around any of them. The usage can be personal, but will most often vary with the region.

65. **Overcrowded classes prevent the individual attention needed to facilitate language development. This drawback can be best overcome by (Skill 9.2, Average Rigor)**

    A. dividing the class into independent study groups.

    B. assigning more study time at home.

    C. using more drill practice in class.

    D. team teaching.

The answer is A. Dividing a class into small groups fosters peer enthusiasm and evaluation, and sets an atmosphere of warmth and enthusiasm. It is much preferable to divide the class into smaller study groups than to lecture, which will bore students and therefore fail to facilitate curricular goals. Also, it is preferable to do this than to engage the whole class in a general teacher-led discussion because such discussion favors the loquacious and inhibits the shy.

66. **Which of the following is not true about the English language? (Skill 9.2, Average Rigor)**

    A. English is the easiest language to learn.

    B. English is the least inflected language.

    C. English has the most extensive vocabulary of any language.

    D. English originated as a Germanic tongue.

The answer is A. Just like any other language, English has inherent difficulties which make it difficult to learn, even though English has no declensions such as those found in Latin, Greek, or contemporary Russian, or a tonal system such Chinese.

67. **What was responsible for the standardizing of dialects across America in the twentieth century? (Skill 9.2, Rigorous)**

    A. With the immigrant influx, American became a melting pot of languages and cultures.

    B. Trains enabled people to meet other people of different languages and cultures.

    C. Radio, and later, television, used actors and announcers who spoke without pronounced dialects.

    D. Newspapers and libraries developed programs to teach people to speak English with an agreed-upon common dialect.

The answer is C. The growth of immigration in the early part of the twentieth century created pockets of language throughout the country. Coupled with regional differences already in place, the number of dialects grew. Transportation enabled people to move to different regions where languages and dialects continued to merge. With the growth of radio and television, however, people were introduced to a standardized dialect through actors and announcers who spoke so that anyone across American could understand them. Newspapers and libraries never developed programs to standardize spoken English.

68. **Which event triggered the beginning of Modern English? (Skill 9.3, Average Rigor)**

    A. Conquest of England by the Normans in 1066

    B. Introduction of the printing press to the British Isles

    C. Publication of Samuel Johnson's lexicon.

    D. American Revolution

The answer is B. With the arrival of the written word, reading matter became mass produced, so the public tended to adopt the speech and writing habits printed in books and the language became more stable.

69. **Which of the following is the least effective procedure for promoting consciousness of audience? (Skill 9.4, Average Rigor)**

    A. Pairing students during the writing process

    B. Reading all rough drafts before the students write the final copies

    C. Having students compose stories or articles for publication in school literary magazines or newspapers

    D. Writing letters to friends or relatives

The answer is B. Reading all rough drafts will not encourage the students to take control of their text and might even inhibit their creativity. On the contrary, pairing students will foster their sense of responsibility, and having them compose stories for literary magazines will boost their self esteem as well as their organization skills.

70. **In literature, evoking feelings of pity or compassion is to create (Skill 10.1, Average Rigor)**

    A. colloquy.

    B. irony.

    C. pathos.

    D. paradox

The answer is C. A very well known example of pathos is Desdemona's death in *Othello*, but there are many other examples of pathos.

71. **Identify the type of appeal used by Molly Ivins in this excerpt from her essay "Get a Knife, Get a Dog, But Get Rid of Guns." (Skill 10.1, Rigorous)**

    As a civil libertarian, I, of course, support the Second Amendment. And I believe it means exactly what it says:

    A well regulated militia being necessary to the security of a free state, the right of the people to keep and bear arms shall not be infringed.

    A. Ethical

    B. Emotional

    C. Rational

    D. Literary

The answer is A. An ethical appeal is using the credentials of a reliable and trustworthy authority. In this case, Ivins cites the Constitution. Pathos is an emotional appeal, and logos is a rational appeal. Literature might appeal to you, but it's not a rhetorical appeal.

72. **Which part of a classical argument is illustrated in this excerpt from the essay "What Should Be Done About Rock Lyrics?" (Skill 10.3, Rigorous)**

> But violence against women is greeted by silence. It shouldn't be. This does not mean censorship, or book (or record) burning. In a society that protects free expression, we understand a lot of stuff will float up out of the sewer. Usually, we recognize the ugly stuff that advocates violence against any group as the garbage it is, and we consider its purveyors as moral lepers. We hold our nose and tolerate it, but we speak out against the values it proffers.
> --"What Should Be Done About Rock Lyrics?" Caryl Rivers

A. Narration

B. Confirmation

C. Refutation and concession

D. Summation

The answer is C. The author refutes the idea of censorship and concedes that society tolerates offensive lyrics as part of our freedom of speech. Narration provides background material to produce an argument. In confirmation, the author details the argument with claims that support the thesis. In summation, the author concludes the argument by offering the strongest solution.

73.   In preparing students for their oral presentations, the instructor provided all of these guidelines, except one. Which is not an effective guideline? (Skill 10.5, Average Rigor)

   A. Even if you are using a lectern, feel free to move about. This will connect you to the audience.

   B. Your posture should be natural, not stiff. Keep your shoulders toward the audience.

   C. Gestures can help communicate as long as you don't overuse them or make them distracting.

   D. You can avoid eye contact if you focus on your notes. This will make you appear more knowledgeable.

The answer is D. Although many people are nervous about making eye contact, they should focus on two or three people at a time. Body language, such as movement, posture, and gestures, helps the speaker connect to the audience.

74.   The arrangement and relationship of words in sentences or sentence structures best describes (Skill 10.6, Rigorous)

   A. style.

   B. discourse.

   C. thesis.

   D. syntax.

The answer is D. Syntax is the grammatical structure of sentences. Style is the manner of expression of writing or speaking. Discourse is an extended expression of thought through either oral or written communication. A thesis is the unifying main idea that can be either explicit or implicit.

75. **Which of the following sentences contains a capitalization error? (Skill 10.7, Average Rigor)**

    A. The commander of the English navy was Admiral Nelson

    B. Napoleon was the president of the French First Republic

    C. Queen Elizabeth II is the Monarch of the British Empire

    D. William the Conqueror led the Normans to victory over the British

The answer is C. Words that represent titles and offices are not capitalized unless used with a proper name. This is not the case here.

76. **In a class of non-native speakers of English, which type of activity will help students the most? (Skill 10.9, Rigorous)**

    A. Have students make oral presentations so that they can develop a phonological awareness of sounds.

    B. Provide students more writing opportunities to develop their written communication skills.

    C. Encourage students to listen to the new language on television and radio.

    D. Provide a variety of methods to develop speaking, writing, and reading skills.

The answer is A. Research indicates that non-native speakers of English develop stronger second language skills by understanding the phonological differences in spoken words.

77. **Oral debate is most closely associated with which form of discourse? (Skill 10.10, Average Rigor)**

    A. Description

    B. Exposition

    C. Narration

    D. Persuasion

The answer is D. It is extremely important to be convincing while having an oral debate. This is why persuasion is so important, because this is the way that you can influence your audience.

78. **Which of the following type of questions will not stimulate higher-level critical thinking? (Skill 10.10, Rigorous)**

    A. A hypothetical question

    B. An open-ended question

    C. A close-ended question

    D. A judgment question

The answer is C. A close-ended question requires a simple answer, like a "yes" or "no." An open-ended question can generate an extended response that would require critical thinking. Both a hypothetical question and a judgment question require deeper thinking skills.

79.   In presenting a report to peers about the effects of Hurricane Katrina on New Orleans, the students wanted to use various media in their argument to persuade their peers that more needed to be done. Which of these would be the most effective? Skill 10.11, Rigorous)

    A.   A PowerPoint presentation showing the blueprints of the levees before the flood and redesigned now for current construction..

    B.   A collection of music clips made by the street performers in the French Quarter before and after the flood.

    C.   A recent video showing the areas devastated by the floods and the current state of rebuilding.

    D.   A collection of recordings of interviews made by the various government officials and local citizens affected by the flooding.

The answer is C. For maximum impact, a video would offer dramatic scenes of the devastated areas. A video by its very nature is more dynamic than a static PowerPoint presentation. Further, the condition of the levees would not provide as much impetus for change as seeing the devastated areas. Oral messages such as music clips and interviews provide another way of supplementing the message but, again, they are not as dynamic as video.

80.   Mr. Ledbetter has instructed his students to prepare a slide presentation that illustrates an event in history. Students are to include pictures, graphics, media clips and links to resources. What competencies will students exhibit at the completion of this project? Skill 10.11, Rigorous)

    A.   Analyze the impact of society on media.

    B.   Recognize the media's strategies to inform and persuade.

    C.   Demonstrate strategies and creative techniques to prepare presentations using a variety of media.

    D.   Identify the aesthetic effects of a media presentation.

The answer is B. Students will have learned how to use various media to convey a unified message.

81. **What is the common advertising technique used by these advertising slogans? (Skill 10.11, Rigorous)**

"It's everywhere you want to be." Visa
"Have it your way." - Burger King
"When you care enough to send the very best" - Hallmark
"Be all you can be" – U.S. Army

A. Peer Approval

B. Rebel

C. Individuality

D. Escape

The answer is C. All of these ads associate products with people who can think and act for themselves. Products are linked to individual decision making. With peer approval, the ads would associate their products with friends and acceptance. For rebelling, the ads would associates products with behaviors or lifestyles that oppose society's norms. Escape would suggest the appeal of getting away from it all.

82. **Which of the following is most true of expository writing? (Skill 11.1, Easy)**

A. It is mutually exclusive of other forms of discourse.

B. It can incorporate other forms of discourse in the process of providing supporting details.

B. It should never employ informal expression.

D. It should only be scored with a summative evaluation.

The answer is B. Expository writing sets forth an explanation or an argument about any subject.

83.   **Explanatory or informative discourse is (Skill 11.1, Average Rigor)**

A. exposition.

B. narration.

C. persuasion.

D. description.

The answer is A. Exposition sets forth a systematic explanation of any subject. It can also introduce the characters of a literary work, and their situations in the story.

84.   **Which of the following is not one of the four forms of discourse? (Skill 11.1, Average Rigor)**

A. Exposition

B. Description

C. Rhetoric

D. Persuasion

The answer is C. Rhetoric is an umbrella term for techniques of expressive and effective speech. Rhetorical figures are ornaments of speech such as anaphora, antithesis, metaphor, etc. The other three choices are specific forms of discourse.

85.　Middle and high school students are more receptive to studying grammar and syntax (Skill 11.2, Average Rigor)

A.　through worksheets and end of lessons practices in textbooks.

B.　through independent, homework assignments.

C.　through analytical examination of the writings of famous authors.

D.　through application to their own writing.

The answer is D. At this age, students learn grammatical concepts best through practical application in their own writing.

86.　**In general, the most serious drawback of using a computer in writing is that (Skill 11.2, Average Rigor)**

A.　the copy looks so good that students tend to overlook major mistakes.

B.　the spell check and grammar programs discourage students from learning proper spelling and mechanics.

C.　the speed with which corrections can be made detracts from the exploration and contemplation of composing.

D.　the writer loses focus by concentrating on the final product rather than the details.

The answer is C. Because the process of revising is very quick with the computer, it can discourage contemplation, exploring, and examination, which are very important in the process of writing.

87. **Modeling is a practice that requires students to (Skill 11.2, Average Rigor)**

    A. create a style unique to their own language capabilities.

    B. emulate the writing of professionals.

    C. paraphrase passages from good literature.

    D. peer evaluate the writings of other students.

The answer is B. Modeling has students analyze the writing of a professional writer and try to reach the same level of syntactical, grammatical and stylistic mastery as the author whom they are studying.

88. **In preparing a report about William Shakespeare, students are asked to develop a set of interpretive questions to guide their research. Which of the following would not be classified as an interpretive question? (Skill 11.2, Rigorous)**

    A. What would be different today if Shakespeare had not written his plays?

    B. How will the plays of Shakespeare affect future generations?

    C. How does the Shakespeare view nature in *A Midsummer's Night Dream* and *Much Ado About Nothing*?

    D. During the Elizabethan age, what roles did young boys take in dramatizing Shakespeare's plays?

The answer is D. This question requires research into the historical facts; Shakespeare in love notwithstanding, women did not act In Shakespeare's plays, and their parts were taken by young boys. A and B are hypothetical questions requiring students to provide original thinking and interpretation. C requires comparison and contrast which are interpretive skills.

89. **In this paragraph from a student essay, identify the sentence that provides a detail. (Skill 11.3 Rigorous)**

> (1) The poem concerns two different personality types and the human relation between them. (2) Their approach to life is totally different. (3) The neighbor is a very conservative person who follows routines. (4) He follows the traditional wisdom of his father and his father's father. (5) The purpose in fixing the wall and keeping their relationship separate is only because it is all he knows.

   A. Sentence 1

   B. Sentence 3

   C. Sentence 4

   D. Sentence 5

The answer is C. Sentence 4 provides a detail to sentence 3 by explaining how the neighbor follows routine. Sentence 1 is the thesis sentence, which is the main idea of the paragraph. Sentence 3 provides an example to develop that thesis. Sentence 4 is a reason that explains why.

90. **If a student uses slang and expletives, what is the best course of action to take in order to improve the student's formal communication skills? (Skill 11.4, Average Rigor)**

   A. Ask the student to paraphrase writing, that is, translate it into language appropriate for the school principal to read.

   B. Refuse to read the student's papers until he conforms to a more literate style.

   C. Ask the student to read his work aloud to the class for peer evaluation.

   D. Rewrite the flagrant passages to show the student the right form of expression.

The answer is A. Asking the student to write for a specific audience will help him become more involved in his writing. If he continues writing to the same audience—the teacher—he will continue seeing writing as just another assignment and he will not apply grammar, vocabulary and syntax the way they should be. By rephrasing his own writing, the student will learn to write for a different public.

91. **Which of the following should not be included in the opening paragraph of an informative essay? (Skill 11.6, Easy)**

    A. Thesis sentence

    B. Details and examples supporting the main idea

    C. Broad general introduction to the topic

    D. A style and tone that grabs the reader's attention

The answer is B. The introductory paragraph should introduce the topic, capture the reader's interest, state the thesis and prepare the reader for the main points in the essay. Details and examples, however, should be given in the second part of the essay, so as to help develop the thesis presented at the end of the introductory paragraph, following the inverted triangle method consisting of a broad general statement followed by some information, and then the thesis at the end of the paragraph.

92. **The following passage is written from which point of view? (Skill 11.8, Easy)**

    > As she mused the pitiful vision of her mother's life laid its spell on the very quick of her being –that life of commonplace sacrifices closing in final craziness. She trembled as she heard again her mother's voice saying constantly with foolish insistence: *Derevaun Seraun*! *Derevaun Seraun*!*
    > * "The end of pleasure is pain!" (Gaelic)

    A. First person, narrator

    B. Second person, direct address

    C. Third person, omniscient

    D. First person, omniscient

The answer is C. The passage is clearly in the third person (the subject is "she"), and it is omniscient since it gives the characters' inner thoughts.

93.   In the phrase "The Cabinet conferred with the President," Cabinet is an example of a/an (Skill 11.9, Rigorous)

        A. metonym

        B. synecdoche

        C. metaphor

        D. allusion

The answer is B. In a synecdoche, a whole is referred to by naming a part of it. A synecdoche can stand for a whole of which it is a part.

94.   Which of the following is not a fallacy in logic? (Skill 11.10, Rigorous)

        A. All students in Ms. Suarez's fourth period class are bilingual.
           Beth is in Ms. Suarez's fourth period.
           Beth is bilingual.

        B. All bilingual students are in Ms. Suarez's class.
           Beth is in Ms. Suarez's fourth period.
           Beth is bilingual.

        C. Beth is bilingual.
           Beth is in Ms. Suarez's fourth period.
           All students in Ms. Suarez's fourth period are bilingual.

        D. If Beth is bilingual, then she speaks Spanish.
           Beth speaks French.
           Beth is not bilingual.

The correct answer is A. The second statement, or premise, is tested against the first premise. Both premises are valid and the conclusion is logical. In B, the conclusion is invalid because the first premise does not exclude other students. In C, the conclusion cannot be logically drawn from the preceding premises--you cannot conclude that all students are bilingual based on one example. In D, the conclusion is invalid because Beth could be bilingual in French and another language besides Spanish.

95. **Which transition word would show contrast between these two ideas? (Skill 11.12, Average Rigor)**

> We are confident in our skills to teach English. We welcome new ideas on this subject.

    A. We are confident in our skills to teach English, and we welcome new ideas on this subject.

    B. Because we are confident in our skills to teach English, we welcome new ideas on the subject.

    C. When we are confident in our skills to teach English, we welcome new ideas on the subject.

    D. We are confident in our skills to teach English; however, we welcome new ideas on the subject.

The answer is D. Transitional words, phrases and sentences help clarify meanings. In A, the transition word *and* introduces another equal idea. In B, the transition word *because* indicates cause and effect. In C, the transition word *when* indicates order or chronology. In D, *however*, shows that these two ideas contrast with each other.

96. **In preparing your high school freshmen to write a research paper about a social problem, what recommendation can you make so they can determine the credibility of their information? (Skill 11.13, Easy)**

    A. Assure them that information on the Internet has been peer-reviewed and verified for accuracy.

    B. Find one solid source and use that exclusively.

    C. Use only primary sources.

    D. Cross check your information with another credible source.

The answer is D. When researchers find the same information in multiple reputable sources, the information is considered credible. Using the Internet for research requires strong critical evaluation of the source. Nothing from the Internet should be taken without careful scrutiny of the source. To rely on only one source is dangerous and short-sighted. Most high school freshmen would have limited skills to conduct primary research for a paper about a social problem.

97.   To determine the credibility of information, researchers should do all of the following except (Skill 11.14, Rigorous)

      A. Establish the authority of the document.

      B. Disregard documents with bias.

      C. Evaluate the currency and reputation of the source.

      D. Use a variety of research sources and methods.

The answer is B. Keep an open mind. Researchers should examine the assertions, facts and reliability of the information.

98.   Which of the following situations is not an ethical violation of intellectual property? (Skill 11.14, Rigorous)

      A. A student visits ten different websites and writes a report to compare the costs of downloading music. He uses the names of the websites without their permission.

      B. A student copies and pastes a chart verbatim from the Internet but does not document it because it is available on a public site.

      C. From an online article found in a subscription database, a student paraphrases a section on the problems of music piracy. She includes the source in her Works Cited but does not provide an in-text citation.

      D. A student uses a comment from M. Night Shyamalan without attribution claiming the information is common knowledge.

The answer is A. In this scenario, the student is conducting primary research by gathering the data and using it for his own purposes. He is not violating any principle by using the names of the websites. In B, students who copy and paste from the Internet without documenting the sources of their information are committing plagiarism, a serious violation of intellectual property. Even when a student puts information in her own words by paraphrasing or summarizing as in C, the information is still secondary and must be documented. While dedicated movie buffs might consider anything that M. Night Shyamalan says to be common knowledge in situation D, his comments are not necessarily known in numerous places or known by a lot of people.

99. For their research paper on the effects of the Civil War on American literature, students have brainstormed a list of potential online sources and are seeking your authorization. Which of these represent the strongest source? (Skill 11.14, Rigorous)

    A. http://www.wikipedia.org/

    B. http://www.google.com

    C. http://www.nytimes.com

    D. http://docsouth.unc.edu/southlit/civilwar.html

The answer is D. Sites with an "edu" domain are associated with educational institutions and tend to be more trustworthy for research information. Wikipedia has an "org" domain which often means it is a nonprofit. While Wikipedia may be appropriate for background reading, its credibility as a research site is questionable. Both Google and the *New York Times* are "com" sites which are for commercial organizations. Even though this does not discredit their information, each site is problematic for researchers. With Internet searches with Google and others, students may well get overwhelmed with hits and may not choose the most reputable sites for their information. The *New York Times* would not be a strong source for historical information.

100. A punctuation mark indicating omission, interrupted thought, or an incomplete statement is a/an (Skill 12.1, Easy)

    A. ellipsis.

    B. anachronism.

    C. colloquy.

    D. idiom.

The answer is A. In an ellipsis, word or words that would clarify the sentence's message are missing, yet it is still possible to understand them from the context.

101.   Which of the following sentences is properly punctuated? (Skill 12.1, Easy)

A. The more you eat; the more you want.

B. The authors—John Steinbeck, Ernest Hemingway, and William Faulkner—are staples of modern writing in American literature textbooks.

C. Handling a wild horse, takes a great deal of skill and patience.

D. The man, who replaced our teacher, is a comedian.

The answer is B. Dashes should be used instead of commas when commas are used elsewhere in the sentence for amplification or explanation--here within the dashes.

102.   Which of the following sentences contains a subject-verb agreement error? (Skill 12.1, Average Rigor)

A. Both mother and her two sisters were married in a triple ceremony.

B. Neither the hen nor the rooster is likely to be served for dinner.

C. My boss, as well as the company's two personnel directors, have been to Spain.

D. Amanda and the twins are late again.

The answer is C. The reason for this is that the true subject of the verb is "My boss," not "two personnel directors."

103. In preparing a speech for a contest, your student has encountered problems with gender-specific language. Not wishing to offend either women or men, he seeks your guidance. Which of the following is not an effective strategy? (Skill 12.3, Rigorous)

    A. Use the generic "he" and explain that people will understand and accept the male pronoun as all-inclusive.

    B. Switch to plural nouns and use "they" as the gender neutral pronoun.

    C. Use passive voice so that the subject is not required.

    D. Use male pronouns for one part of the speech and then use female pronouns for the other part of the speech.

The answer is A. No longer is the male pronoun considered the universal pronoun. Speakers and writers should choose gender neutral words and avoid nouns and pronouns that inaccurately exclude one gender or another.

104. Which aspect of language is innate? (Skill13.1, Rigorous)

    A. Biological capability to articulate sounds understood by other humans

    B. Cognitive ability to create syntactical structures

    C. Capacity for using semantics to convey meaning in a social environment

    D. Ability to vary inflections and accents

The answer is A. Language ability is innate, and the biological capability to produce sounds lets children learn semantics and syntactical structures through trial and error. Linguists agree that language is first a vocal system of word symbols that enable a human to communicate his/her feelings, thoughts, and desires to other human beings.

105.   **To understand the origins of a word, one must study the (Skill 13.2, Easy)**

        A. synonyms

        B. inflections

        C. phonetics

        D. etymology

The answer is D. Etymology is the study of word origins. A synonym is an equivalent of another word and can substitute for it in certain contexts. Inflection is a modification of words according to their grammatical functions, usually by employing variant word-endings to indicate such qualities as tense, gender, case, and number. Phonetics is the science devoted to the physical analysis of the sounds of human speech, including their production, transmission, and perception.

106.   **Which of the following would be the most significant factor in teaching Homer's *Iliad* and *Odyssey* to any particular group of students? (Skill 13.2, Average Rigor)**

        A. Identifying a translation on the appropriate reading level

        B. Determining the students' interest level

        C. Selecting an appropriate evaluative technique

        D. Determining the scope and delivery methods of background study

The answer is A. Students will learn the importance of these two works if the translation reflects both the vocabulary that they know and their reading level. Greece will always be foremost in literary assessments due to Homer's works. Homer is the most often cited author, next to Shakespeare. Greece is the cradle of both democracy and literature. This is why it is so crucial that Homer be included in the works assigned.

107. **Writing ideas quickly without interruption of the flow of thoughts or attention to conventions is called (Skill 13.4, Easy)**

  A. brainstorming.

  B. mapping.

  C. listing.

  D. free writing.

The answer is D. Free writing for ten or fifteen minutes allows students to write out their thoughts about a subject. This technique allows the students to develop ideas that they are conscious of, but it also helps them to develop ideas that are lurking in the subconscious. It is important to let the flow of ideas run through the hand. If the students get stuck, they can write the last sentence over again until inspiration returns.

108. **If a student has a poor vocabulary, the teacher should recommend first that (Skill 13.7, Average Rigor)**

  A. the student read newspapers, magazines and books on a regular basis.

  B. the student enroll in a Latin class.

  C. the student write the words repetitively after looking them up in the dictionary.

  D. the student use a thesaurus to locate synonyms and incorporate them into his/her vocabulary

The answer is A. It is up to the teacher to *help* the student choose reading material, but the student must be able to choose what provides the reading pleasure indispensable for enriching vocabulary.

109. **Which of the following responses to literature typically give middle school students the most problems? (Skill 13.8, Average Rigor)**

        A. Interpretive

        B. Evaluative

        C. Critical

        D. Emotional

The answer is B. Middle school readers will exhibit both emotional and interpretive responses. In middle/junior high school, organized study models enable students to identify main ideas and supporting details, to recognize sequential order, to distinguish fact from opinion, and to determine cause/effect relationships. Also, a child's being able to say why a particular book was boring or why a particular poem made him/her sad evidences critical reactions on a fundamental level. It is a bit early for evaluative responses, however. These depend on the reader's consideration of how the piece represents its genre, how well it reflects the social/ethical mores of a given society, and how well the author has approached the subject for freshness and slant. Evaluative responses are made only by a few advanced high school students.

110.

110   **What type of reasoning does Henry David Thoreau use in the following excerpt from "Civil Disobedience"? (Skill 13.8, Rigorous)**

Unjust laws exist; shall we be content to obey them, or shall we endeavor to amend them, and obey them until we have succeeded, or shall we transgress them at once? Men generally, under such a government as this, think that they ought to wait until they have persuaded the majority to alter them. They think that, if they should resist, the remedy would be worse than the evil. But it is the fault of the government itself that the remedy *is* worse than the evil. ... Why does it always crucify Christ, and excommunicate Copernicus and Luther, and pronounce Washington and Franklin rebels?

--"Civil Disobedience" by Henry David Thoreau

A. Ethical reasoning

B. Inductive reasoning

C. Deductive reasoning

D. Intellectual reasoning

The answer is C. Deductive reasoning begins with a general statement that leads to the particulars. In this essay, Thoreau begins with the general question about what should be done about unjust laws. His argument leads to the government's role in suppressing dissent.

111. **Which of the following is an example of the post hoc fallacy? (Skill 13.8, Rigorous)**

    A. When the new principal was hired, student reading scores improved; therefore, the principal caused the increase in scores.

    B. Why are we spending money on the space program when our students don't have current textbooks?

    C. You can't give your class a 10-minute break. Once you do that, we'll all have to give our students a 10-minute break.

    D. You can never believe anything he says because he's not from the same country as we are.

The correct answer is A. A post hoc fallacy assumes that because one event preceded another, the first event caused the second event. In this case, student scores could have increased for other reasons. B is a red herring fallacy in which one raises an irrelevant topic to sidetrack from the first topic. In this case, the space budget (federal funds) and the textbook budget (state or local funds) have little effect on each other. Response C is an example of a slippery slope, in which one event is followed precipitously by another event. Response D is an ad hominem ("to the man") fallacy in which a person is attacked rather than the concept or interpretation.

112. **The new teaching intern is developing a unit on creative writing and is trying to encourage her freshman high school students to write poetry. Which of the following would not be an effective technique? (Skill 13.9, Average Rigor)**

> A. In groups, students will draw pictures to illustrate "The Love Song of J. Alfred Prufrock" by T.S. Eliot.
>
> B. Either individually or in groups, students will compose a song, writing lyrics that try to use poetic devices.
>
> C. Students will bring to class the lyrics of a popular song and discuss the imagery and figurative language.
>
> D. Students will read aloud their favorite poems and share their opinions of and responses to the poems.

The answer is A. While drawing is creative, it will not accomplish as much as the other activities to encourage students to write their own poetry. Furthermore, "The Love Song of J. Alfred Prufrock" is not a freshman-level poem. The other activities involve students in music and their own favorites, which will be more appealing.

113. **Which teaching method would best engage underachievers in the required senior English class? (Skill 13.9, Average Rigor)**

> A. Assign use of glossary work and extensively footnoted excerpts of great works.
>
> B. Have students take turns reading aloud the anthology selection
>
> C. Let students choose which readings they'll study and write about.
>
> D. Use a chronologically arranged, traditional text, but assigning group work, panel presentations, and portfolio management

The answer is C. It will encourage students to react honestly to literature. Students should take notes on what they're reading so they will be able to discuss the material. They should not only react to literature, but also experience it. Small-group work is a good way to encourage them. The other answers are not fit for junior-high or high school students. They should be encouraged, however, to read critics of works in order to understand criteria work.

114. **In the paragraph below, which sentence does not contribute to the overall task of supporting the main idea? (Skill 13.12 Easy)**

> 1) The Springfield City Council met Friday to discuss new zoning restrictions for the land to be developed south of the city. 2) Residents who opposed the new restrictions were granted 15 minutes to present their case. 3) Their argument focused on the dangers that increased traffic would bring to the area. 4) It seemed to me that the Mayor Simpson listened intently. 5) The council agreed to table the new zoning until studies would be performed.

    A. Sentence 2

    B. Sentence 3

    C. Sentence 4

    D. Sentence 5

The answer is C. The other sentences provide detail to the main idea of the new zoning restrictions. Because sentence 4 provides no example or relevant detail, it should be omitted.

115. **For students to prepare for a their roles in a dramatic performance, (Skill 14.1, Rigorous)**

    A. they should analyze their characters to develop a deeper understanding of the character's attitudes and motivations.

    B. they should attend local plays to study settings and stage design

    C. they should read articles and books on acting methodology.

    D. they should practice the way other actors have performed in these roles.

The answer is A. By examining how their characters feel and think, the students will understand the characters' attitudes and motivation.

116.   Among junior-high school students of low-to-average readability levels, which work would most likely stir reading interest? (Skill 14.3, Easy)

    A. *Elmer Gantry*, Sinclair Lewis

    B. *Smiley's People*, John Le Carre

    C. *The Outsiders*, S.E. Hinton

    D. *And Then There Were None*, Agatha Christie.

The answer is C. The students can easily identify with the characters and the gangs in the book. S.E. Hinton has actually said about this book: "*The Outsiders* is definitely my best-selling book; but what I like most about it is how it has taught a lot of kids to enjoy reading."

117.   Most children's literature prior to the development of popular literature was intended to be didactic. Which of the following would not be considered didactic? (Skill 14.3, Average Rigor)

    A. "A Visit from St. Nicholas" by Clement Moore

    B. McGuffy's Reader

    C. Any version of Cinderella

    D. Parables from the Bible

The answer is A. "A Visit from St. Nicholas" is a cheery, non-threatening view of "The Night before Christmas." Didactic means intended to teach some lesson.

118. **Children's literature became established in the (Skill 14.3, Average Rigor)**

 A. seventeenth century

 B. eighteenth century

 C. nineteenth century

 D. twentieth century

The answer is A. In the seventeenth century, authors such as Jean de La Fontaine and his fables, Pierre Perreault's tales, Mme d'Aulnoy's novels based on old folktales and Mme de Beaumont's "Beauty and the Beast" all created a children's literature genre. In England, Perreault was translated and a work allegedly written by Oliver Smith, *The Renowned History of Little Goody Two Shoes*, also helped to establish children's literature in England.

119. **Which author did not write satire? (Skill 14.3, Rigorous)**

 A. Joseph Addison

 B. Richard Steele

 C. Alexander Pope

 D. John Bunyan

The answer is D. John Bunyan was a religious writer, known for his autobiography, *Grace Abounding to the Chief of Sinners*, as well as other books, all religious in their inspiration, such as *The Holy City*, or the *New Jerusalem* (1665), *A Confession of My Faith*, and *A Reason of My Practice* (1672), or T*he Holy War* (1682).

120. **The most significant drawback to applying learning theory research to classroom practice is that (Skill 14.3, Rigorous)**

    A. today's students do not acquire reading skills with the same alacrity as when greater emphasis was placed on reading classical literature.

    B. development rates are complicated by geography and culture. In analyzing literature and in looking for ways to bring a work to life for an audience, the use of comparable themes and ideas from other pieces of literature and from one's own life experiences, including from reading the daily newspaper, is important and useful.

    C. homogeneous grouping has contributed to faster development of some age groups.

    D. social and environmental conditions have contributed to an escalated maturity level than research done twenty or more years ago would seem to indicate.

The answer is D. Because of the rapid social changes, topics which did not used to interest younger readers are now topics of books for even younger readers. There are many books dealing with difficult topics, and it is difficult for the teacher to steer students toward books which they are ready for and to try to keep them away from books whose content, although well-written, is not yet appropriate for their level of cognitive and social development. There is a fine line between this and censorship.

121.	After watching a movie of a train derailment, a child exclaims, "Wow, look how many cars fell off the tracks. There's junk everywhere. The engineer must have really been asleep." Using the facts that the child is impressed by the wreckage and assigns blame to the engineer, a follower of Piaget's theories would estimate the child to be about (Skill 14.3, Rigorous)

A.	ten years old.

B.	twelve years old.

C.	fourteen years old.

D.	sixteen years old.

The answer is A. According to Piaget's theory, children seven- to eleven-years old begin to apply logic to concrete things and experiences. They can combine performance and reasoning to solve problems. They have internalized moral values and are willing to confront rules and adult authority.

122.	Which of the following is a formal reading-level assessment? (Skill 14.5, Average Rigor)

A.	A standardized reading test

B.	A teacher-made reading test

C.	An interview

D.	A reading diary

The answer is A. If assessment is standardized, it has to be objective, whereas B, C and D are all subjective assessments.

123.   Based on the excerpt below from Kate Chopin's short story "The Story of an Hour," what can students infer about the main character? (Skill 14.5, Rigorous)

> She did not stop to ask if it were or were not a monstrous joy that held her. A clear and exalted perception enabled her to dismiss the suggestion as trivial. She knew that she would weep again when she saw the kind, tender hands folded in death; the face that had never looked save with love upon her, fixed and gray and dead. But she saw beyond that bitter moment a long procession of years to come that would belong to her absolutely. And she opened and spread her arms out to them in welcome.

A. She dreaded her life as a widow.

B. Although she loved her husband, she was glad that he was dead for he had never loved her.

C. She worried that she was too indifferent to her husband's death.

D. Although they had both loved each other, she was beginning to appreciate that opportunities had opened because of his death.

The answer is D. Dismissing her feeling of "monstrous joy" as insignificant, the young woman she realizes that she will mourn her husband who had been good to her and had loved her. But that "long procession of years" does not frighten her; instead she recognizes that this new life belongs to her alone and she welcomes it with open arms.

124. **The English department is developing strategies to encourage all students to become a community of readers. From the list of suggestions below, which would be the least effective way for teachers to foster independent reading? (Skill 14.6, Average Rigor)**

    A. Each teacher will set aside a weekly 30-minute in-class reading session during which the teacher and students read a magazine or book for enjoyment.

    B. Teacher and students develop a list of favorite books to share with each other.

    C. The teacher assigns at least one book report each grading period to ensure that students are reading from the established class list.

    D. The students gather books for a classroom library so that books may be shared with each other.

The answer is C. Teacher-directed assignments such as book reports appear routine and unexciting. Students will be more excited about reading when they can actively participate. In A, the teacher is modeling reading behavior and providing students with a dedicated time during which time they can read independently and still be surrounded by a community of readers. In B and D, students share and make available their reading choices.

125. **Written on the sixth grade reading level, most of S. E. Hinton's novels (for instance, *The Outsiders*) have the greatest reader appeal with (Skill 14.7, Average Rigor)**

    A. sixth-graders.

    B. ninth-graders.

    C. twelfth-graders.

    D. adults.

The answer is B. Adolescents are concerned with their changing bodies, their relationships with each other and adults, and their place in society. Reading *The Outsiders* makes them confront different problems that they are only now beginning to experience as teenagers, such as gangs and social identity. The book is universal in its appeal to adolescents.